Local History and Genealogy Abstracts from Marion, Indiana Newspapers 1865-1870

Ralph D. Kirkpatrick, Ph.D.

HERITAGE BOOKS
2009

HERITAGE BOOKS
AN IMPRINT OF HERITAGE BOOKS, INC.

Books, CDs, and more—Worldwide

For our listing of thousands of titles see our website at
www.HeritageBooks.com

Published 2009 by
HERITAGE BOOKS, INC.
Publishing Division
100 Railroad Ave. #104
Westminster, Maryland 21157

Copyright © 2001 Ralph D. Kirkpatrick, Ph.D.

All rights reserved. No part of this book may be reproduced or transmitted in any form or by any means, electronic or mechanical, including photocopying, recording or by any information storage and retrieval system without written permission from the author, except for the inclusion of brief quotations in a review.

International Standard Book Numbers
Paperbound: 978-0-7884-1832-7
Clothbound: 978-0-7884-8227-4

TABLE OF CONTENTS

Foreword	v
Abbreviations and Conventions	vii
Local History and Genealogy Abstracts From Marion, Indiana Newspapers 1865-1870	1
Maiden Name Index	191

FOREWORD

The first newspapers published in Marion, Grant County, Indiana may have appeared as early as 1840. The earliest extant issue of a Marion newspaper is one from August 18, 1865. It is truly unfortunate that the newspapers published during the Civil War did not survive to tell us about day to day happenings. That war served to awaken the then-remote village of Marion. Men came in from the surrounding small farm clearings, forests and prairies to enlist in the State Volunteer Regiments that were formed to force the Confederate States back into the Union. Men left their parents, wives and children to march away and give battle to the Secessionists. Too many of the Grant County men and boys either left their bodies on bloody southern fields or they returned home severely handicapped in mind or body. No longer boys or naive men, the returning men had a greater appreciation of the possibilities for building a better life for themselves and their families right here in Marion and Grant County.

The early-1860's found the farmers forced to take their produce to market on flatboats down the Mississinewa River or to moving their produce overland to the canal to the north of Grant County. The very poor roads, impassable during spring and much of the winter, did not necessarily go where the pioneers needed or wanted to go.

The years covered by the abstracts in this book saw the coming of the railroads and telegraph, the construction of new roads, and the appearance of industries in Marion that would provide a market for the products of the nearby forests and farms. It is exciting to read about the changes occurring in Grant County.

Ralph D. Kirkpatrick, Ph.D.
Osage Farm

ABBREVIATIONS AND CONVENTIONS

AB - Bachelor of Arts
ac - acres
Addn - Addition
admin - administers or administrator
agric - agricultural
AM - Master of Arts
anniv - anniversary
Assn - Association
asst - assistant
atty - attorney
att - attended or is attending
b - born on or born at
bd - board
bldg - building
blk - block
bur - buried at
ca - circa or about
Cem - Cemetery
Ch - Church
CH - Courthouse
Coll - College
Co - company or county name, if not followed by a state name
    is an Indiana county
comm - commission or commissioner
Conv - Convention
corr - corresponding
CW - Civil War
d - died at or died on
da - days
dec - deceased
dir - director
dt - daughter of
Esq - Esquire
est - established
exor - executor
f - former or formerly
F&AM - Free & Accepted Masons, a lodge
Friends or Friends Meeting - a certain Protestant denomination
ft - foot or feet
grad - graduate or graduate of

ABBREVIATIONS AND CONVENTIONS

HS - high school
Inf - Infantry
IOGT - Independent Order of Good Templars, a lodge
IOOF - Independent Order of Odd Fellows, a lodge
JP - Justice of the Peace
KIA - killed in action
m - married or month
manuf - manufacture or manufacturing
mbr - member of
M.E. - Methodist Episcopal Church
MH - Meetinghouse, a building used for religious services
mi - mile or miles
M.P. - Methodist Protestant Church
(Name) - maiden surname of married woman or widow
'Name' - nickname
Name - name this person was known by or 'went by'
pres - president
prob - probably
prop - proprietor
rd - road
Regt - Regiment
Rep - Republican, a member of a certain political party
s - son of
sch - school
secy - secretary
serv - served in or served as
Soc - Society
SS - Sunday School
St - Street or Streets
tchr - teacher
treas - treasurer
Twp - Township; township name not followed by a county
    name is in Grant County, Indiana
U.B. - United Brethren Church
Vol - Volunteers
WIA - wounded in action
wk - week
y or yr - years
yg - young

LOCAL HISTORY AND GENEALOGY ABSTRACTS FROM MARION, INDIANA NEWSPAPERS 1865 - 1870

ACHOR(S), Caroline - owns land in Green Twp (1/8/68)

ACHOR, W[illiam] H. - Dec 1869 buys license to m M[ary] J. Wood (1/5/70)

ADAMS, Ellen Adelia - is att Marion Public Sch (11/6/67); - see William GUNDER

ADAMS, George - is att Marion Public Sch (11/6/67)

ADAMS, Mrs. M.E. - 1867-68 tchr, Marion Public Sch (9/25/67); is on faculty of Academic Institute, Marion (3/4/68)

ADAMS, Mary E. - sells 40 ac in Center Twp (10/27/69)

ADAMS, Rev. Samuel L. - mbr IOOF; dec (9/22/69)

ADAMS, Sarah J. - 1867 buys a Marion lot (1/8/68)

ADAMS, Thomas - dec; owned land in Pleasant Twp (1/6/69)

ADAMSON, Jonathan - 1868 Liberty Twp landowner (1/12/70); prop of a sawmill in Independence (4/6/70)

ADAMSON, Moses - 1867 buys 62 ac in Van Buren Twp from Dr. Lavanner Corey (4/2/68)

ADKINS, Wyatt M. - sells land in Liberty Twp (11/10/69)

ADSIT, Olive M. - Jefferson Twp landowner (1/6/69)

ALDERDICE, Rev. Thomas H. - 1842 preached in Grant Co CH on at least one Sunday (7/13/70)

ALLEN, J. D[avis] - 1 Jun 1869 m Martha E. Moore (6/2/69)

ALLEN, James - is att Marion Public Sch (11/6/67)

ALLEN, James - owns property in Fairmount (1/8/68); 1861 sells land in Franklin Twp to Pleasant Foster & 1863 sells 80 ac in Franklin Twp to Pleasant Foster (5/14/68)

ALLEN, James M. - buys 40 ac in Sims Twp (9/28/70)

ALLEN, John W. - buys 40 ac in Washington Twp (5/18/70)

ALLEN, Joseph - Sims Twp landowner (1/8/68); Aug 1869 buys license to m Mary Allen (9/8/69)

ALLEN, Miss Mary - & Miss Maggie Kinneer, props, Millinery & Fancy Goods Shop, Pierce Bldg, N side of CH Square, Marion (4/9/68); - see Joseph ALLEN

ALLEN, Solomon D. - Washington Twp Assessor (10/19/70)

AMMONS, Francis E. - sells 30 ac in Pleasant Twp to James M. Props (2/26/68); Monroe Twp landowner (1/6/69); sells 42 ac in Pleasant Twp to James Sweetser (11/10/69)

AMMONS, George W. - Sims Twp delegate to State Rep Conv (2/9/70)

AMMONS, J.M. - f of Marion; moved to Mason, MI; now moves to Chillicothe, MO (3/3/69); is putting in his vegetable garden in Chillicothe (4/28/69)

AMMONS, Jane A. - owns property in Marion (1/6/69)

AMMONS, Capt. John M. - 1867 sells property in Marion (1/29/68); dec; owned land in Pleasant Twp (1/8/68)

ANCIL, Catherine - Pleasant Twp landowner (1/8/68)

ANDERSON, Asbury - buys Fairmount lots (2/9/70)

ANDERSON, Isaac - Van Buren Twp dir, Grant Co Agric Soc Fair (7/29/68; 8/3/70); organizes support in Van Buren Twp for the proposed GR,W&C RR (11/3/69); att Old Settlers meeting (6/8/70)

ANDERSON, Sarah A. - sells 40 ac in Van Buren Twp (1/29/68)

ANDERSON, William - Monroe Twp landowner (1/8/68; 1/6/69)

ANDREWS, Jehu - JP, Center Twp (10/19/70)

ANDREWS, Robert - of Center Twp; CW vet (1/19/70)

ANTRIM, Thomas - 1869 sells 80 Washington Twp ac (1/5/70)

APEANY(?), Willis - Jun 1868 buys license to m Esther Asbery (7/1/68)

ARCANA, Town of - in Monroe Twp; has a Post Office (11/30/70)

ARMSTRONG, Ann E. - Sims Twp landowner (1/6/69)

ARNETT, Elwood - buys 40.25 ac in Liberty Twp (2/9/70)

ARNETT, Levi A. - JP, Franklin Twp (9/18/67)

ARNOLD, Andrew - 1868-71 owns property in Mier (1/12/70)

ARNOLD, Samuel - buys 1 lot in Marion (4/30/68)

ARTHURHULTS, David - Pleasant Twp landowner (1/6/69)

ATKINSON, Joseph - buys 10 ac in Monroe Twp (12/25/67)

AYRES, I.L., Esq - f of Marion; now lives in Warsaw (10/12/70)

AYRES, Dr. Stephen D. - sells property in Marion to Henry Wade (4/13/70); his saddle horse, 'Charley', d last wk, at age 26; Ayres had 'Charley' for 23 yr (11/16/70)

AYRES, William H. - a dir, Liberty Twp Pike Co (4/28/69)

BABB, Enoch - 1869 Franklin Twp landowner (12/21/70)

BABB, Henry - sells 47 ac in Franklin Twp (10/27/69)

BAGLEY, Sarah J. - 1869 Richland Twp landowner (12/21/70)

BABB, Samuel - Mar 1869 buys license to m Mary C. Cochran (4/7/69)

BAILEY, Rufus W., Esq - new atty in Marion; late of Godman & Bailey of Marion, OH (7/1/68); buys a lot on Washington St from Leo F. Duff & buys 8 more Marion lots (11/10/69)

BAILEY, Thomas - a carpenter; is injured when he fell from a ladder while working on the barn of Moses Bradford (8/12/68)

BAILEY, William S. - lives 2.5 mi NW of Roseburg (9/18/67); Mar 1869 buys license to m Sarah A. Haines (4/7/69)

BAKER, Aaron - 1869 Sims Twp landowner (12/21/70)

BAKER, Henry - 1869 Sims Twp landowner (12/21/70)

BALDWIN, Addison M. - buys 3 Fairmount lots (4/30/68)

BALDWIN, Arthur - is att Marion Public Sch (12/18/67)

BALDWIN, David - Fairmount Twp landowner (1/6/69)

BALDWIN, Edward - sells 1.25 ac near Marion (11/2/70); sells 40 ac in Franklin Twp to John Ruff (12/7/70); to sell his personal property 24 Nov 1870 & move to KS (11/16/70)

BALDWIN, Hannah H. - age 24y, 1m, 13da; dt J.W. & S.J. Baldwin; d 17 Jun 1870 (7/6/70)

BALDWIN, Jonathan - Oct 1852 lays out 22 lots in Baldwin's Addn, Fairmount; Oct 1857 lays out 20 lots in Baldwin's 2nd Addn, Fairmount; Jan 1859 lays out 6 lots in Baldwin's 3rd Addn, Fairmount (4/23/68); organizes Fairmount Twp support for proposed GR, W&C RR (11/3/69); sells Fairmount lots (11/24/69; 12/15/69); is on committee to fight alcohol in Fairmount (12/29/69); 1869 sells Fairmount lots to Isaac Smithson (1/5/70), to Asbury Anderson (2/9/70), & to Joel B. Wright (11/30/70)

BALDWIN, Joseph W. - left for Washington, D.C. this wk to att inauguration of pres Grant (3/3/69); viewer for a rd in Center Twp (3/11/69); buys 60 ac in Fairmount Twp (11/10/69)

BALDWIN, Lancaster D. - Trustee, 5th Ward, Jonesboro (5/11/70); JP, Mill Twp (10/19/70); is Grant Co Deputy Sheriff (11/16/70)

BALDWIN, Mary - owns property in Jonesboro (1/8/68); buys 2 lots in Marion from Moses Bradford (4/27/70)

BALDWIN, Micah - buys property in Fairmount (2/2/70)

BALDWIN, Moses - sells 80 ac in Pleasant Twp (12/29/69)

BALDWIN, S.T. - Postmaster at Jonesboro (5/11/70)

BALDWIN, Thomas - dec; John Ratliff is exor for his estate (1/13/69)

BALL, John W. - buys 120 ac in Jefferson Twp (9/14/70)

BALLARD, James - of Washington Twp is dec; Emily Ballard admin his estate (8/18/65)

BALLARD, W[illiam] - Dec 1869 buys license to m E[lizabeth] V. Shinholt (1/5/70)

BALLENGER, David - 5 Mar 1869 in Marion m Martha Jane Jacks (3/11/69; 4/7/69)

BALLINGER, David - sells 40 ac in Jefferson Twp (2/26/68)

BALLINGER, Elijah - 1869 Monroe Twp landowner (12/21/70)

BALLINGER, Isaac - 1867 sells 1.25 ac in Jefferson Twp to U&L RR Co for $1 (6/25/68)

BALLINGER, Jesse - Jefferson Twp landowner (1/6/69)

BANNISTER, John - losing candidate for JP, Liberty Twp (10/19/70)

BARGERY, William - Mar 1869 buys license to m Mary McNamara (4/7/69)

BARLEY, Aaron R. - Mar 1868 buys license to m Emily Pulley (4/2/.68); organizes support for proposed GR,W&C RR (11/3/69)

BARLEY, Miss Arta - is att Marion Public Sch (12/18/67)

BARLEY, C.S. - prop, Union House at corner of Clay & Branson St (4/2/68)

BARLEY, Conrad - dec; owned Washington Twp land (1/6/69)

BARLEY, Guy - infant s Clinton Barley; d Marion 11 Aug 1868 (8/19/68)

BARLEY, Jackson - Nov 1867 buys license to m Sarah Seford (12/11/67)

BARLEY, Jacob S. - buys half interest in the Marshall Mill in Pleasant Twp at Sheriff's auction (5/14/68)

BARLEY, John H. - 1868 Monroe Twp landowner (1/12/70)

BARLEY, Martin - 23 Feb 1869 was m to Amanda Campbell by Elder James Maple (2/24/69; 3/3/69)

BARLEY/BURLEY, Noah - Jun 1869 buys license to m A[nnie] Fitzsimmons (7/7/69)

BARLEY, Sarah J. - 1867 buys a lot in Marion (1/8/68)

BARLEY, Valentine - age 29; d 17 May 1868 (5/21/68)

BARLOW, Rev. George W. - late of Lane Seminary; 19 May 1868 in Presbyterian Ch of Erie (Vienna) MI, m Amanda, only dt of Rev. A. Sanford (5/28/68)

BARNARD, A.L. - a dir of Jonesboro & Kokomo Gravel Rd Co (5/7/68); mbr, IOOF, Jonesboro (3/24/69); 1869 sells a lot in Jonesboro to C.R. Jones (1/5/70)

BARNARD, Jacob M. - 1Jan 1868 m Mary C. Beck in Jonesboro (1/8/68); 1867 buys a lot in Jonesboro (1/29/68)

BARNARD, Lewis - 1867 sells 1 New Cumberland lot (2/12/68)

BARNES, George W. - sells 73 ac in Liberty Twp (4/16/68)

BARNES, Joshua - sells 89 ac in Richland Twp (11/10/69)

BARNET, M.J. - Liberty Twp landowner (1/8/68)

BARNETT, Wellington - 1867 sells 5 Liberty Twp ac (1/22/68)

BARNGROVER, Solomon D. - sells 50 ac in Sims Twp to John Lyon & buys 80 ac in Sims Twp from John R. Kob (1/12/70)

BARNHOUSE, Henry - Fairmount Twp landowner (1/8/68)

BARNHOUSE, John - owns property in Fairmount (1/8/68)

BARRETT, M.J. - Liberty Twp landowner (1/6/69)

BARTHOLOMEW, Ephraim - his Liberty Twp home burned last wk (2/12/68)

BARTHOLOMEW, William - buys 2 Fairmount lots (12/15/69)

BARTLETT, Joseph - Oct 1870 buys a license to m Phebe Bradfield (11/2/70)

BARTLETT, William K. - 1869 buys a lot in Marion from Mary Doty (1/5/70), where he now has a jewelry store (3/30/70); age 58; moved to Seneca Co, OH 1832; moved to Marion 1869; mbr Marion M.E. Ch; d Fostoria, OH 30 May 1870 (6/8/70)

BASLER, Ephraim - sells 3 ac in Sims Twp (3/30/70)

BASS, Jacob - owns land in Center Twp (1/6/69)

BATES, Aaron D. - sells 45 ac in Fairmount Twp (11/3/69); Mill Twp taxpayer (1/26/70); buys 1 ac lot in Jonesboro (4/27/70)

BATES, Mrs. Eliza A. - officer, Rebekah Lodge, Jonesboro (4/28/69)

BATES, Dr. James H. - att Rush Medical Coll in Chicago during Fall & Winter Terms 1867-68; recently set up practice in Jonesboro (4/30/68); mbr, Grant Co Medical Soc (5/21/68); mbr, IOOF, Jonesboro (3/24/69)

BATES, John W. - 1864 sells 197.73 ac in Mill Twp (5/14/68)

BATES, William - of Jonesboro is agent for sale of a certain book (5/14/68)

BAYLESS, Daniel, Sr. - Nov 1853 laid out the original 16 lots in the Grant Co part of Independence (4/23/68)

BAYLESS, John - admin estates of John Powell, dec (8/18/65; 12/11/67), & of Hugh Hamilton, dec (3/24/69); sells 72 ac in Liberty Twp to James A. Stephenson (12/28/70)

BAYLESS, S.L. - buys the Maion clothing store of Morgan H. Zeller, dec (8/18/65)

BEACH, __ - age ca 15; s Stephen Beach of Richland Twp; killed 30 Jun 1868 when harnessed horse he was riding ran through a wheat field, he fell off, entangled in the harness and he was dragged to death (7/8/68)

BEALL, Anna M. - of Jonesboro; d 26 Nov 1867 (12/4/67)

BEALL, Thomas C. - Trustee, Mill Twp (9/18/67); of Jonesboro; age 48; b Preble Co, OH 1819; m; Charter Mbr, Amana Lodge, No. 92, IOOF; 1860 joined M.E. Ch; d 11 Mar 1869 (3/24/69); 1868 owned property in Harrisburg (1/12/70)

BEALS, Enoch - is on committee to fight alcohol in Fairmount (12/29/69); buys 3 ac near Fairmount (12/7/70)

BEAM, Cephas I. - sells 80 ac in Franklin Twp (4/13/70)

BEAM, Margaret - age 62; wife of Samuel Beam; d 16 Apr 1868 (5/7/68)

BEARD, John H. - Sims Twp landowner (1/8/68); sells 160 ac in Sims Twp to James Sweetser (4/2/68)

BEATTY, __ - age ca 7; s J.D. Beatty of Jonesboro; 29 Jun 1868 drowned at Back Creek dam (7/1/68)

BEATTY, Robert, Esq - Marshal, Grant Co Live Stock Assn (8/5/68); Center Twp taxpayer (1/26/70); Rep candidate for Co Comm (7/13/70); owns a rental farm 3 mi S of Marion (9/14/70)

BEATTY, Samuel - losing candidate for JP, Franklin Twp (10/19/70)

BEAUCHAMP, Curtis - dec; 1869 owned land in Franklin Twp (12/21/70)

BEAVER, John - Green Twp landowner (1/8/68)

BECHT, Jehu/John - owns Jonesboro property (1/6/69); sells a lot in Jonesboro to R.B. Hawley (4/27/70)

BECHTEL, Samuel - buys 80 ac in Pleasant Twp (11/10/69)

BECK, Eli - Jun 1868 buys license to m Nancy J. Cloud (7/1/68)

BECK, Henry - sells 160 ac in Monroe Twp (11/16/70)

BECK/BECKET, Jehu - Apr 1868 buys license to m Ann E. Johnson/Johnston (5/14/68)

BECK, Michael - buys from George Wine 2 Marion lots & an adjoining 2.23 ac (4/2/68); sells Marion lot (4/30/68)

BECK, Richard - is att Marion Public Sch (11/6/67)

BECK, Samuel H. - buys 80 ac in Van Buren Twp (2/2/70)

BECKFORD, Dr. L.C. - mbr Grant Co Medical Soc (7/13/69)

BEDSAUL, Isaac - f a leading Marion businessman; ca 1848 moved to Magnolia, IA; is now visiting in Marion (5/14/68)

BEDWELL, Samuel - dec; owned property in Marion (1/6/69)

BEHYMER, Daniel - buys 40 ac in Green Twp (10/19/70)

BEHYMER, William - Liberty Twp landowner (1/8/68)

BELL, Christopher - buys 100 ac in Washington Twp (10/5/70)

BELL, Evan - buys 126 ac in Sims Twp (4/9/68)

BENAKER, Elizabeth - owns property in Brownsville (1/6/69)

BENBOW, Charity - owns property in Jonesboro (1/6/69)

BENBOW, Enos - 1869-71 Center Twp landowner (12/21/70)

BENBOW, Evan - viewer for a rd in Grant Co (6/23/69)

BENBOW, Stephen - buys property in Jonesboro (12/7/70)

BENNETT, J.K. - buys 40 ac in Liberty Twp (3/30/70); sells 80 ac in Liberty Twp to Thomas Brookshire (8/17/70)

BENNETT, Joseph - buys 48 ac in Liberty Twp (4/30/68)

BENSON, George T. - 30 Sep 1867 m Rosetta Turner (10/1/67)

BESHORE, Jacob 'Jake' W. - Trustee, Center Twp (9/18/67; 10/19/70); v pres, Marion Literary Soc (1/15/68); Rep candidate for re-election as Trustee (2/17/69); is a Marion businessman (9/8/69); last wk was accidentally shot in face with birdshot while out hunting, is recovering (11/10/69); CW vet (1/19/70); buys property in Marion (6/29/70); his large house on 3rd St just W of Sweetser's Bank burned last Sunday; it was the f home of the late Abraham Oppy (8/17/70); buys 40 ac in Sims Twp (9/7/70); raises hogs (11/2/70)

BESHORE, L.C. - & Bro. sell cooking stoves on S side of Square (9/29/69; 11/2/70)

BESHORE, Martha - is att Marion Public Sch (11/13/67)

BESHORE, Samuel B. - is att Marion Public Sch (12/18/67)

BESHORE, Sarah E. - sells a lot in Marion (12/28/70)

BEVARD, David - 1869 sells 2 ac in Monroe Twp (1/5/70)

BEVARD, Robert - 3 Apr 1870 m Mary A. Kunkel (4/6/70)

BIDDLE, Horace P./T. - Judge, Grant County Circuit Court (9/18/67), held this position in 1864 (6/9/69)

BIGELOW, Capt. A. - prop, Marion Omnibus Line (1/5/70); contracts to carry mail from Post Office to RR depot (11/2/70); & H.C. Lanckton are putting up ice in the old wagon shop at ft of Washington St, the ice is 6" thick and is clear (12/28/70)

BILLINGS, Joseph - 1869 Green Twp landowner (12/21/70)

BINFORD, Calvin - 1868 owns property in Jonesboro (1/12/70)

BIRD, Lafayette - is att Marion Public Sch (12/18/67)

BIRD, Miss Lou - is att Marion Public Sch (11/6/67)

BIRD, Robert W. - Green Twp landowner (1/6/69)

BIRELEY, Joseph D. - buys a lot in Marion (4/2/68)

BIRTNER, Thomas - Green Twp landowner (1/6/69)

BISH, David A. - buys 80 ac in Van Buren Twp (7/13/70)

BISH, Sarah [(Stout)] - age 39; wife of David Bish; d 18 Aug 1868 near Marion (8/19/68)

BITEZEL, George - Mar 1869 buys license to m Rebecca McGee (4/7/69)

BITNER, Isaac N. - sells 40 ac in Green Twp (12/7/70)

BITNER, William H. - Green Twp landowner (1/8/68)

BLACK, Joseph - Dec 1868 buys license to m Margaret Payne (1/6/69)

BLESSING, William - Green Twp landowner (1/8/68)

BLINN, Henry Z. - 1867 buys 50 ac in Franklin Twp (1/22/68); & Samuel Blinn admins estate of Samuel Blinn, dec (10/23/67); 9 Jan 1868 m Sarah C. Eby in Washington Twp (1/15/68); sells 4 ac in Franklin Twp (2/26/68)

BLINN, Samuel - dec (10/23/67)

BLINN, Samuel A. - & Henry Z. Blinn admin estate of Samuel Blinn, dec (10/23/67)

BLUE, Isaiah - sells 80 ac in Washington Twp (1/22/68)

BLUMENTHAL, M. - buys 1 lot in Marion from George Cubberly (6/1/70); is a Democrat (8/31/70)

'BOB' - CW warhorse of Col. David Shunk (6/9/69); - see CIVIL WAR

BOBBS, Dr. Andrew J. - physician & surgeon with office on Adams St 2 blk above Square (1/8/68; 9/7/70); 1867 buys Marion property (1/15/68); sells 1 Marion lot (2/26/68); buys cem lot from Trustees of IOOF Lodge for $28.33 (4/2/68)

BOCOCK, James - 1869 Monroe Twp landowner (1/6/69)

BOGANWRIGHT, John - 1869 Van Buren Twp landowner (12/21/70)

BOGUE, Amos H. - sells 20 ac in Liberty Twp (1/12/70)

BOGUE, Jesse - buys/sells land in Franklin Twp (4/2/68); 21 Jan 1869 m Nancy Wilson (1/27/69)

BOGUE, Jonathan - buys 40 ac in Franklin Twp (4/2/68)

BOGUE, Millie - 1868 sells 40 ac in Franklin Twp to Jesse Bogue (4/2/68); buys a lot in Fairmount from Eli Neal (11/10/69)

BOGUE, Robert - 1867 buys a Fairmount lot from Jonathan P. Winslow (3/4/68); buys 40 Franklin Twp ac (1/8/68; 4/2/68)

BOGUE, Thomas - buys land in Franklin Twp (1/8/68; 4/2/68)

BOGUE, William P. - 6 Oct 1870 m Mary J. Shugart (10/12/70; 11/2/70)

BOLE, Lorenzo - 1864 buys 2 ac in Mill Twp from William Phillips (4/9/68); 1869 Mill Twp landowner (12/21/70)

BOLLER, Benjamin - serv 130th Regt Ind Vol Inf during CW, crippled in war; Rep candidate for Land Appraiser of Grant Co (3/4/68); of Van Buren Twp; his house burned last wk (11/16/70)

BOLLER, James - Monroe Twp landowner (1/8/68); Mar 1868 buys license to m Susannah Haines (4/2/68); 1869 Washington Twp landowner (12/21/70)

BOLLER, John - buys property in Van Buren Twp (10/5/70)

BOND, __ - partner in Ward & Bond Sawmill, located 3 mi N of New Cumberland; sawmill boiler exploded 7 Aug 1868 killing Mr. Ward and the engineer, Mr. Shelton; Mr. Bond was injured but will recover (8/12/68)

BOND, Benjamin - Rep candidate, Land Appraiser of Grant Co (3/4/68); Supt, Morris Chapel SS (5/26/69); CW vet (1/19/70)

BOND, E.L. - lives on farm 1.5 mi NW of Jonesboro (8/31/70)

BOND, Lt. Joseph - secy, Morris Chapel SS (5/26/69); assesses lands for constructing Marion & Liberty Twp Turnpike (6/23/69); of Washington Twp; CW vet (1/19/70)

BOND, Levi L. - buys 80 ac in Jefferson Twp (7/13/70); admin estate of Leander Ward, dec (7/20/70)

BONE, William - viewer for new rd in Jefferson Twp (3/11/69)

BONHAM, Frank W. - of Monroe Twp; CW vet (1/19/70); losing candidate for JP, Monroe Twp (10/19/70)

BOOKOUT, Calvin - 1869 Jefferson Twp landowner (12/21/70)

BOOKOUT, Reuben - 14 Mar 1870 m Mrs. Nancy Terrell in Fairmount Twp (4/6/70)

BOOSEY, John - 1866 buys 1 lot near Fairmount (4/30/68)

BOOTS, Martin - & David Branson platted Marion Feb 1832; May 1838 lay out Boots Addn to Marion (4/16/68)

BOWEN/ROWEN, George R. - 2 Jan 1869 m Mary E. Hite, m by Rev. Henry L. Brown (1/20/69)

BOWERS, John L. - Jun 1868 buys license to m Rebecca J. Snyder/Saider (7/1/68)

BOWERS, Mary E. - 1866 sells 1 lot near Fairmount (4/30/68)

BOWERS, Samuel - sells 40 ac in Fairmount Twp (1/26/70)

BOWMAN, George - 1868 owns property in Marion (1/12/70)

BOWMAN, Isaac C. - Washington Twp landowner (1/8/68)

BOWMAN, Lavina - 1868 owns property in Marion (1/12/70)

BOWMAN, Peter - & C.W. Bowman sell lime by the bushel 3.5 mi NW of Marion (11/6/67); 1867 sells 1 lot in Marion to Elizabeth J. Bowman (5/14/68)

BOXELL, James - of Monroe Twp; recently found a stray horse (11/20/67)

BOXELL, Thomas - Van Buren Twp landowner (1/8/68)

BOYD, James M. - Mar 1868 buys license to m Melissa Burden (4/2/68)

BOYD, Samuel R. - 1869 Franklin Twp landowner (12/21/70)

BOYD, William - buys 80 ac in Jefferson Twp (10/27/69)

BOYDEN, Myron J. - sells 1 lot in Fairmount (5/14/68)

BRADDOCK, M[ichael] C. - Oct 1870 buys license to m Mary A. Miller (11/2/70)

BRADFIELD, B.T. - dec; owned land in Fairmount Twp & in Jefferson Twp (1/8/68)

BRADFIELD, Mary - Fairmount Twp landowner (1/8/68)

BRADFORD, __ - yg dt of Moses Bradford; fell from a horse and broke an arm in two places (7/8/68)

BRADFORD, Henry - 1866 sells 2 ac in Washington Twp (4/2/68); sells 76 ac in Washington Twp (10/27/69)

BRADFORD, Isaac - organizes support in Washington Twp for the proposed GR,W&C RR (11/3/69)

BRADFORD, John S. - owns property in Fairmount (1/6/69)

BRADFORD, Leonard - is dec (8/18/65)

BRADFORD, Mrs. Lucy G. - see Thomas D. THARP

BRADFORD, M. - SS tchr, Salem Ch (5/5/69); injured while shearing sheep on his farm near Marion, is recovering (6/8/70)

BRADFORD, Moses - sells 7 ac in Washington Twp (2/26/68); of Marion; is in Washington, D.C. as a witness in the trial of pres Andrew Johnson (3/26/68); repairing his barn (8/12/68); lays out a new addn of 80 lots just E of his home; sells bldg lots for $125 each (7/7/69); sells Marion lots to James A. Cotton (10/27/69), to Rufus W. Bailey (11/10/69), to Nathan Haines (1/12/70), to Mary Baldwin (4/27/70), to William C. DeLong (10/5/70), & to Nathan Haines (11/2/70)

BRADFORD, Oliver M. - Mar 1868 buys license to m Dulcena H. Hamaker (4/2/68)

BRADFORD, Sarah E. [(Culbertson)] - Chorister, Morris Chapel SS (5/26/69)

BRADLEY, John - Dec 1868 buys license to m S[usan] J. [Johnson] (1/6/69)

BRAFFIT, Silas - dec Grant Co farmer; William Wood admin his estate (9/25/67)

BRAGG, Henderson - dec; 1868 his heirs own property in Farmington (1/12/70)

BRAGG, Henry - 22 Sep 1870 m Angeline C. Westfall (9/28/70)

BRAGG, John W. - buys 40 ac in Jefferson Twp (4/27/70)

BRANDON, Mollie - is att Marion Sch (1/12/70); Marion HS student (12/23/70)

BRANSON, David - & Martin Boots platted Marion Feb 1832 (4/16/68); dec; owned land in Center Twp (1/6/69)

BRANSON, Nathan - Jan 1840 lays out Branson's Addn to Marion (4/16/68)

BREWER, H[esekiah] - Dec 1867 buys license to m Nancy E. Bennett (1/8/68)

BREWER, M[ilton] - Aug 1869 buys a license to m R[achel] E. Osborn (9/8/69)

BRIDGELAND, John A. - owns property in Jonesboro (1/8/68)

BRIGGS, Henderson - dec; owned property in Farmington (1/6/69)

BRIGHT, William - buys 40 ac in Monroe Twp from Reuben Hodson (1/26/70); sells 132 ac in Richland Twp (4/13/70)

BRILEY (or Riley?), Mrs. Sarah - age 77; mbr M.E. Ch; d 6 Aug 1868 (8/12/68)

BRODERICK, Case - 1868 Jefferson Twp landowner (1/12/70)

BROOKS, Noah - sells 40 ac in Mill Twp to Joseph M. Little & sells another 40 ac in Mill Twp to David Emel (10/5/70)

BROOKS, T[homas] L. - Aug 1869 buys a license to m M[ary] A. Richards (9/8/69)

BROOKS, William - is att Marion Public Sch (1/12/70)

BROOKS, William - April 1868 buys license to m M[ary] E. Allen (5/14/68)

BROOKSHIRE, Thomas - buys 80 ac in Liberty Twp (8/17/70)

BROWN, Rev. Henry L. - pastor, Marion Presbyterian Ch (9/18/67); his home on Branson St is for sale since he is moving to Minnesota (7/13/69)

BROWN, J.H. - buys 123 ac in Pleasant Twp (2/2/70)

BROWN, James W. - 1851 is Clerk, Grant Co Courts (8/17/70)

BROWN, Mrs. M.O. - pres, Sewing Soc, Marion Presbyterian Ch (2/3/69)

BROWN, Serena - Sims Twp landowner (1/6/69)

BROWN, William A. - 1867 buys Fairmount Twp ac (4/30/68)

BROWN, William D. - Apr 1849 lays out 16 lots in Brownsville (4/23/68)

BROWNFIELD, Samuel - dec; 1869 owned land in Richland Twp (12/21/70)

BROWNLEE, Charles - is att Marion Sch (11/6/67; 1/12/70)

BROWNLEE, Hiram, Esq - secy, Grant Co Livestock Assn (8/5/68); buys/sells a Marion lot (11/3/69; 7/13/70)

BROWNLEE, James, Esq - 1847 is ed, 'Marion Telegraph' (7/6/70), & Grant Co Auditor (7/20/70); 1850 Whig candidate for Grant Co Auditor (8/18/69); replaces Davidson Culbertson as Grant Co Treas (8/18/65); sells 1 Marion lot (2/12/68); is a dir, LM,W&C RR (3/3/69); admin estate of James C. Fleming, dec (3/11/69); buys Monroe Twp ac (12/29/69)

BROWNLEE, John, Esq - sells 80 ac in Richland Twp (1/12/70)

BROWNLEE, John Q., Esq - 1867 sells property in Marion & in Franklin Twp (1/15/68); & Daniel Hopkins Mar 1868 laid out Haws & Hopkin's Addn, Marion (4/16/68); buys land in Fairmount Twp (5/14/68); left today for his new home in Lincoln, NE (8/18/69); is joint owner of the 'Nebraska State Journal' with __ Butler, Governor of Nebraska (11/17/69)

BROWNLEE, Robert 'Robbie' - is att Marion Sch (1/12/70); Marion HS student (12/23/70)

BROWNLEE, Miss Rose - is att Marion Sch (11/6/67)

BROWNLEE, William - is att Marion Sch (1/12/70); Marion HS student (12/23/70)

BROWNSVILLE, Town of [may have been in SE 1/4 of Section 16, Pleasant Twp??] - Apr 1849, a plat of 16 lots is laid out by William D. Brown (4/23/68)

BROYLES, G.H. - & Simon Kaufman, A. Kaufman & Moses Kaufman May 1855 lay out Kaufman & Broyles' Addn, Jonesboro (4/23/68)

BRUMFIEL, Jacob - 1867 sells 6 ac in Jefferson Twp to U&L RR Co for $1 (6/25/68)

BRUMLEY, Samuel - 1869 owns Jonesboro property (12/21/70)

BRUSHWILLER, John - owns property in Jonesboro (1/8/68)

BRUSHWILLER, Maria - 1869 owns property in Jonesboro (12/21/70)

BRUSHWILLER, R[obert] A. - Jun 1868 buys license to m M[ary] A. Hanmore/Hannon (7/1/68)

BRUSS, Saloma - is dec; A.B. Reeves admin her estate (8/18/65)

BRYANT, Samuel R. - sells part of a Marion lot to William Lomax (4/30/68); 1868 Monroe Twp landowner (1/12/70)

BUCHANAN, A. - Sheriff, Grant County (1/8/68); is Rep candidate for re-election as Sheriff (2/17/69); buys a lot in Marion from Sarah E. Beshore (12/28/70)

BUCHANAN, James - is att Marion Public Sch (11/13/67)

BUCKLES, James - Judge, Grant Circuit Court (10/16/67)

BUGHER, Jacob - admin estate of Zachariah Hayden, dec (8/18/65); 1867 sells 7 ac in Jefferson Twp to U&L RR Co for $1 (6/25/68); 30 Sep 1867 lays out the 48 lots in Upland (4/23/68); sells Upland lots to Jeremiah Jacks (3/26/68), to John Palmer (10/27/69), to David Horner (2/9/70), & to S.M. Knight (10/5/70)

BULL, John J. - Fairmount Twp taxpayer (1/26/70)

BULLER, Adam - dec; 1869 Van Buren Twp landowner (12/21/70)

BULLER, Andrew - buys 1 ac in Fairmount from Nixon Winslow (2/9/70); sells 80 ac in Fairmount Twp (8/17/70)

BULLER, Franklin - buys 40 ac in Fairmount Twp (10/27/69)

BULLER, Harmon - buys 20 ac in Liberty Twp (1/12/70)

BULLER, John - Fairmount Twp landowner (1/8/68); 21 Sep 1869 m Lydia C. Scott (9/29/69); 1869 Van Buren Twp landowner (12/21/70)

BULLOCK, E.H. - is att Marion Sch (1/12/70); Marion HS student (12/23/70)

BUNDY, Edwin T. - sells 80 ac in Liberty Twp (4/6/70)

BURAKER, Joshua - Sims Twp landowner (1/6/69)

BURDEN, Austin - dec; 1868 his heirs own land in Liberty Twp (1/12/70)

BURDEN, Emma - sells 40 ac in Liberty Twp (5/14/68)

BURDEN, Francis M. - 1867 buys 40 Liberty Twp ac (5/14/68); buys/sells Liberty Twp ac (4/30/68; 4/16/68)

BURIS, Margaret - buys 40 ac in Van Buren Twp (11/3/69)

BURKE, Robert - 1869-71 Fairmount Twp landowner (1/6/69)

BURNS, Henry - buys 40 ac in Sims Twp (1/26/70)

BURNS, John - owns property in New Cumberland (1/6/69)

BURNS, Joseph - 14 Oct 1869 m Sarah A. Hutchins (11/3/69)

BURNS, Michael P. - Apr 1868 buys license to m M[ary] A. Sullivan (5/14/68)

BURSON, Jane - and David Palmer buy m license in March 1868 (4/2/68); buys 30 ac in Monroe Twp (4/9/68)

BURSON, Thomas - 1867 buys 0.4 ac in Franklin Twp (1/15/68); Pleasant Twp landowner (1/6/69)

BUSH, James M. - Nov 1867 buys license to m Mary M. Palmer (12/11/67)

BUSHMILLER, John - 1863 sells 1 lot in Jonesboro (2/12/68)

BUSING, John - buys 1 lot in Fairmount (5/14/68)

BUSINGER, W. - Dec 1868 buys license to m Auracy Willcuts (1/6/69)

BUSK, Michael - buys 85 ac in Richland Twp (4/6/70)

BUSKET, Daniel - sells 40 ac in Liberty Twp (5/14/68)

BUTLER, C.H. - dec; owned property in Marion (1/6/69)

BUTLER, Jesse - 1868 Green Twp landowner (1/12/70); is on committee to fight alcohol in Fairmount (12/29/69)

BUTLER, Miss Queeny - is att Marion Sch (11/6/67)

BYRD, Edwin - is att Marion Sch (1/12/70)

BYRD, James C. - Green Twp landowner (1/8/68)

BYRD, Lou - is att Marion Public Sch (1/12/70)

CALDWELL, Train - organizes support in Liberty Twp for the proposed GR,W&C RR (11/3/69)

CALLOWAY, Cyrus - sells 1 lot in Independence (3/4/68)

CALLOWAY, James - Green Twp landowner (1/8/68)

CALLAWAY, Lydia E. - 1866 buys Independence lots (3/4/68)

CALLOWAY, William - a businessman in Independence (6/16/69); prop, Calloway Stave Factory (1/19/70)

CALLENTINE, Henry - buys 80 Washington Twp ac (2/26/68)

CALLENTINE/CALENTINE, Joseph - 1869 Van Buren Twp landowner (12/21/70)

CALLENTINE/CALENTINE, Sarah - dec; M.D. Marsh admin her estate (12/11/67)

CAMBLIN, E[noch] E. - losing candidate for JP, Van Buren Twp (10/19/70)

CAMMACK, Willis - 1865 buys 120 Liberty Twp ac (4/30/68); dir, Jonesboro & Kokomo Gravel Rd Co (5/7/68); 1865 buys 80 Liberty Twp ac (5/14/68); Liberty Twp dir, Grant Co Agric Soc Fair (7/29/68); dir, Liberty Twp Pike Co (4/28/69); viewer of a

Franklin Twp rd (7/23/69); organizes Liberty Twp support for the proposed GR,W&C RR (11/3/69); elected Liberty Twp Trustee (10/19/70)

CAMPBELL, Charles - owns property in Brownsville (1/6/69); 1868 Pleasant Twp landowner (1/12/70); buys 49 ac in Pleasant Twp from C.W.M. Smith (12/16/70)

CAMPBELL, Enoch - dec; owned Van Buren Twp ac (1/8/68)

CAMPBELL, George W. - sells 40 Monroe Twp ac (12/16/70)

CAMPBELL, John P. - of Pleasant Twp; CW vet (1/26/70)

CAMPBELL, Susan - Richland Twp landowner (1/6/69)

CAMPBELL, Thomas - Richland Twp landowner (1/6/69)

CANDY, Jacob - buys 80 ac in Mill Twp (6/25/68)

CANESVILLE/CARRIENSVILLE - in Grant Co on the Muncie Rd; Mr. __ Carriens (dec several yr ago) kept a 'half-way house' there for several yr; is shown as 'Canesville' on an Indiana map (7/6/70)

CANTWELL, John - admin estate of Rebecca Marshall, dec (12/11/67)

CAPPER, Charles J. - 1868 Jefferson Twp landowner (1/12/70)

CAREINS, George - m; dec; David Heal admin his estate (4/2/68)

CAREY, Elias - sells 10 ac in Franklin Twp (11/24/69)

CAREY, Isaac - 1867 sells 80 ac in Fairmount Twp (1/22/68)

CAREY, James E. - 7 Oct 1869 m Jennette Baldwin, both of Grant Co (10/27/69)

CAREY, John - sells 50 ac in Fairmount Twp (10/27/69)

CAREY, Liston D. - and brother are props, Eagle Shoe Store (12/25/67); buys property in Marion (4/2/68)

CAREY, Lucy M. - age 23; dt Col. O.H.P. Carey; d recently while visiting in Ft. Wayne; bur Marion (8/18/65)

CAREY, Col. O[liver] H.P. - 1867 sells 1 ac near Marion (1/22/68); sells 30 ac in Center Twp to William Morehead (12/29/69); Jun 1870 att Old Settlers meeting (6/8/70)

CAREY, S.B. - prop, Carey Photography (4/2/68)

CAREY, Volney S. - sells property in Marion (4/2/68)

CARLSON, Frank - Aug 1869 buys a license to m C[atharine] Lacy (9/8/69)

CARPENTER, H[enry] M. - Jun 1869 buys license to m H[ester] A. Malone (7/7/69)

CARR, Miss Hattie - b 29 Nov 1852; d near Jonesboro 30 May 1869 (7/23/69)

CARROLL, Benjamin - 1868 owns Marion property (1/12/70)

CARROLL, George - is att Marion Sch (12/18/67)

CARROLL, Jacob - of Monroe Twp; CW vet (1/19/70); buys 80 ac in Monroe Twp from William Simons (4/27/70)

CARROLL, Miss Mary - is att Marion Sch (11/6/67)

CARTER, Asa - sells 2 lots in Fairmount (11/10/69)

CARTER, James A. - Green Twp landowner (1/6/69)

CARTER, Elijah - 1867 buys 1 lot in Jonesboro (2/12/68); Trustee, Jonesboro Schs (3/11/69); officer, Rebekah Lodge, Jonesboro (4/28/69)

CARTER, Ira J. - losing candidate for JP, Jefferson Twp (10/19/70)

CARTER, Isaac J. - sells 40 ac in Fairmount Twp (12/25/67)

CARTER, Isaac W. - buys/sells Liberty Twp ac (11/3/69; 9/14/70)

CARTER, John H. - is elected Jefferson Twp Trustee (10/19/70)

CARVER, Henry - 1868 Van Buren Twp landowner (1/12/70)

CARVER, Levi - 1869 Green Twp landowner (12/21/70)

CARVER, William - 1869 Green Twp landowner (12/21/70)

CASE, Eli - Dec 1868 buys license to m Catharine Thorn (1/6/69)

CASEY, George - Liberty Twp landowner (1/8/68)

CASKEY, John C.F. - 1869 owns Jonesboro property (12/21/70)

CASTLE, Orland G. - of Urbank, OH; 19 Sep 1867 m Mary Lowe of Grant Co (9/25/67)

CEMETERIES
ODD FELLOWS/IOOF - lot owners are called to a meeting (4/6/70); partition between Friends' Cem and Odd Fellows' Cem is now removed (9/14/70)

CENTER TOWNSHIP - Jake W. Beshore, Trustee (9/18/67); John Hodge, Twp Assessor (1/6/69; 1/12/70)

CENTER TOWNSHIP, Schools of - 340 school children reside in Twp, not including Marion (11/17/69)
ACADEMIC INSTITUTE - in Marion, sch bldg is being painted and/or whitewashed; faculty: A.H. Harritt, AM & S. Haggerty, AB & Mrs. Sarah McLain & Mrs. M.E. Adams; spring term begins 9 Mar 1868, lasts for 16 wk; tuition ranges from $1 to $3 per m depending on curriculum chosen by student (3/4/68)
DISTRICT # 6 - site of a meeting of persons forming the Marion & Liberty Rd Co (4/14/69)

CERTAIN, George W. - 21 May 1870 m Ellen Felton (5/25/70)

CHAMBERS, D.W. - Rep candidate, Circuit Prosecutor (7/13/70)

CHAMNESS, Eli - 1869 owns property in Jonesboro (12/21/70)

CHAMNESS, Mary - dec; Enoch P. Jones admin her estate (3/3/69)

CHANEY, Miss Alice - is att Marion Public Sch (11/6/67)

CHARLES, Albert S. - buys 40 ac in Monroe Twp (11/2/70)

CHARLES, Dr. Henry - mbr, Grant Co Medical Soc (11/20/67; 7/13/69); chairs temperance meeting in Fairmount (12/29/69); practices in Fairmount (2/9/70)

CHARLES, James - buys 7.34 ac in Washington Twp (2/26/68)

CHARLES, P. - of Pleasant Twp; raises hogs (11/2/70)

CHARLES, William - contracts with John Secrist to furnish timber for new Grant Co jail (3/11/69)

'CHARLEY' - Dr. S.D. Ayres' saddle horse, d last wk at age 26; Ayres owned him 23 yr (11/16/70)

CHAVIS, Ann - 1869 Liberty Twp landowner (12/21/70)

CHAWNER, Chalkey A. - Van Buren Twp landowner (1/8/68)

CHOPSON, [Elizabeth] - age 107; [m William Chopson]; d in Liberty Twp recently (2/9/70)

CHRISTMAN, Jacob H. - sells Washington Twp ac (1/22/68)

CHURCHES
BACK CREEK FRIENDS - Friends of Grant, Wabash & Miami Co will meet here 14 - 16 Aug 1868; the 3 da of meetings will be att by a committee of the Indiana Yearly Meeting of Friends (8/5/68); 20 Mar 1869 Northwestern [Northern] Quarterly

Meeting met here; the MH which is very large, was completely filled; "There were several good sermons preached, much salutary advice given, and many appropriate prayers, some of them by mere children. Friends were urged to attend the election on the 23rd, and as one nominee for Senator now occupies the platform of equality that the Soc has stood upon for more than a half century, and as they now had an opportunity to show their "faith by their works" it was deemed advisable to vote accordingly. In Friends business meetings, preparative, monthly, quarterly, and yearly meetings they have no delegates whose exclusive right it is to speak and do business: but any member has a right to speak, to make propositions and argue the point, if necessary. And in the meetings for worship, any one may preach, pray, exhort, &c., and finally, the women have the same right, and the same privilege to speak that the men have, and their rights and privileges in the Ministry of the Gospel are on an equality with that of the men. Once more, their platform is 'Equality of Right' all the way through." (3/24/69); 19 Jun 1870 a group living near Independence, while returning home from Meeting, had the tongue of their wagon break frightening the horses; the team ran away and threw all of the party from the wagon, more or less injuring everyone (6/29/70)

FAIRMOUNT FRIENDS - in the MH 20 May 1868, William S. Elliott m Alice C. Radley (6/11/68)

FAIRMOUNT WESLEYAN METHODIST (W.M.) - Joseph M. Little recently m Millie Brooks here (1/20/69)

JONESBORO METHODIST EPISCOPAL (M.E.) - Rev. William E. Pierce, pastor (1/15/68)

LUGAR CREEK CHRISTIAN - 6 mi SE of Marion; Elder __ Tripp, pastor (7/22/68)

MARION CHRISTIAN - Aug 1849, Rev. Enoch Harvey will preach here next Sunday evening (8/3/70); on Washington St between Monroe St & Harrison St; Elder James Maple, pastor (9/18/67); Ch was est here in Oct(?) 1864 (6/9/69)

MARION FRIENDS - the Friends took an active part in the union meeting held yesterday in Shugart's Grove (7/1/68)

MARION METHODIST EPISCOPAL (M.E.) - is on Clay St between Washington St and Boots St; Rev. F.A. Sale, pastor (9/18/67), is now replaced as pastor by Rev. A. Greenman (4/30/68); vacant lots on Washington St were recently purchased as a future bldg site (2/10/69); Rev. Greenman moves

to Springfield, MO (4/21/69); Rev. E.F. Hasty, new pastor (4/28/69)
MARION PRESBYTERIAN - on Clay St between Adams St and Branson St; Rev. H.L. Brown, pastor (9/18/67); Rev. Samuel Sawyer is a f pastor (4/28/69); lady mbrs are having a Fair in Academy Hall (7/23/69); blue stone for foundation of new Ch bldg is obtained from the Sanders Quarry on the E side of the river ca 1 mi N of (below) Marion, work on foundation begins; the old Ch bldg is moved to the Marion sch grounds just S of the Academy Bldg for sch use (6/22/70; 7/13/70); Ch Trustees D.P. Cubberly, Joseph L. Custer, J.H. Fishell appoint Daniel Mowrer to collect funds to erect new Ch. bldg (8/17/70); brick for the new bldg is made by Jacob Coon (10/19/70); work on the new bldg is suspended for the winter (11/30/70)
MARION UNITED BRETHREN (U.B.) - mbr Mrs. J. Sperbeck d 29 May 1868 (6/4/68); has SS of 100 scholars in neighborhood adjoining NE Marion (7/1/68); is 2.5 mi NE of Marion; to have SS picnic 15 Aug 1868 (8/12/68)
MARION WESLEYAN METHODIST (W.M.) - is on Washington St (12/11/67); to have services Sunday 29 Mar 1868 in charge of Rev. E. Marsh, pastor (3/26/68); a SS is organized (5/5/69)
METHODIST PROTESTANT (M.P.) - located in Sims Twp; bldg was almost completed by contractor J.B. Mark when it burned 22 Oct 1870; cause of fire may be accidental (11/2/70)
METHODIST PROTESTANT (M.P.) - is in Washington Twp; Rev. _ Fulton, pastor; 49 persons, converted in this Ch last yr, are baptized in Mississinewa River on Sunday (7/13/69)
MORRIS CHAPEL - SS is reorganized for the summer with officers F.M. Helm, B. Hamaker, Benjamin Bond, Joseph Bond, Samuel McCan, Benjamin Gaines, John Sears, Sarah Bradford, Elizabeth Kelley; tchrs are James Otis, Bethuel Smith, John Otis, Lydia Kelley, Lucy Malotte, Dorcas Culbertson, Matilda Thompson and Eliza Culbertson (5/26/69)
NEW CUMBERLAND PRESBYTERIAN - is being built; will be finished 1 Mar 1869 (2/3/69)
NORTHERN QUARTERLY MEETING OF FRIENDS - was held 18 & 19 Dec 1870 with about 650 in attendance; mbr C.S. Ratliff, in a letter to the Ed, suggests that the 2nd da's meeting succumbed to religious fervor with 2 persons speaking at a time and several persons speaking several times each, 25 to 30 different persons prayed, each meeting session lasted 3 to 4

hours; Ratliff suggests that the Elders should control the religious frenzy (12/21/70)
PLEASANT VIEW CHRISTIAN - 14 Feb 1868 buys 1 ac from Lewis F.R. Morgan (2/26/68)
ST. MARY'S ROMAN CATHOLIC (R.C.) - is on Branson St (6/25/68); soon will build a new Ch, use the old Ch for a sch (11/2/70)
SALEM UNITED BRETHREN (U.B.) - is in Washington Twp; Rev. J.Y. Parlett organized a SS here 2 May 1869 with D. Hillshammer, Supt; R.F. Lenfesty, secy; W. Stout, asst; Samuel Secrist, librarian; W. Hix, song leader; M. Myers, sexton; tchrs are C. Murphy, J. Hix, S. Shinhalt, W.S. Conn, R. Stout, L.N. Stout, T. Steele, S.A. Tinkle, M. Bradford and E. Woolman; SS here last summer had as many as 110 att (5/5/69)
SOUTH MARION FRIENDS - a new Ch in grove in southern suburb of Marion (11/2/70)

CIVIL WAR - Nathaniel T. Davis serv Co K, 40th Ind Regt Inf, was severely WIA in hip at Battle of Spring Hill; John F. Furnish serv Co F, 34th Regt Ind Vol Inf during CW, lost arm in war; Isaac Hamilton serv as 1st Lieut., 12th Ind Battery; Benjamin Boller serv 130th Regt Ind Vol Inf, crippled in war (3/4/68); John L. Hummell serv 8th Ind Regt Inf; John Hull Power serv 36th Regt Ind Vol Inf, WIA at Chickamauga, laid on battlefield for 7 da with no medical attention, was brought home June 1864, was an invalid until death in Fairmount 29 Feb 1868, bur by GAR Post No. 3 (4/2/68); Joseph M. Little serv in 89th Ind Vol Inf (1/20/69); Stephen W. Moore serv 4 y as a soldier (2/17/69); while serv with the 8th Regt, Col. [David] Shunk purchased the warhorse 'Bob' who had been captured in 1863 in the rear of Vicksburg; 'Bob' was stolen from Col. Shunk shortly after his purchase, was re-sold to the US government & branded on the shoulder with 'U.S.'; Col. Shunk recognized him in New Orleans and reclaimed him; Col. Shunk rode him for rest of CW, traveling over 12,000 mi with him; during Battle of Cedar Creek, a spent cannon shot hit 'Bob' on the shoulder or neck, glanced off & struck Col. Shunk in chest, causing Shunk's eventual death [at home in Marion 21 Feb 1865]; Samuel McClure, exor of Col. Shunk's will, sold 'Bob' to Capt. Ridgeway in Savannah, GA in 1865; Ridgeway brought 'Bob' to Grant Co and sold him to B.H. Jones; 'Bob' is 20 yr old, looks fine, but has impaired gait; 'Bob' was recently stolen W of

Marion and was found wandering near the County Poor Farm, perhaps the thief released him when his age was discovered (6/9/69); Deacon Smith, of Marion, serv/d in war (1/5/69); Grant Co CW vets include Robert Andrews, J.W. Beshore, Benjamin Bond, Joseph Bond, Frank Bonham, Jacob Carroll, Joseph Corey, Albert Cotterell, E.W. Creviston, Capt. D.P. Cubberly, J.L. Custer, Foster Davis, Morris Fankboner, Jasper Flaner, Amos Fowler, M.S. Friend, Lieut. Isaac Hamilton, John Hamilton, Capt. S.H. Hamilton, John Hardacre, Sylvester Harnden, Gabriel Hayes, Oliver Hix, Benjamin Holt, J.A. Howard, James S. Jennings, G.W. Jump, Abraham Kelley, Alpheas Leas, Capt. E.S. Lenfesty, J.W. Linder, Joseph Lugar, William McNeal, G.W. Modlin, J.C. Nottingham, John Riffle, George Ruminus, William B. Russell, John Shields, John Smiley, Isaac Smithson, Clark Spears, Capt. James A. Stretch, Jeremiah Strickler, L.D. Swan, G.L. Swope, Capt. T.D. Tharp, S.W. Titus, J.B. Wells, Capt. J.M. Wells, Capt. W. Woods, Marion Wright (1/19/70), John A. Smith, W.R. Vooris, John P. Campbell (1/26/70), William T. Hess (dec) (11/30/70)

CLAIR, John - buys 85 ac in Sims Twp (4/16/68)

CLANIN, Samuel - 1867 buys 80 ac in Richland Twp (1/8/68)

CLANIN, William H. - 19 Nov 1870 m Lydia Buraker, both of Sims Twp (11/23/70)

CLARK, F.J.F. - officer, Rebekah Lodge, Jonesboro (4/28/69)

CLARK, J.H. - dissolves his partnership in City Drugstore with J. Davis; may go into lumber business (10/30/67)

CLARK, James H. - Jun 1870 att Old Settlers meeting (6/8/70)

CLARK, Simon B. - owns property in Jonesboro (1/6/69)

CLARK, Mrs. Susie D. - officer in Rebekah Lodge, Jonesboro (4/28/69); mbr IOGT Lodge, Jonesboro (6/22/70)

CLARKE, Lyman P. - of Pleasant Twp; recently found a stray horse (12/11/67)

CLEAVELAND, Miss M. - Marion Grammar Sch tchr (9/14/70)

CLEVENGER, Cimon/Simon - sells 40 ac in Sims Twp to Evan Myers (4/27/70); buys 40 ac in Sims Twp (10/26/70)

CLEVENGER, William - Mar 1869 buys a license to m B[arbara] A[nn] White (4/7/69)

CLIFTON, M.F. - owns property in Jonesboro (1/6/69)

CLOON, Philip B. - of Cincinnati, OH; 10 Aug 1865 m Evaline Pierce of Marion (8/18/65); dir, Grant Co Live Stock Assn (8/5/68)

CLOTHIER, Henry - sells property in Marion (6/29/70)

CLOUD, Jonathan - Jun 1869 buys license to m R[achel] E. Scott (7/7/69)

CLOUSE, Joseph - buys 81 ac(?) in Franklin Twp (9/14/70)

CLOWSER, N.D. - buys a Harrisburg lot (7/13/70)

CLUNK, George - is att Marion Public Sch (12/18/67)

CLUNK, Henry F. - sells a lot in Marion (1/12/70)

CLUNK, Mary 'Mollie' E. - is att Marion Public Sch (11/6/67); see Henry D. THOMAS

COAN, James W. - Richland Twp delegate to State Rep Conv (2/9/70); Richland Twp dir, 1870 Grant Co Fair (8/3/70)

COAN, Washington - 1869 Sims Twp landowner (12/21/70)

COATS, William - buys/sells Marion lots (2/9/70)

COBB, Calvin - buys 10 ac in Franklin Twp (11/24/69)

COCHRAN, Caroline - Pleasant Twp landowner (1/6/69)

COFFEL/COFFOLD, Jacob - 1866 sells 10 ac in Green Twp to Thomas O. McLain (2/2/70)

COFFIN, Levi - owns property in Jonesboro (1/6/69)

COGGESHALL, Eli - buys 23 Franklin Twp ac (1/8/68; 4/2/68)

COGGESHALL, Nathan - appraises the benefits & damages of Wild Cat Prairie Ditch (3/12/68); Mill Twp dir, Grant Co Agric Soc Fair (7/29/68); a dir, Liberty Twp Pike Co (4/28/69); organizes Mill Twp support for proposed GR,W&C RR (11/3/69); moves to Marion from Mill Twp (11/17/69); buys 30 ac in Center Twp (1/12/70), & sells 182 ac in Mill & Franklin Twp's (5/11/70)

COLE, Philip - of near Jonesboro; is arrested & jailed on suspicion of attempting to derail a train on the C&CI tracks on 10 Dec 1867 (2/12/68)

COLEMAN, D[aniel] - viewer of a rd between Jonesboro and Harrisburg (7/23/69)

COLEMAN, James F. - admin estate of William Coleman, dec (10/23/67)

COLEMAN, Thomas - v pres of Old Settlers meeting (6/8/70)

COLEMAN, William - dec; James F. Coleman admin his estate (10/23/67)

COLLINS, George W. - 11 Feb 1869 m Laura Hamilton of Liberty Twp (2/17/69; 3/3/69)

COLLINS, James - Jefferson Twp landowner (1/8/68)

COLLINS, William S. - a Rep of Liberty Twp (6/8/70)

COLVILLE, John H. - buys 40 ac in Liberty Twp (10/19/70)

COLVER, F.T. - telegrapher, Atlantic & Pacific Telegraph Line, Marion (12/15/69); his wife is dt William K. Bartlett (dec) (6/8/70)

COMER, Lilburn H. - 1869 Richland Twp landowner (12/21/70)

COMPTON, Alex W. - Mar 1869 buys a license to m M[ary] A. Hahn (4/7/69)

COMPTON, J.W. - f of Piqua, OH; prop, Compton Furniture Store (8/24/70)

COMPTON, Joseph D. - Sims Twp landowner (1/8/68); is elected JP, Sims Twp (10/19/70)

CONARD, John - Mar 1868 buys license to m Rebecca Harl (4/2/68)

CONAWAY, Mary M. - 1869 Sims Twp landowner (12/21/70)

CONES, Robert - Liberty Twp landowner (1/8/68)

CONGER, Calvin - Monroe Twp landowner (1/8/68)

CONN, Ephraim - sells 71 ac in Van Buren Twp (1/22/68)

CONN, Ezra - buys 40 ac in Washington Twp (2/12/68)

CONN, George - 1869 Washington Twp landowner (12/21/70)

CONN, W.S. - SS tchr, Salem Ch (5/5/69)

CONNELLY, J[ohn] - Aug 1869 buys a license to m E[mily] Ballinger (9/8/69)

CONNER, Eva - Franklin Twp landowner (1/6/69)

CONNER, Ezra - Franklin Twp landowner (1/8/68)

CONNER, Isaiah, Esq - 1867-68 buys lots in Jalapa (1/22/68)

CONNER, Jack - a pauper (3/11/69); d recently in Grant Co Asylum [poor farm] (2/9/70)

CONNER, Nelson - Apr 1838 lays out Conner's Addn, Marion (4/16/68); 1867 sells 40 ac in Liberty Twp (1/22/68); organizes Pleasant Twp support for proposed GR,W&C RR (11/3/69)

CONNER, Sylvanus - 1868 Richland Twp landowner (1/12/70)

CONNER, William - 11 Feb 1869 m Margaret J. Tucker (2/17/69; 3/3/69)

CONNER, William - 3 Feb 1870 m Mrs. Margaret J. Conner (2/9/70)

COOK, George K. - Washington Twp landowner (1/8/68)

COOK, J.D. - 1849 is publ of 'Marion Western Union' (7/6/70); now lives in Toledo, OH (8/3/70)

COOK, James - Liberty Twp landowner (1/8/68)

COOK, James C. - Feb 1869 buys license to m Lorinda Bole (3/3/69)

COOK, John M. - sells 30.97 ac in Pleasant Twp to Henry Miller (1/29/68); Pleasant Twp landowner (1/6/69)

COOK, Joseph - buys 40 ac in Franklin Twp (1/29/68)

COOK, Mary A. - sells a Marion lot (1/29/68)

COOK, Milton - sells 40 ac in Jefferson Twp (3/30/70)

COON, George W. - sells 2 lots in Marion (6/29/70)

COON, Jacob - of near Marion; elderly; d recently (2/2/70)

COON, Jacob - of N of Marion; made the bricks used to build the new Marion Presbyterian Ch (10/19/70)

COPPOCK, Calvin - 1867 sells Jonesboro property (1/15/68); owns property in Jonesboro (1/6/69); of Jonesboro; is a Rep candidate for Sheriff (2/17/69); 11 Aug 1870 m Elizabeth A. Anderson (8/17/70); is elected JP, Mill Twp (10/19/70)

COPPOCK, David M. - sells 40 ac in Richland Twp (4/27/70)

CORDER, Jacob - Fairmount Twp landowner (1/6/69)

CORDER, Robert - 1868 owns property in Jonesboro (1/12/70)

COREY, Joseph - of Van Buren Twp; CW vet (1/19/70)

COREY, Dr. Lavanner - mbr, Grant Co Medical Soc (11/20/67); 1866 buys 62 ac in Van Buren Twp & 1867 sells 62 ac in Van Buren Twp to Moses Adamson (4/2/68)

COREY, William D. - buys 120 ac in Van Buren Twp (3/4/68)

CORN, J.F. - viewer of a rd in Jefferson Twp (7/23/69)

CORPORAL, A[nthony] - Mar 1870 buys license to m M[ary] L. Johnson (4/6/70)

COTTAGE CORNER - is about midway between Fairmount & Independence; has a blacksmith, a cooper, a shoemaker, photograph gallery; a small grist mill is attached to a steam sawmill, cutting lumber for Behimer's; Goodwin & Fankboner, f of Jonesboro, have a general store and run a huckster wagon; there is no post office here (6/16/69)

COTTERELL, Albert - is on Co bd to assess property (1/5/70); CW vet (1/19/70); is Franklin Twp Assessor (10/19/70)

COTTON, James A. - buys 9 lots in Marion (10/27/69; 5/11/70)

COUNTS, Elijah - 1867 sells 40 Washington Twp ac (4/30/68)

COVALT, Abraham - buys 40 ac in Green Twp (4/13/70)

COWGILL, F.A. - sells 203 ac in Mill Twp (1/26/70)

COX, J.W. - Dec 1868 buys license to m Sarah A. Antrim (1/6/69)

COX, Nathan - Jun 1869 buys license to m Jennie Fisher (6/2/69; 7/7/69)

COX, Nathanial - buys 40 ac in Liberty Twp (1/29/68)

COX, Oliver - sells 40 ac in Washington Twp (5/18/70)

CRABB, Henry - Fairmount Twp landowner (1/8/68)

CRAIG, George - 1869 Green Twp landowner (12/21/70)

CRANDLE, Sarah - Monroe Twp landowner (1/6/69)

CRANSTON, Archibald - Apr 1869 buys license to m Angeline Harper (5/5/69)

CRAWFORD, Hugh - Jefferson Twp landowner (1/8/68)

CRAWFORD, John - admin for estate of Noah Hardy, dec (8/18/65); sells Jefferson Twp ac (4/27/70; 12/7/70)

CREEKS
BIG DEER CREEK - in Liberty Twp; "previous to draining, was a vast expanse of water, with no perceptible current. Since ditching, the water is confined to the channel most of the time..." (2/9/70)
PIPE CREEK - Co Comm gave $150 to Pleasant Twp Trustee to aid in constructing a bridge over Pipe Creek and also over Taylor's Creek, both on the Delphi State Rd (3/11/69)

CRETSINGER, David - buys 80 Washington Twp ac (9/14/70)

CREVISTON, Daniel - sells 120 Washington Twp ac (6/29/70)

CREVISTON, E.W. - of Washington Twp; CW vet (1/19/70); a Rep (6/8/70)

CREVISTON, Elijah - Nov 1867 buys license to m Lida A. Whinney (12/11/67)

CREVISTON, Julietta - buys 2 lots in Marion (2/26/68)

CRIM, Noah - buys 40 ac in Fairmount Twp & sells 40 ac in Fairmount Twp to Franklin Buller (10/27/69)

CRIST, Jacob - buys 303 ac in Van Buren Twp (1/15/68)

CRIST, Morris H. - Trustee, Richland Twp (9/18/67; 10/19/70); last wk while threshing his wheat with a horse-powered machine, a fire burned almost all of his wheat crop and the threshing machine (8/18/69)

CRISWELL, Elizabeth - Franklin Twp landowner (1/6/69)

CROOK, Sally - 1867 buys 6.18 ac in Franklin Twp (3/26/68)

CROSS, Jeremiah - Green Twp landowner (1/8/68)

CROSSON/CROSSEN, Lashla - Jun 1868 buys license to m M[ary] A. Patterson (7/1/68)

CROW, Joseph - sells 100 ac in Monroe Twp (10/26/70)

CROW, William - of Jefferson Twp; recently found 5 stray hogs (12/11/67)

CROWELL, Benjamin - Rep candidate for Coroner (7/13/70); Grant Co Coroner (11/23/70)

CRULL, H.H. - 1869 Center Twp landowner (12/21/70)

CRUMRINE, William - is att Marion Public Sch (11/6/67)

CUBBERLY, Major __ - f of Marion; lives in Chillicothe, MO (4/7/69), where he is making & selling brick (4/28/69)

CUBBERLY, Capt./Dr. David P. - Aug 1849 is dentist in Marion (8/3/70); dentist here since 29 Dec 1865; his dental office is over Swayzee & Co store on W side of Square (9/18/67); Sch Trustee for Marion Schs (7/1/68); secy, Grant Co Agric Soc Fair (7/29/68; 8/3/70); CW vet (1/19/70); att Old Settlers meeting (6/8/70); Trustee, Marion Presbyterian Ch (8/17/70)

CUBBERLY, Eddie - s George and Sarah Cubberly; d 6 Jan 1868 (1/22/68)

CUBBERLY, George - sells 1 lot in Marion (6/1/70)

CUBBERLY, Lewis - is att Marion Sch (11/13/67; 1/12/70)

CULBERTSON, C.T. - buys 9 ac in Green Twp (11/2/70)

CULBERTSON, Davidson - is replaced by James Brownlee as Grant Co Treas (8/18/65); sells 40 ac in Liberty Twp (3/30/70)

CULBERTSON, Dorcas - tchr, Morris Chapel SS (5/26/69)

CULBERTSON, Eliza - tchr, Morris Chapel SS (5/26/69)

CULBERTSON, Lucinda - 1869-71 Center Twp landowner (12/21/70)

CURLESS, Marion - Nov 1867 buys license to m Angeline Covalt (12/11/67)

CUSTER, __ - s M/M J.L. Custer; last wk his mother saw him fall into a well on the lid of the well, water in the well is 15 ft deep and comes to within 10 ft of the surface; he laid on the floating wooden lid until rescued by Mr. __ Maddux (8/4/69)

CUSTER, Joseph L., Esq - atty; office is over Carey's Bookstore on N side of CH Square (9/18/67); moves his office to above/ over the Post Office (10/16/67); treas, Marion Literary Soc (1/15/68); candidate for State's atty, Common Pleas Court (8/5/68; 7/13/70); forms law partnership with G.W. Harvey with an office in White's Bldg (6/9/69); CW vet (1/19/70); Trustee, Marion Presbyterian Ch (8/17/70); Prosecutor, Common Pleas Court (8/31/70)

CUTTING, Adolphus - Van Buren Twp landowner (1/6/69)

DAILEY, Dennis - dec; owned Washington Twp land (1/8/68)

DAILEY, Joseph S. - Mar 1870 buys license to m E[mma] Gutelius (4/6/70)

DALBY, Nathan - 1 Jan 1868 m Nancy Murray in Jonesboro (1/8/68)

DANIEL, Margaret - buys 40 ac in Jefferson Twp (12/21/70)

DARBY, Samuel - b Butler Co, OH; age 62; m; 1846 came to IN; mbr M.E. Ch; 8 Sep 1870 d at his home near Xenia (10/5/70)

DAVIDSON, Isaiah - dec; owned Fairmount Twp land (1/6/69)

DAVIS, Caleb B. - buys 40 ac in Franklin Twp (12/25/67)

DAVIS, David F. - manuf & sells grain cradles near bridge in Marion (6/16/69; 4/19/71); prop of a wagon shop (11/23/70)

DAVIS, Delilah - Sims Twp landowner (1/8/68)

DAVIS, Elwood - sells 84 ac in Mill Twp (10/19/70)

DAVIS, Foster - 1867 sells Fairmount property (1/15/68; 4/2/68); of Fairmount Twp; CW vet (1/19/70)

DAVIS, George - Jun 1870 att Old Settlers meeting (6/8/70)

DAVIS, Henry - sells 40.25 ac in Liberty Twp (2/9/70)

DAVIS, Henry, Jr. - Liberty Twp landowner(1/8/68)

DAVIS, Jacob O. - lives on rd. to Jonesboro 1.5 mi from Marion (8/18/65)

DAVIS, Job - Apr 1869 buys license to m Keziah Felton (5/5/69); 1869 sells 40 ac in Liberty Twp (1/5/70)

DAVIS, John - sole prop, City Drugstore after he dissolves his partnership with J.H. Clark (10/30/67)

DAVIS, Kelly W. - sells 40 ac in Liberty Twp (11/3/69)

DAVIS, Lorena A. - Washington Twp & Franklin Twp landowner (1/8/68)

DAVIS, Nathaniel T. - serv Co K, 40th Ind Regt Inf during CW; severely WIA in hip at Battle of Spring Hill, is now unable to make a living by manual labor; Union Party candidate for Grant Co Recorder (3/4/68)

DAVIS, Prichard - buys/sells Franklin Twp ac (7/20/70)

DAVIS, Samuel - buys 80 ac in Van Buren Twp (9/14/70)

DAVIS, W[illiam] F. - is elected JP, Liberty Twp (10/19/70)

DAVIS, Wyllys - buys a lot in Jonesboro (7/6/70)

DAWSON, John H. - Pleasant Twp landowner (1/8/68)

DEAN, Patrick H. - buys 1 lot near Fairmount (4/30/68)

DEBOLT, Charles F. - 1869-71 owns property in Jalapa (12/21/70); sells a lot near Jalapa (12/16/70)

DEEREN, Olen H. - sells 40 ac in Van Buren Twp (4/13/70)

DEEREN, Richard - buys 2 lots in Upland (2/9/70)

DELAHAY, R.A. - buys a lot in Jonesboro (8/17/70)

DeLONG, Dominie - is att Marion Sch (11/6/67)

DeLONG, J.A. - 1869 buys 1 lot in Marion (1/5/70)

DeLONG, Mollie - is att Marion HS (12/23/70)

DeLONG, Portius - is att Marion Sch (1/12/70); Marion HS student (12/23/70)

DeLONG, William C. - prop, DeLong Store (10/30/67); buys a lot in Marion (10/5/70; 10/19/70)

DeVORE, Elbridge - Green Twp landowner (1/8/68)

DICKEN, George - May 1868 buys license to m M[artha] A. Creviston (6/4/68)

DICKERSON, R.H. - sells 40 ac in Jefferson Twp (4/27/70)

DICKEY, Benjamin F. - buys 160 ac in Liberty Twp (4/27/70)

DICKEY, Benjamin W. - sells 80 ac in Liberty Twp for $1,860 to John A. Stuckey (12/25/67); Liberty Twp landowner (1/6/69)

DICKEY, James - of NE Madison Co; son-in-law of Emily Wells (3/12/68)

DICKEY, Jasper - 1868 Liberty Twp landowner (1/12/70)

DICKEY, Joseph - of NE Madison Co (3/12/68)

DICKEY, Lucretia - 1868 owns Independence property (1/12/70)

DICKEY, Newton - 1869 Liberty Twp landowner (12/21/70)

DICKEY, Oliver H. - 1866 sells 40 ac in Liberty Twp (5/14/68)

DILL, Isaac H. - 1869 Green Twp landowner (12/21/70)

DILLON, Albert Y., MD - [23 Jan 1869 m Mary M. Marsh]; recently came to Van Buren Twp; claims to be a MD; last wk was arraigned before Esq A. Diltz on a charge of bigamy; bail is set at $500, but he is released from custody (2/3/69); case is dismissed because charges are false (3/3/69); moves back to his native WV (4/21/69)

DILLON, James - buys 40 ac in Washington Twp (7/6/70)

DILLON, Jesse - dec; owned land in Fairmount Twp (1/6/69)

DILLON, Margaret - Fairmount Twp landowner (1/6/69)

DILLON, Sarah - buys 1 lot in Marion (2/9/70)

DILLON, William B. - buys property in Jonesboro from Hiram S. Simons (4/30/68); sells property in Jonesboro (10/26/70)

DILTZ, Andrew - JP, Center Twp (10/19/70)

DITCHES
BIG DEER CREEK DITCHING CO - dir are James Scott, E.M. Kimes and Thomas E. Rush (9/18/67)

WILD CAT PRAIRIE DITCH - is in Green Twp; B.H. Jones petitions for this ditch; Joshua Marshall, Nathan Coggshall and Sidney Harvey are appointed to appraise the benefits & damages of this ditch (3/12/68)

DOAN, Col. Thomas - age 37; serv 101st Ind Vol Regt during CW; d 10 Aug 1865 (8/18/65); Sarah E. Doan admin his estate (7/20/70)

DODD, John W. - Aug 1849 was in stove business in Marion; more recently was Indiana State Auditor (8/3/70)

DOGGETT, M[artin] V. - Mar 1869 buys a license to m M[ary J.] Haines (4/7/69)

DOLAN, Thomas F. - 26 May 1868 was m to Julia Ann Dillon by Rev. Charles Mangin (6/4/68; 6/11/68)

DOLLAR, John - 1867 buys 40 ac in Jefferson Twp from Otho Hardy (4/2/68); Jefferson Twp landowner (1/6/69)

DOLMAN, John - owns property in Jonesboro (1/6/69); sells property in Jonesboro to Stephen Benbow (12/7/70)

DOLMAN, William A. - 9 Jan 1869 is m to Mrs. Mary A. Kester by W.M. Pierce in Jonesboro M.E. parsonage (1/6/69; 1/13/69)

DONAHUE, Michael - 1869 owns Marion property (12/21/70)

DOOLEY, Samuel - a yg man of W of Marion accused of placing logs on the RR track 4 mi W of Marion; his relatives intend sending him to KS to escape punishment by the railroaders (6/8/70)

DOOLY, David R. - buys 40 ac in Franklin Twp from Jacob Druckemiller (1/12/70); is elected JP, Franklin Twp (10/19/70)

DOTY, Mrs. Mary - 1869 sells a lot in Marion (1/5/70)

DOUGHERTY, E. - b in Maryland; a yg man; reared as a Roman Catholic; mbr Friends; d 20 Jul 1868 (7/29/68)

DOUGLASS, John L. - 1869 Franklin Twp landowner (12/21/70)

DOWNARD, Catharine C. - buys 1 ac in Center Twp (4/2/68)

DOWNING, John - Green Twp landowner (1/6/69)

DOWNS, Abraham - sells 40 ac in Green Twp (10/19/70)

DOWNS, James - Mar 1870 buys license to m S[usan] Kelley (4/6/70)

DOYLE, T[homas] B. - of Van Buren Twp; is on a Co bd to assess property (1/5/70)

DOYLE, William - of Van Buren Twp; 3 Nov 1870 m Sarah J. Hays, dt William Hays (11/2/70)

DOYLE, William E. - prop, New Cash Store (8/12/68)

DRAPER, Hugh - buys 40 ac in Jefferson Twp (12/25/67)

DRAPER, John - dec; 1869 owned Center Twp land (12/21/70)

DROOK, Alfred - viewer for new rd in Richland Twp (3/11/69)

DROOK, James M./W. - 8 Aug 1869 m Mary Buraker (8/11/69; 9/8/69)

DRUCK, Jacob - Richland Twp landowner (1/6/69); sells 40 ac in Richland Twp to John Irvine (12/15/69)

DRUCK/DROOK, William - Sims Twp landowner (1/8/68); 1867 buys 40 ac in Sims Twp from Lewis Harter (1/29/68)

DRUCKEMILLER, Jacob - organizes Franklin Twp support for the proposed GR,W&C RR (11/3/69); sells 40 ac in Franklin Twp to David R. Dooly (1/12/70)

DRUCKEMILLER, John - Franklin Twp dir, 1870 Grant Co Fair (8/3/70)

DRUCKEMILLER, Mahala - Franklin Twp landowner (1/8/68)

DRUCKEMILLER, W[illiam] A. - Dec 1868 buys license to m M[ary] Lloyd (1/6/69)

DRULEY, Ransom - Franklin Twp landowner (1/8/68)

DRULY, Daniel - Jun 1870 att Old Settlers meeting (6/8/70)

DUFF, Leo F. - sells a Marion lot to Rufus W. Bailey (11/10/69)

DUGAN, Robert - tenant on farm of Robert Beatty 3 mi S of Marion; a brown mare is stolen from his stable (9/14/70)

DULING, Edmund - 1864 is a Grant Co Comm (6/9/69); buys a lot in Jonesboro (3/30/70)

DULING, Elijah - 1864 buys 80 ac in Jefferson Twp (12/25/67)

DULING, Joel - 1862 buys 80 ac in Fairmount Twp (12/25/67); May 1868 buys license to m Mary C. Roush (6/4/68)

DULING, John W. - buys 40 ac in Fairmount Twp (12/25/67)

DULING, Solomon - 1862 sells 80 ac in Fairmount Twp; 1864 sells 80 ac in Jefferson Twp (12/25/67); Trustee, Jefferson Twp (9/18/67)

DUNCAN, Andrew - 16 Mar 1870 m Elvira Bowman in Marion (4/6/70)

DUNKLE, William - Marshal, Jonesboro (5/11/70)

DUNN, Alexander - f of Grant Co; d 10 May 1870 at his home near Leroy, Coffee Co, KS (5/25/70)

DUNN, George F., Esq - a Grant Co farmer (7/23/69); Jun 1870 att Old Settlers meeting (6/8/70); Pleasant Twp dir, 1870 Grant Co Fair (8/3/70); elected JP, Pleasant Twp (10/19/70); raises hogs (11/2/70); has a litter of 18 pigs (11/23/70)

DUNN, Mrs. Lucinda - see Thomas GREGG

DUNSETH, M[arion] A. - Feb 1868 buys license to m M[elissa] A. Harmon (3/4/68)

DUNWOODY, Alex - 1868 owns property in Marion (1/12/70)

EAKINS, Johnson - Trustee, Green Twp (9/18/67)

EAKINS, William S. - Nov 1867 buys license to m Phoebe C. Echelbarger (12/11/67)

EARL, Edward - buys a lot in Harrisburg (1/12/70)

EARL, Isaac T. - sells 85 ac in Sims Twp to John Clair (4/16/68); Sims Twp landowner (1/6/69)

EATON, John - buys 100 ac in Liberty Twp (2/2/70)

EBBERT, Enoch - Liberty Twp landowner (1/8/68)

EBY, Jacob G. - 25 Mar 1869 m Sarah E. Blinn (3/24/69; 4/7/69); sells property in Marion (12/29/69); buys 80 ac in Franklin Twp (4/13/70)

ECHELBARGER, Christian - Nov 1867 buys license to m Mary A. Matchett (12/11/67)

ECKFIELD/ECKFELD, George N. - 1864 sells 1 lot in Marion to Sarah Thomas (4/16/68); sells a lot in Fairmount (12/15/69)

EDDINGTON, William - Liberty Twp landowner (1/6/69)

EDWARD(S), John W. - Center Twp landowner (1/6/69)

ECKHART/EKHART, Eden - Sims Twp landowner (1/6/69)

ELLIOTT, Dr. D[avid] S. - mbr, Grant Co Medical Soc; recently traveled to Europe (11/20/67); grad, Medical Dept., Univ of Michigan; had medical practice in Fairmount; mbr Quaker Ch; 5 Jun 1869 d at his father's home near Richmond (7/13/69)

ELLIOTT, Isaac - Center Twp taxpayer (1/26/70)

ELLIOTT, J.N. - is elected Fairmount Twp Assessor (10/19/70)

ELLIOTT, Jacob R. - owns property in Jalapa (1/6/69)

ELLIOTT, Lewis H. - Sheriff of Grant County (9/18/67); sells 200 ac in Washington Twp to Elias W. McKinney (4/6/70)

ELLIOTT, Samuel - 1867 buys 10 ac in Liberty Twp (4/30/68)

ELLIOTT, William S. - s Reuben and Rebecca Elliott; in Fairmount Friends MH 20 May 1868 m Alice C. Radley, dt Samuel and Mary Radley, f of Essex Co, England (6/11/68)

ELLIS, J.W. - Liberty Twp landowner (1/8/68)

ELLIS, Jehu J. - Oct 1854 lays out Ellis' Addn, Jonesboro (4/23/68)

ELWOOD, D.R. - is Van Buren Twp Assessor (10/19/70)

EMBREE, Jesse - sells 80 ac in Monroe Twp to Jonathan C. Hays (3/26/68); Center Twp taxpayer (1/26/70)

EMEL, David - buys 40 ac in Mill Twp (10/5/70)

EMERSON, Major W.C. - business agent/manager for the RR in Marion, built & has charge of new Marion Depot (7/1/68)

ENGLAND, Sephronia - Green Twp landowner (1/8/68)

ENTZMINGER, David - buys Jonesboro lot (3/12/68); viewer for new Jefferson Twp rd (3/11/69); Mill Twp taxpayer (1/26/70)

ENYART, Allen - Franklin Twp landowner (1/8/68)

ENYART, Samuel - sells 40 ac in Pleasant Twp (4/30/68)

ERTLE, Charles - owns land in Green Twp (1/6/69)

ESHELMAN, Annie - is att Marion Public Sch (11/6/67)

ESHELMAN, Peter - sells a lot in Marion (6/29/70)

EVANS, Calvin J. - sells 60 ac in Mill Twp to Seth Gordon & buys a lot in Jonesboro from [Dr.] T.A. Lucas (4/2/68)

EVANS, Fountain - 1867 buys ac in Liberty Twp (1/8/68)

EVANS, George - Center Twp landowner (1/6/69)

EVANS, Henry - is att Marion Public Sch (11/6/67)

EVANS, John C. - 9 Mar 1869 in Jonesboro m Mary E. Smith (3/11/69; 4/7/69)

EVANS, Piner - is a Grant Co Comm (10/1/67)

EVANS, William - 1865 buys 80 ac in Van Buren Twp; 1867 buys 80 ac in Van Buren Twp from Jane H.H. Todd (1/8/68)

EVANS, William M. - buys 12 ac in Center Twp from Ira Schooley (8/17/70); sells 8 ac in Center Twp (11/30/70)

EVISTON, George E. - 1867 buys 1 lot in Jonesboro from James A. Moore & buys 2 lots in Harrisburg (6/25/68)

EVISTON, Mrs. S.E. - officer, Rebekah Lodge, Jonesboro (4/28/69)

EWARD, Dorcas - owns property in Marion (1/6/69)

EWARD, John W., Esq - publ of 'Marion Journal' (8/18/65); 1868 owns Center Twp land (1/12/70)

EWING, Sam - has a collection of old coins (7/7/69)

EWING, Thomas - buys 40 ac in Liberty Twp (4/13/70)

EYESTONE, Asbury - Mar 1868 buys license to m F[rances] D. Clark (4/2/68)

EYESTONE, George W. - 1 Jan 1868 m Hattie A. Buchanan, dt A. Buchanan (1/8/68); sells his interest in 'Stove Depot' to Jesse

Iams; intends move to KS (2/17/69); and D. Eyestone now are in Girard, KS where they have a hardware & stove business (5/5/69; 1/19/70)

EYESTONE, Jonathan W. - and wife of near Marion celebrated their 50th wedding anniv 20 Jan 1870; their youngest dt, [Florence O.,] was also m on that date (1/26/70); Jun 1870 att Old Settlers meeting (6/8/70); wife is Nancy (10/26/70)

FAIRMOUNT, Town of - 28 Dec 1850 original plat of 45 lots is laid out by David Stanfield; 6 Oct 1852 Jonathan Baldwin lays out 22 lots of Baldwin's Addn; 29 Oct 1857 Jonathan Baldwin lays out 20 lots of Baldwin's 2nd Addn; 14 Jan 1859 Jonathan Baldwin lays out 6 lots of Baldwin's 3rd Addn; 2 Aug 1859(?) David Stanfield lays out 8 lots of Stanfield's Addn (4/23/68); town has 3 drygoods stores, 1 grocery store, 1 drugstore, 1 harness shop, 1 boot & shoe store, 1 tin shop, 3 physicians; has no saloon; has a 3-wheeled velocipede that is too large to be run on the sidewalk (7/21/69); is on E bank of Back Creek; streets are dry & clean; has ca 400 people, Quaker element predominates, "much of the simple beauty and attractiveness of the place is due to these plain, good people"; town has 3 drygoods, 2 provision/grocery stores, 2 millinery, one drugstore, 1 saddlery shop, 2 boot/ shoe makers, 1 tinshop, 1 blacksmith/ wagonmaker's shop, 1 hotel, 1 steam 'grist' mill, 1 woolen mill, a Friends Ch, a Wesleyan Methodist Ch, a large seminary with a good sch with 3 tchrs and 120 pupils; there are 4 medical men, Dr's. Charles, Horn, Henley and Wright (2/9/70)
BALDWIN & SMITH GROCERY - mentioned (2/9/70)
BOGUE MERCANTILE - a new store (2/9/70)
BUSING GROCERY - John Busing, prop (2/9/70)
ELLIOTT & WILSON DRUGSTORE - mentioned (9/25/67)
FAIRMOUNT FLOURING MILL/WINSLOW MILL - J.P. Winslow, prop; a steam 'grist' mill (2/9/70)
WILSON, WILSON & CO - Micajah Wilson, prop (2/9/70)
WINSLOW, OAKLEY & ELLIOTT STORE - a new store; J.N. Elliott is a prop (2/9/70)

FAIRMOUNT SCHOOLS - tchrs for fall session of the HS are H.A. Hutchins, B.C. Harris & Miss Mollie Winslow (8/3/70)

FAIRMOUNT TOWNSHIP - sometime after 1847 Fairmount Twp was formed from Union Twp (which ceased to exist) and a 2 mi wide strip taken from the E edge of Liberty Twp (7/20/70); J.P. Winslow, Trustee (9/18/67); Morgan O. Lewis, Trustee (6/29/70)

FAIRMOUNT TOWNSHIP, Schools of - 617 school children reside in Twp (11/17/69)

FALLIS/FOLLIS, Amos L. - Feb 1868 buys license to m Mary Hayden (3/4/68)

FANKBONER, George W. - 1867 sells 1 lot in Jonesboro to Elijah Carter (2/12/68); sells 1 lot in Jonesboro to John W. Shideler (4/30/68); viewer for a rd in Grant Co (6/23/69)

FANKBONER, John, Sr. - sells 30 ac in Mill Twp (7/20/70)

FANKBONER, Levi L. - sells 1/3 interest in two mills at Jonesboro to Sylvester R. Fankboner (3/12/68); buys 160 ac in Fairmount Twp from Zimri Richardson (4/27/70)

FANKBONER, Mary E. - 1869 owns property in Jonesboro (12/21/70)

FANKBONER, Morris - admin estate of Drucilla Hiatt,dec (9/18/67); Trustee, Jonesboro Schs; Constable, Mill Twp (3/11/69); of Jonesboro; CW vet (1/19/70); mbr Jonesboro Masonic Lodge (5/18/70); sells property in Jonesboro to E.P. Jones (7/13/70)

FANKBONER, Sylvester R. - buys 1/3 interest in two mills at Jonesboro from Levi L. Fankboner (3/12/68)

FANN, James - buys a lot in Marion (11/10/69)

FANNING, C[olumbus] - Aug 1869 buys license to m M[ahala] J. Moorman (9/8/69)

FANNING, Marinda [(Rood)] - 1869 owns property in Farmington (1/6/69; 12/21/70)

FANSLER, Margaret - 1867 buys 20 ac in Green Twp (1/8/68)

FANSLER, William - 1869 Franklin Twp landowner (12/21/70)

FARMINGTON, Town of - was laid out with 26 lots on 4 Apr 1848 by Benjamin Hillman (4/23/68); a number of lots are vacated by order of Grant Co Comms (6/23/69)

FARR, John N. - Mar 1869 buys a license to m Susannah Farr (4/7/69)

FAULKNER, Thomas B. - sells 40 ac in Monroe Twp (11/2/70)

FEAR, George W. - Apr 1869 buys license to m Elizabeth Daniels (5/5/69)

FEAR, James E. - sells 5 ac in Fairmount Twp (12/29/69)

FEE, John G. - 1867 sells 160 ac in Franklin Twp to William Lomax (1/15/68); Franklin Twp landowner (1/6/69)

FEIGHNER, Adam - sells 40 ac in Washington Twp to Adam J. Feighner (5/14/68); is Washington Twp Trustee (10/19/70)

FELTON, Charles - m; last wk his house, 1.25 mi NW of Center Sch, Liberty Twp, burned (11/23/70)

FELTON, George - Liberty Twp landowner (1/6/69)

FELTON, John - 1842 buys 44.25 ac in Liberty Twp from Larkin Hall; 1857 buys 44.25 ac in Liberty Twp (1/15/68)

FERGUSON, J.H. - & C.A. Ferguson buy 40 ac in Monroe Twp from James F. Hultz (11/10/69)

FERGUSON, Josiah - buys 30 ac in Monroe Twp (5/14/68)

FERREE, Oliver S. - 27 May 1869 m Mary 'Molly' L. Miles, dt W.C. Miles of Marion (6/2/69)

FIANT, Jesse - 3 Dec 1868 m Sarah E. Pence, both of Richland Twp (1/6/69)

FIELDS, Nancy - sells land in Pleasant Twp (4/30/68)

FIELDS, William - is dec (8/18/65)

FIELDS, William L. - Pleasant Twp landowner (1/6/69)

FIGLEY, Meredith J. - is att Marion Public Sch (12/18/67)

FINE, David M. - sells 40 ac in Monroe Twp (1/22/68)

FINK, James C. - buys 120 ac in Liberty Twp from E. Osborn (12/15/69); is a Liberty Twp blacksmith who can make a "shucking peg" or "remodel a steam boiler" (2/9/70)

FINLEY & ALLEN STEAM MILL/LITTLE RIDGE MILLS - is at W end of the completed part of the Little Ridge Gravel Rd; is stationary mill with upright saw in Liberty Twp 1 mi E of Big Deer Creek; it cuts up large quantities of lumber & has a set of burrs attached that, one da each wk, grinds corn (2/9/70)

FINLEY, Edward H. - of Little Ridge Mills; is severely injured at Deer Creek Hill when his spring wagon upset (6/29/70)

FINNEY, John, Sr. - 1866 sells 24 rods(?) in Monroe Twp to Monroe Twp Trustee [for schoolyard (?)] for $10 (5/14/68)

FISHELL, Belle - 1869 owns property in Marion (12/21/70)

FISHELL, J.H. - sells Grover & Baker Sewing Machines from his residence on Branson St opposite the Catholic Ch (6/25/68); Trustee, Marion Presbyterian Ch (8/17/70)

FISHER, Daniel - Richland Twp landowner (1/6/69)

FISHER, Jonathan - Richland Twp landowner (1/6/69)

FITZGERALD, William - recently m Anna C. Grindle (2/12/68; 3/4/68)

FLANER, Jasper - of Liberty Twp; CW vet (1/19/70)

FLEENER, Jonathan 'John' - of just W of Independence; his house recently burned (1/13/69)

FLEENER, Martha - 1869 owns property in Independence (12/21/70)

FLEMING, Archibald - Jefferson Twp landowner (1/6/69)

FLEMING, James C. - dec; James Brownlee admin estate (3/11/69); Abner Holloway now admin his estate (3/17/69; 7/20/70)

FLEMING, Nathan R. - age 37; m; mbr Mt. Etna Masonic Lodge; d Mt. Etna 19 Oct 1867 (11/13/67)

FLINN, John W. - 1850 is Whig candidate for Grant Co Treas (8/18/69); candidate for Co Treas (3/26/68); sells 6 Franklin Twp ac (5/14/68); 24 Mar 1869 m Naomi Bloxin (3/24/69; 4/7/69); sells 80 ac in Franklin Twp to B. Anderson (9/14/70), & sells a lot in Marion (10/19/70)

FLINN, Peter G. - owns property in Jonesboro (1/8/68); 1867 sells 6.18 ac in Franklin Twp to Sally Crook (3/26/68)

FLOYD, Sarah A. - buys 20 ac in Sims Twp (3/4/68)

FLUMMER, Jacob - sells 80 ac in Sims Twp (9/7/70)

FORD, Capt. J.H. - f of Marion; opens his law office in Jonesboro (10/23/67); Jonesboro Town Clerk (5/11/70); mbr Jonesboro Masonic Lodge (5/18/70)

FOREST, Hezekiah - 1868 owns Independence property (1/12/70)

FOREST, Hiram - 1869 Washington Twp landowner (12/21/70)

FOSTER, Andrew - Feb 1869 buys license to m Sarah E. Early (3/3/69)

FOSTER, George - a yg man of W of Marion; recently had a leg broken while loading logs (7/6/70)

FOSTER, John - losing candidate for JP, Liberty Twp (10/19/70)

FOSTER, Lottie - is att Marion Public Sch (1/12/70)

FOSTER, Pleasant - 1861 buys land in Franklin Twp & 1863 buys 80 ac in Franklin Twp from James Allen (5/14/68)

FOSTER, Sarah - Van Buren Twp landowner (1/8/68); 1866 sells 40 ac in Van Buren Twp to P.C. Williamson (4/2/68)

FOWLER, Amos D. - May 1868 buys license to m Rachel J. Hiatt (6/4/68); of Franklin Twp; CW vet (1/19/70)

FOWLER, Powell H. - Trustee, Franklin Twp (9/18/67; 10/19/70); Franklin Twp delegate to State Rep Conv (2/9/70)

FOX, John - dec; 1868 his heirs own Pleasant Twp land (1/12/70)

FRANKLIN TOWNSHIP - Powell H. Fowler, Trustee (9/18/67); Levi S. Arnett, JP (9/18/67)

FRANKLIN TOWNSHIP, Schools of - 504 school children reside in Twp (11/17/69)

FRANTZ, Michael - prop, Frantz Drugstore, Jalapa (9/25/67); sells Jalapa lots (1/22/68); elected JP, Pleasant Twp (10/19/70)

FRAZIER, Elizabeth - Franklin Twp landowner (1/8/68)

FRAZIER, M.J. - & Bros. buys 145 ac in Franklin Twp (8/17/70)

FRAZIER, Nathan W. - a quarry of bldg stone is being worked on his farm 4 mi below Marion (7/15/68); Center Twp taxpayer (1/26/70)

FRAZIER, Robert - 1868 Liberty Twp landowner (1/12/70)

FREE, Orvin - 1867 sells 2 lots in Marion to C&IC RR (1/29/68)

FREEMAN, W[ilson T.] - Feb. 1868 buys license to m S[arah] F. Rogers (3/4/68)

FREESTONE, Amos - 1868 owns Jonesboro property (1/12/70)

FRIEND, Mathias S., Esq - JP, Liberty Twp (2/12/68); of Liberty Twp; CW vet (1/19/70); Liberty Twp delegate to State Rep Conv (2/9/70); is elected JP, Liberty Twp (10/19/70)

FRIERMOOD, Jacob - 1869 sells 60 ac in Sims Twp to Joseph B. Mark & buys 40 ac in Sims Twp from Joseph B. Mark (1/5/70)

FRIERMOOD, Z[achariah] T. - 1869 sells 20 ac in Sims Twp & buys 40 ac in Sims Twp from Joseph B. Mark (1/5/70)

FRITZ, Harrison M. - buys 34 ac in Green Twp (11/16/70)

FRY, Mark - 11 Aug 1870 m Mollie E. Huggins (8/17/70)

FULTON, Rev. [Samuel] - pastor, M.P. Ch in Washington Twp (7/13/69)

FURGUS, Edwin - buys 40 ac in Jefferson Twp (3/30/70)

FURNISH, A[bsolom] G. - Dec 1867 buys license to m Sarah E. Richards (1/8/68)

FURNISH, B.W. - dec; owned land in Jefferson Twp (1/6/69)

FURNISH, John F. - serv Co F, 34th Regt Ind Vol Inf during CW, lost arm during war; has diploma from Indianapolis Commercial Coll; Union Party candidate for Grant Co Recorder (3/4/68); Doorkeeper, Ind State Senate (1/13/69); buys 2 Marion lots (11/10/69); sells a Marion lot (1/12/70); is Rep candidate for Co Auditor (7/13/70)

FURNISH, Joseph - dec; 1869 owned land in Fairmount Twp (12/21/70)

FURNISH, M.J. - buys property in Marion (1/26/70), & sells a lot on Branson St, Marion to C.W. Hill, Jr. (10/5/70)

FUTRELL, Abe - sells 80 ac in Franklin Twp (10/26/70)

FUTRELL, M[ichael] - Dec 1869 buys license to m Martha Pierce (1/5/70); sells 40 ac in Monroe Twp to Jordon Futrell (2/2/70)

GABRIEL, J. Frank - Liberty Twp landowner (1/8/68)

GAINES, Benjamin - Apr 1868 buys license to m Catherine Williams (5/14/68); treas, Morris Chapel SS (5/26/69)

GALATIA, Town of - has been vacated by the Co bd of Comm (4/23/68)

GALBREATH, Jacob - 1867 sells 0.5 ac in Liberty Twp to Liberty Twp for $1.00 [for a sch?] (4/2/68)

GALBREATH, William, Sr. - buys 40 Liberty Twp ac (5/14/68)

GARD, Edmund S. - sells 160 ac in Green Twp (12/25/67)

GARD, Jason - Sims Twp landowner (1/6/69)

GARNER, George W. - buys 80 Van Buren Twp ac (4/16/68)

GARNER, Joseph H. - Feb 1868 buys license to m Nellie Ogle (3/4/68)

GARNER, Riley - sells 40 ac in Liberty Twp to Charles Howell (2/9/70), & buys 80 ac in Liberty Twp (4/6/70)

GARRETSON, Rev. O[wen] C. - of Madison Co; 8 Aug 1865 m Mrs. R[ebecca] L. Shaw of Grant Co (8/18/65)

GARRISON, H[enry W.] - Dec 1869 buys license to m E[lizabeth] E. Mitchener (1/5/70)

GARRISON, Reuben - 30 Aug 1870 m Bathsheba Wright (8/31/70)

GARVER, William - 1851 is candidate for Prosecuting Atty (8/17/70); Rep candidate for Common Pleas Judge (7/13/70); now a Judge in Noblesville; his wife d 15 Dec 1870 (12/21/70)

GASKIN, Nathan - 1867 buys 5 ac in Liberty Twp from Wellington Barnett & 1868 sells 2 ac in Liberty Twp to William Milton (1/22/68); 1869 Liberty Twp landowner (12/21/70)

GAUNTT, Reuel J., Esq - of Liberty Twp; Rep candidate for Grant Co Treas (3/4/68; 7/13/70); Grant Co Treas (11/2/70)

GEMMILL, A. - buys 7 ac in Green Twp (10/5/70)

GERARD, T.J. - is elected Center Twp Constable (10/19/70)

GIBBONS, Rodney - buys 40 ac in Monroe Twp (12/16/70)

GIBBS, Rufus H. - at Fairview, Fayette Co 15 May 1869 m Minerva Reeves, dt Dr. A.B. Reeves, f of Grant Co (6/2/69)

GIBSON, Elizabeth - Liberty Twp landowner (1/8/68)

GIBSON, Elkanah - owns property in Independence (1/6/69)

GIBSON, George W. - Nov 1867 buys license to m Louisa J. Welch (12/11/67); 1868 Liberty Twp landowner (1/12/70)

GIBSON, James - buys 1 lot in Harrisburg (5/14/68)

GIFFORD, J[ohn] H. - May 1868 buys license to m Lydia Foutche (6/4/68)

GIFFORD, James, Jr. - Green Twp landowner (1/6/69)

GILBERT, John - 1842 is ed of the 'Marion Democratic Herald' (7/6/70), & later was Grant Co Auditor (7/13/70)

GILBREATH, Samuel - 2 Aug 1869 m Sarah A. Wise (8/11/69; 9/8/69)

GILLAND, James E. - 28 Mar 1870 m Nancy A. Parson (3/30/70; 4/6/70)

GILLESPIE, James - Monroe Twp landowner (1/6/69); age 72 (7/13/71)

GILLIMORE, David W. - buys 40 ac in Liberty Twp (9/7/70)

GILPIN, John - Richland Twp landowner (1/6/69)

GINNEY, Catherine - 1868 owns property in Marion (1/12/70)

GITHENS, Lemuel - 1869 Green Twp landowner (12/21/70)

GLEASON, Newell - 1869 Richland Twp landowner (12/21/70)

GLESSNER, B. - assesses benefits/damages of a Franklin Twp ditch (6/23/69)

GLIDEWELL, Robert - viewer for a Jefferson Twp rd (7/23/69)

GOLDING, Aaron - m; lives on Washington St N of the river (12/21/70)

GOLDING, William L. - 2 Oct 1867 m Delight Price (10/9/67)

GOLDTHAIT, Cimon - 1851 is Marion Postmaster (8/17/70); & D.S. Hogin are props, Hogin & Goldthait Drygoods Store (12/29/69); 1869 sells Marion lots to James Hummel & to Caroline Murry & to Elias C. Murry (1/5/70), & to Mary J. McIlwain (1/12/70), & to William Coats (2/9/70); Jun 1870 att Old Settlers meeting (6/8/70); sells 2 Marion lots (7/13/70)

GOLDTHAIT, Edgar - is att Marion Sch (12/18/67)

GOLDTHAIT, James - is att Marion Sch (12/18/67; 1/12/70)

GOLDTHAIT, Simon - is att Marion Public Sch (11/6/67); gave a temperance speech at Christian Ch recently (12/18/67)

GOODRICH, Isaac - sells 40 ac in Sims Twp (11/10/69)

GOODWIN, Carlos - 1868 Monroe Twp landowner (1/12/70)

GOODWIN, Eli - owns property in Jonesboro (1/6/69)

GOODWIN, L.W. - Prosecutor, Grant Co (10/16/67)

GORDON, Nathan W., Esq - atty; office is on W side of CH Square (9/18/67); buys a Marion lot from A.C. Swayzee (9/7/70), & sells 40 ac in Sims Twp (9/7/70)

GORDON, Seth - buys/sells Mill Twp property (4/2/68; 9/14/70); viewer for a rd in Grant Co (6/23/69)

GORDON, William L. - of Liberty Twp; recently found a stray roan heifer (1/13/69)

GORHAM, William - Green Twp landowner (1/6/69)

GOSSOM, William - Feb 1868 buys license to m Cynthia A. Clark (3/4/68)

GOURLEY, Thomas M. - Mar 1868 buys license to m E[lizabeth] Ballinger (4/2/68)

GRAND ARMY of the REPUBLIC (GAR) Post No. 3 - had charge of burial of John Hull Power (4/2/68)

GRANDY, Samuel M. - buys 5.77 ac in Franklin Twp (5/14/68)

GRANT COUNTY - 1842 the 1st newspaper publ in Grant Co prob was 'Marion Democratic Herald' with Jeremiah Harry, publ, & John Gilbert, ed (7/6/70); 1864 Co Comm are C.S. Tibbits, John Spears & Edmund Duling (6/9/69); Davidson Culbertson is replaced by James Brownlee as Co Treas (8/18/65); Co Officers are Joseph Morrow, Clerk; William Neal, Auditor; John C. Nottingham, Recorder; Lewis H. Elliott, Sheriff; Anderson Overman, Surveyor; Nicholas Holman, Coroner (9/18/67); George W. Harvey, Sch Examiner, examines/tests prospective sch tchrs (9/25/67); fence around CH is in disrepair, livestock often go through fence and defile the enclosure; also someone is using the enclosure at night as a horse pasture (11/13/67); fence around CH is being repaired (12/11/67); CH is dilapidated, window blinds in cupalo are down & ragged, and the horse rack is old and broken-down (4/23/68); a new county jail is being built on N side of Monroe St just E of the CH Square in Marion; Co comm John Secrist is the contractor (1/13/69), new jail to be 44' X 70' with sheriff's residence in front part of bldg (2/24/69); William Charles contracts to furnish timber for new

Co jail (3/11/69); jail construction progresses; Hulley & Hulley are the iron contractors & are preparing the cell bars (6/23/69); to cost over $3,000 to pave sidewalks around Square (7/21/69); last stone for jail is laid (11/10/69); the log house standing on Nathan Coggshall's property near the head of Washington St was once the County CH, Nathan is tearing it down and using the logs as firewood (11/24/69); cells are being installed in the new jail (1/5/70); the 1st prisoner in the new jail is __ Hollowell, who is partly crazy & partly drunk; the Co Poor Farm has a 2-story brick house with a 1-story wooden addn; the house is 58' long with 7 rooms on the lower floor varying in size from 10' X 6.25' to 12' X 18'; the upper story is divided into 2 rooms, 12' X 18' each; these 9 rooms must accommodate the inmates & the superintendent and his family; veranda on S side is 28' long; usual number of inmates is 25 but there are presently only 5 males & 7 females, including 3 insane, a male & 2 females; the insane male is kept in chains (6/29/70); there are 15 post offices in the county; the old county jail, built on Boots St by Samuel McClure yr ago & used as a jail until ca 1869, was taken down; outside it was 20' X 30' and was made of hewn timber; walls were 2.5' thick & consisted of 3 layers, the middle layer being hewn timbers set upright & the other layers being horizontal; the floor & ceiling were each also 3 layers of hewn timber; inside were 2 rooms with but 1 door to the outside; each 'cell' had a small aperture covered with iron bars; the Co comm sold the site to John Kiley who intends to erect a brick residence thereon (7/13/70); heavy stone pavement, 4' X 8' X 6", is being laid in front of the hitching racks around the Square to keep tied horses from stamping mud holes (10/26/70); Sheriff Jones moves into the new jail residence (12/21/70)

GRANT COUNTY, Schools of - 5,312 of the 6,333 Grant Co children, between the ages of 6 and 21 years, att sch; 115 sch houses are in co, with sch being taught in all but one; average length of sch term is 60 da; in primary schools are 88 male tchrs & 34 female tchrs; in HS are 5 male & 3 female tchrs (1/27/69); average pay for common sch tchrs is $1.50 to $2 (4/6/70)

GRANT COUNTY AGRICULTURAL SOCIETY - 23-26 Sep 1868 will hold its 14th annual exhibition (7/22/68); officers: James Sweetser, pres; Henry Shugart, v pres; D.P. Cubberley, secy; J.N. Turner, treas; dir are: J. Hummel, Washington Twp; Isaac

Anderson, Van Buren Twp; J. Lugar, Pleasant Twp; N. Overman, Richland Twp; George W. Hultz, Monroe Twp; William Wharton, Jefferson Twp; Moses Larkin, Fairmount Twp; Willis Cammack, Liberty Twp; Hugh Hamilton, Green Twp; J.S. Harris, Franklin Twp; Washington Smith, Sims Twp; Nathan Coggshall, Mill Twp; Jacob Smith, Center Twp (7/29/68)

GRANT COUNTY FAIR - 1870 officers: Henry Shugart, pres; D.R. Seegar, v pres; D.P. Cubberly, secy; J.N. Turner, treas; Twp dir: Isaac Anderson, Van Buren; John Hummell, Washington; George F. Dunn, Pleasant; James W. Coan, Richland; G. Strange, Monroe; William Wharton, Jefferson; J.R. Rodgers, Liberty; John Druckamiller, Franklin; Joseph Spurgeon, Sims; D.R. McKinney, Center; Samuel Moore, Mill (8/3/70)

GRANT COUNTY INFIRMARY/POOR FARM - has 13 inmates (1/27/69); John A. Slover is re-appointed supt (3/11/69)

GRANT COUNTY LIVESTOCK ASSOCIATION - has park/grounds near Marion; 2nd annual Exhibition of Imported and American Bred Horses' will be held 1-3 Sep 1868; Assn Officers are Elam Hiatt, pres; F.J. Leas, v pres; Hiram Brownlee, secy; W.C. Webster, treas; Robert Beatty, marshal; dir are Jason Willson, Philip B. Cloon, D.B. Sweetser, and L.P. Hess (8/5/68)

GRANT COUNTY MEDICAL SOCIETY - existed in Jun 1850 (8/18/69); pres, Dr. Samuel S. Horne; mbrs: Dr's. Albert C. Irwin, J.A. Meek, Henry Charles, D. Palmer, Alpheas Henley, Lavanner Corey, D.S. Elliott, Lewis Williams, William Lomax & Constantine Lomax (11/20/67); new mbrs: L.M. Jackson, James H. Bates & J.C. Neal; William Lomax, secy (5/21/68); mbrs: L.P. Hess, Abner D. Kimball, H.D. Reasoner, James S. Shively, L.C. Beckford, C.E. Riggs, Samuel S. Horne, Jr. (7/13/69)

GRAY, Daniel - 1869 sells 40 ac in Washington Twp (1/5/70)

GRAY, Elizabeth - 1868 Fairmount Twp landowner (1/12/70)

GREEN, Jesse - sells a lot in Harrisburg (1/12/70)

GREEN, John - 1864 is Judge, Grant Co Common Pleas Bench (6/9/69)

GREEN, Robert - Liberty Twp landowner (1/8/68)

GREEN, Wilkerson - 1868 Richland Twp landowner (1/12/70)

GREEN TOWNSHIP - Johnson Eakins, Trustee (9/18/67); 1868 buys 0.25 ac from Andrew Miller for $25 (4/2/68)

GREEN TOWNSHIP, Schools of - 368 school children reside in Twp (11/17/69)

GREENMAN, Rev. A. - replaces Rev. Sale as pastor, Marion M.E. Ch (4/30/68); came here from Union City (5/7/68), now moves to Springfield, MO (4/21/69)

GREGG, Thomas - [16 Aug 1868] m Lucinda (Line) Dunn, dt Jacob Line, Esq (8/19/68)

GREY, Elizabeth - 1866 sells 80 ac in Fairmount Twp (4/2/68)

GRICE, Edward C. - 1867 sells 0.5 Van Buren Twp ac (4/2/68)

GRIFFIN, Dennis - Dec 1867 buys license to m Catherine Genney (1/8/68)

GRIFFIN, Martin - Center Twp taxpayer (1/26/70)

GRIFFIN, Robert - Center Twp taxpayer (1/26/70)

GRIFFITH, J.K. - of Jonesboro; his 5-yr. old small, iron-gray mare has strayed (10/27/69)

GRIFFITH, Joseph - Dec 1869 buys license to m M[ary] J. Futrell (1/5/70)

GRINDLE, George W. - buys 70 ac in Pleasant Twp (1/15/68)

GRINDLE, Jacob - 1869 buys 2 ac near Mier from Benjamin Harnden (1/5/70); buys 1 lot in Mier (2/9/70)

GRINDLE, Mary - 1868 Franklin Twp landowner (1/12/70)

GRINDLE, Samuel - of Green Twp; is on a Co bd to assess property (1/5/70)

GRYHALS, William - sells 70 ac in Pleasant Twp (1/15/68)

GUNDER, Daniel - opens his new grocery on Adams St on corner of 1st blk above Square, next door to Marion Marble Works (6/4/68); is returning to his grocery business in Marion after being a yr in Wapekong, Miami Co (8/3/70)

GUNDER, William - 30 Jun 1870 m Adelia Adams (7/20/70)

GUTHRIE, M. - has a business on N side of Square (6/2/69)

GUT(T)SHALL, Moses - Franklin Twp landowner (1/6/69)

GUTSHALL, Polly - 1868 Franklin Twp landowner (1/12/70)

HAAS, David - is att Marion Public Sch (11/6/67)

HACKLEMAN - name of a Post Office proposed for Liberty Twp; to be named for General __ Hackleman, a Hoosier who was killed at Battle of Corinth during the CW (6/16/69)

HADLEY, George W. - Sims Twp landowner (1/8/68); buys 80 ac in Monroe Twp from John Zimmerman (4/27/70)

HAGGERTY, Robert I. - 1869 owns Marion property (12/21/70)

HAGGERTY, S. - has AB academic degree; is on faculty of Academic Institute, Marion (3/4/68)

HAHN, Ezra - sells part of lot in Jonesboro (3/12/68)

HAINES, Alex - Dec 1868 buys license to m Elvira Blackburn (1/6/69)

HAINES, Nathan - is appraiser on route of Liberty Twp Pike (8/4/69); Monroe Twp delegate to State Rep Conv (2/9/70); buys 2 Marion lots (1/12/70), & buys 2 lots in Marion & buys 1.25 ac near Marion from Ed Baldwin (11/2/70)

HAINES, Milton - Marion HS student (12/23/70)

HAISLEY, Cyrus - 1867 buys land in Fairmount Twp (2/12/68)

HAISLEY, Eli - is on committee to fight alcohol in Fairmount (12/29/69); Fairmount Twp taxpayer (1/26/70)

HAISLEY, Elwood - buys Fairmount property (4/27/70)

HAISLEY, Eri - sells 13 ac in Liberty Twp (11/10/69); 2 Jun 1870 riding a wild yg horse home from Oak Ridge while carrying a broad-ax, he was thrown and the ax severed the arteries in his neck, killing him very quickly (6/8/70)

HAISLEY, John - buys 10 ac in Liberty Twp (4/9/68)

HAISLEY, Mary A. - 1866 buys 10 ac in Liberty Twp from William K. Mendenhall (1/22/68)

HALE, James - 1868 Pleasant Twp landowner (1/12/70)

HALE, James H. - Dec 1867 buys license to m June Arthurhultz (1/8/68)

HALE, Virgil - organizes Green Twp support for the proposed GR,W&C RR (11/3/69)

HALE, W[illiam] A. - Oct 1870 buys a license to m Martha Berry (11/2/70)

HALEY, Charles - Franklin Twp landowner (1/8/68); dec; his heirs sell 40 ac in Franklin Twp to William Michael (6/8/70)

HALL, Mrs. B. - age 84; m; d 28 Jan 1868 (1/29/68)

HALL, H.H. - of Peru; is teaching penmanship at the Academy bldg on Adams St (2/12/68)

HALL, Larkin - 1842 sells 44.5 ac in Liberty Twp (1/15/68)

HALL, Levi - Dec 1869 buys license to m M[artha] B. Brushwiller (1/5/70)

HALL, Robert - Jun 1868 buys license to m M[ary] H. Mauller (7/1/68)

HALL, William - 6 Sep 1870 m Sarah J. Hall (9/7/70)

HALL, William - 1865 sells 30.6 ac in Fairmount Twp (2/12/68); 1867 sells 10 ac in Liberty Twp to Samuel Elliott (4/30/68); secy of a temperance meeting in Fairmount (12/29/69)

HALLETT, Lucinda - 1868 Van Buren Twp landowner (1/12/70)

HAMAKER, Alice - is att Marion Public Sch (11/6/67)

HAMAKER, B. - librarian, Morris Chapel SS (5/26/69)

HAMAKER, Jeremiah - 1866 buys 2 Washington Twp ac from Henry Bradford (4/2/68)

HAMDEN, Benjamin - Mar 1864 lays out the 38 lots of Hamden's Addn to Mier (4/23/68)

HAMILTON, Hugh - Green Twp landowner (1/8/68); sells lot in Independence (3/4/68); buys 40 ac in Green Twp (4/2/68); Green Twp dir, Grant Co Agric Soc Fair (7/29/68); dec; John Bayless & Samuel Titus admin his estate (3/24/69)

HAMILTON, Isaac - serv 1st Lieut., 12th Ind Battery during CW; Union Party candidate for Land Appraiser of Grant Co (3/4/68); of Jalapa (1/19/70); now a Rep of Pleasant Twp (6/8/70)

HAMILTON, J. [James?] F. - Green Twp landowner(1/8/68)

HAMILTON, John - of Mill Twp; CW vet (1/19/70)

HAMILTON, Capt. S.H. - CW vet (1/19/70)

HAMILTON, William - 1867 buys 20 ac in Green Twp from Harrison Horine (1/8/68); sells 20 ac in Green Twp (2/2/70)

HANMORE/HAMMON, Thomas - Feb 1868 buys license to m Mariah Connoty/Connaty (3/4/68)

HANNA O[liver] H.P. - sells Monroe Twp ac (12/29/69)

HANNAH, John R. - 1866 sells 40 ac in Green Twp (1/8/68); Green Twp landowner (1/13/69); as exor of estate of J.J. McLain (dec), sells 40 ac in Green Twp to J.E. Hannah (10/27/69); is elected JP, Green Twp (10/19/70)

HANNAN, James W. - 1866 buys 40 ac in Jefferson Twp from Jacob Newberger (4/30/68)

HANTER, William T. - sells 40 ac in Liberty Twp (4/30/68)

HARDACRE, H[enry] B. - Oct 1870 buys a license to m E[sther] A[nn] Grindle (11/2/70)

HARDACRE, John - of Sims Twp; CW vet (1/19/70); sells 40 ac in Sims Twp to Henry Burns (1/26/70)

HARDACRE, Margaret - 1869 owns Mier property (12/21/70)

HARDY, Noah - dec; John Crawford admin his estate (8/18/65); owned land in Jefferson Twp (1/8/68)

HARDY, Otho - 1867 sells 40 ac in Jefferson Twp (4/2/68); organizes Jefferson Twp support for the proposed GR,W&C RR (11/3/69); losing candidate for JP, Jefferson Twp (10/19/70)

HARE, J.C. - viewer for a rd in Sims Twp (6/23/69)

HARLAN, A[ndrew] J. - 1842 is an atty in Marion (7/13/70)

HARLAN, Amanda - dec; Phineas Skinner admin her estate (7/20/70)

HARLAN, John C. - Van Buren Twp landowner (1/8/68); recently sells his Franklin Twp farm, may move to Chillicothe, MO (4/7/69); is now living in Chillicothe with his family and is employed there; is putting in his vegetable garden (4/28/69)

HARLAN, Samuel - 1868 owns property in Marion (1/12/70)

HARMAN, J.M. - buys 40 ac in Pleasant Twp (1/22/68)

HARMAN, Luther H. - sells 120 ac in Pleasant Twp (11/10/69)

HARNDEN, Benjamin - 1867 sells 2 ac in Richland Twp to C&IC RR (6/25/68); 1869 sells 2 ac near Mier (1/5/70); sells 1 lot in Mier (2/9/70), & sells 1 ac near Mier (4/6/70)

HARNDEN, Jonathan - 1867 sells 1 lot & part of 2 lots in Mier to C&IC RR Co (6/25/68)

HARNDON, Sylvester - viewer for new rd in Richland Twp (3/11/69); CW vet (1/19/70)

HARPER, M[oses] P. - Green Twp delegate to State Rep Conv (2/9/70)

HARRIS, Benajah C. - Rep candidate for Co Surveyor (7/13/70); Fairmount HS tchr, fall session 1870 (8/3/70)

HARRIS, Elam T. - sells 70 ac in Mill Twp (8/17/70)

HARRIS, G[eorge] W. - Mar 1869 buys a license to m Sarah Hollis (4/7/69)

HARRIS, Jesse B. - 1869 sells 120 ac in Franklin Twp (1/5/70)

HARRIS, John S. - May 1857 laid out original plat of 97 Harrisburg lots; Apr 1868 he lays out 29 lots of Harris' 1st Addn, Harrisburg (4/23/68); 1867 sells Harrisburg lots (1/15/68; 6/25/68; 5/14/68); Franklin Twp dir, Grant Co Agric Soc Fair (7/29/68); sells lots in Harrisburg (10/27/69; 11/24/69; 2/2/70; 7/6/70); of Franklin Twp, he owns ca 1,000 ac (7/13/70)

HARRIS, Newton W. - 27 Feb 1869 m Elmina Bogue of near Marion (3/3/69)

HARRIS, Thomas - Franklin Twp landowner (1/8/68), & taxpayer (1/26/70); buys 2 ac in Mill Twp (9/14/70); b NC; age 74;

came to IN ca 1830; came to Grant Co 1834; mbr Friends; d 5 Oct 1870, bur Deer Creek Friends Cem (10/5/70)

HARRIS, Zachariah M. - Rep candidate, Grant Co Recorder (3/4/68); agent for Phoenix Insurance Co, Hartford, CT (9/29/69); buys Marion lots (1/12/70); sells property in Marion (1/26/70); of Center Twp, recently finds a stray 2-yr old heifer (12/8/69); buys 19 ac near Marion from M.M. Hill (10/5/70)

HARRISBURG, Town of - 25 May 1857 is laid out in 97 lots by John S. Harris, then on 10 Apr 1868 he lays out the 29 lots in Harris' 1st Addn (4/23/68)

HARRISON, Lewis - dec; 1869 owned land in Fairmount Twp (12/21/70)

HARRITT, Prof. A.H. - 1867-68 Principal, Marion Sch (9/25/67); also is prop, Book, Stationary & Notion Store (10/23/67); has AM academic degree; is on faculty of Academic Institute, Marion (3/4/68)

HARROLD, Jeremiah - Oct 1870 buys a license to m Victoria Bocock (11/2/70)

HARRY, Allen - Dec 1868 buys license to m Matilda Reece (1/6/69)

HARRY, J. - & E. Harry are wallpaper hangers & painters (9/18/67)

HARRY, Jeremiah - Dec 1842 is publ of the 'Marion Democratic Herald' (7/6/70)

HARTER, Miss Emma - Marion HS tchr (9/14/70)

HARTER, George M. - 1868 Van Buren Twp landowner (1/12/70)

HARTER, Lewis - 1867 sells 40 ac in Sims Twp (1/29/68); Mar 1870 buys license to m Jane Horton (4/6/70)

HARTER, Dr. Milton G. - sells part of a lot in Marion (4/2/68)

HARTER, Solomon - dec, Charles W.M. Smith is exor of his estate (3/24/69)

HARTER, William - 26 Mar 1870 m Mary J. Junken (4/6/70)

HARTLEY, John W. - Green Twp landowner (1/13/69)

HARVEY, Rev. Enoch - Aug 1849 will preach at Marion Christian Ch next Sunday evening (8/3/70)

HARVEY, George W., Esq - Sch Examiner, examines/tests prospective sch tchrs (9/25/67; 8/3/70); & also inspects county schs; pres, Marion Literary Soc (1/15/68); forms law partnership with J.L. Custer with office in White's Bldg (6/9/69); enters law firm of Steele & St. John which becomes Steele, St. John & Harvey (12/16/70)

HARVEY, Henry - Mill Twp taxpayer (1/26/70)

HARVEY, Mahlon - of Liberty Twp; a pack of dogs recently killed several of his sheep (11/20/67); assesses lands for constructing Marion & Liberty Twp Turnpike (6/23/69); sells 40 ac in Liberty Twp (12/15/69; 12/29/69)

HARVEY, Sidney - appraises the benefits/damages of Wild Cat Prairie Ditch (3/12/68); viewer of a Franklin Twp rd (7/23/69)

HARVEY, Stephen - 1869 Richland Twp landowner (12/21/70)

HARVEY, Thomas - & Solomon Knight lay out Knight & Harvey's Addn to Jonesboro (4/23/68); b 13 Dec 1795 near Ashborough, NC; s Jesse and Keziah Harvey; was m nearly 53 yr; mbr Friends; d 3 Feb 1868 in Fairmount while visiting friends; Rev. Thomas Jay had charge of his funeral (2/26/68)

HASTY, Rev. E.F. - new pastor, Marion M.E. Ch (4/28/69)

HATTAWAY, H[enry] C. - 8 Dec 1869 m L[aura] J. Buchanan (12/15/69; 1/7/70)

HAVENS, James C. - sells 45 ac in Franklin Twp (6/8/70)

HAWES, Alfred - dec; owned property in Marion (1/6/69)

HAWKINS, Hillard - buys 40 ac in Liberty Twp (11/24/69)

HAWLEY, R.B. - buys a lot in Jonesboro (4/27/70)

HAYDEN, Stephen - dec; 1869 owned Sims Twp land (12/21/70)

HAYDEN, Zachariah - dec; Jacob Bugher admin his estate (8/18/65)

HAYES, Gabriel - of Richland Twp; CW vet (1/19/70)

HAYNE, Nancy J. - sells 40 ac in Pleasant Twp (5/14/68)

HAYNE, William H. - buys 65.87 ac in Pleasant Twp (4/2/68)

HAYNES, L. - dec; 1869 owned Fairmount Twp ac (12/21/70)

HAYNES, S.P. - Washington Twp landowner (1/8/68)

HAYS, Basil D. - sells land in Sims Twp to O. Phillips (2/12/68); buys property in Marion from Luther P. Hess (4/13/70)

HAYS, Gabriel - viewer for new rd in Richland Twp (3/11/69)

HAYS, Jonathan C. - 1867 buys 40 Monroe Twp ac (2/12/68); buys Monroe Twp ac (3/26/68; 11/30/70)

HAYS, Nelson - buys 40 ac in Monroe Twp (2/26/68)

HAYS, William - Van Buren Twp delegate to State Rep Conv (2/9/70)

HAYWARD, William - Feb. 1868 buys license to m Louisa Payne (3/4/68)

HAZZARD, Samuel - of Independence; argued with Charles Leer during a card game in Liberty Twp near Antioch Sch; Leer threatened to hit him with a club and Hazzard shot him in the hand with a revolver; Hazzard mounted his horse and fled, supposedly for Elwood (5/18/70); captured in Rush Co, he was returned to Independence where he appeared before Esq __ Wallace & was acquitted on grounds of self defence (6/1/70)

HEADLEY, B[enjamin] F. - Jul 1868 buys license to m M[aris] E. Sirtine (8/5/68)

HEADLEY, James M. - Mar 1869 buys a license to m Abigail Ogle (4/7/69)

HEAL, David - admin estate of George Cariens, dec (4/2/68)

HEAL, James N. - of Jefferson Twp; recently found 2 stray steers (12/11/67)

HEAVERLAND, Joseph - dec; owned Mier property (1/6/69)

HEDRICK, Charles - dec; owned property in Marion (1/6/69)

HEDRICK, Jacob J. - 1867 buys ac in Van Buren Twp (4/2/68)

HEDRICK, William O. - owns property in Marion (1/6/69)

HEFFNER, J. - sells beef & ice in Marion (7/13/70)

HEFFNER, Margaret - 1868 owns Marion property (1/12/70)

HELM, Francis 'Frank' M. - Trustee, Washington Twp (4/7/69); asst supt, Morris Chapel SS (5/26/69)

HENDERSON, James - 2 Jun 1868 m Margaret Brown of Jefferson Twp (7/1/68; 7/8/68)

HENDRICKS, G.W. - dec; owned land in Sims Twp (1/6/69)

HENDRICKS, William E. - buys a cemetery lot for $28.70 from the Trustees of IOOF Lodge NO. 96 (4/2/68)

HENLEY, Dr. Alpheas - Grant Co Medical Soc mbr (11/20/67); 2 Sep 1869 m by Rev. James Maple to Louisa J. Baldwin (9/8/69); practice is in Fairmount (2/9/70)

HENLEY, Jesse M. - sells property in Fairmount Twp to Cam T. Schooley (2/26/68; 3/4/68)

HERBERT, August, Sr. - sells 47 ac in Sims Twp to August Herbert, Jr. & sells 40 ac in Richland Twp (12/25/67)

HERMAN, John W. - 1868 owns property in Farmington (1/12/70); 1869 Jefferson Twp landowner (12/21/70)

HERRON, Isaac - owns property in Jonesboro (1/6/69)

HESS, Dr. Luther P. - 1864 is in Marion (6/9/69); physician & surgeon (8/18/65); has office on Washington St S of New York Clothing Store (9/18/67); a dir, Grant Co Live Stock Assn (8/5/68); lives 2nd door E of Spencer House (1/6/69); Grant Co Medical Soc mbr (7/13/69); has franchise for making Prof. Warren's New Soap in Grant & nearby counties (12/29/69); sells property in Marion to Basil D. Hays (4/13/70)

HESS, William T. - b Grant Co 11 May 1840; m; serv in army during CW; mbr M.E. Ch; d 23 Nov 1870 at his home near Marion (11/30/70)

HESTER, Amos - Van Buren Twp landowner (1/6/69)

HESTER, Esther - sells 80 ac in Van Buren Twp (2/2/70)

HESTER, Philip W. - 1866 buys 80 Fairmount Twp ac (4/2/68)

HIATT, Alfred - 1868 Franklin Twp landowner (1/12/70)

HIATT, B.C. - & Obadiah Jones in 1852 lay out Jones & Hiatt's Addn to Jonesboro (4/23/68)

HIATT, B.O. - dec; owned land in Mill Twp (1/8/68)

HIATT, Daniel, Sr. - owns property in Jonesboro (1/6/69)

HIATT, Daniel S. - May 1867 lays out Hiatt's Addn to Jonesboro (4/23/68); sells a lot in Jonesboro (3/30/70); Jun 1870 att Old Settlers meeting; b IN, moved to Grant Co area in 1827 (6/8/70); sells Jonesboro lots (7/6/70; 8/17/70)

HIATT, Daniel W. - sells 80 ac in Mill Twp (5/14/68)

HIATT, Drucilla - dec; Morris Fankboner admin her estate (9/18/67)

HIATT, Elam - sells land in Monroe Twp (4/30/68); pres, Grant Co Live Stock Assn (8/5/68); buys/sells Mill Twp property & buys property in Marion from Joseph Morrow (12/29/69; 1/5/70); Mill Twp taxpayer (1/26/70)

HIATT, Jacob - 16 Oct 1870 m Mary J. Behymer (10/19/70; 11/2/70)

HIATT, Lee M. - prop, Feed & Livery Stable, 1 blk S of Spencer House, Marion (1/12/70)

HIATT, Lemuel - owns property in Jonesboro (1/6/69); sells 1 lot in Jonesboro to Daniel S. Hiatt (4/6/70)

HIATT, William A. - Apr 1869 buys license to m Anna Patterson (5/5/69)

HICKS, J.N. - is att Marion Public Sch (11/6/67)

HIGHLEY, D[avid] F. - Oct 1870 buys a license to m Sarah V. Stair (11/2/70)

HIGHLEY, James - of Richland Twp; 18 Oct 1867 two of his horses were stolen and were not recovered (4/7/69)

HIGHLEY, John - buys 80 ac in Richland Twp (5/14/68)

HILL, Charles W., Jr. - buys a lot in Marion (10/5/70)

HILL, Charles W. - sells his part of a Marion planing mill to F.S. McKinney (7/6/70), & sells 1.65 ac near Marion (11/16/70)

HILL, Ezra C. - 1868 owns property in Jalapa (1/12/70)

HILL, J. Monroe - s C.W. Hill of Marion; telegrapher for Atlantic & Pacific Telegraph Line, North Judson (12/15/69)

HILL, Joseph W. - 1867 sells land in Fairmount Twp (2/12/68)

HILL, Martha M. - 1869 Center Twp landowner (12/21/70); sells 19 ac near Marion to Z.M. Harris (10/5/70)

HILL, Thomas - Liberty Twp landowner (1/6/69)

HILLMAN, Benjamin - Apr 1848 lays out the 26 lots of the town of Farmington (4/23/68)

HILLMAN, Daniel H. - buys 80 ac in Mill Twp (5/14/68)

HILLMAN, W.R. - is elected JP, Jefferson Twp (10/19/70)

HILLSHAMMER, D[avid] - supt, Salem Ch SS (5/5/69)

HILLSHAMMER, Mark - of Washington Twp; 2 Sep 1869 his yg son was playing with matches in the barn burning it down with all of its contents; the boy was rescued from the burning barn by his sister (9/8/69)

HILLSPAUGH, William - sells ac in Jefferson Twp (12/16/70)

HILTON, L.P. - buys a lot in Mier from John R. Lewis (5/18/70)

HINCHMAN, Robert - Liberty Twp landowner (1/6/69)

HINELINE, Abram - May 1868 buys license to m Emeline Needler (6/4/68)

HINSHAW, Amos - is att Marion HS (12/23/70)

HINSHAW, George I. - buys 40 ac in Liberty Twp (11/10/69)

HINTON, Reuhama J. - buys 80 ac in Green Twp (11/10/69)

HISS, Jacob - Van Buren Twp landowner (1/8/68)

HITE, Basil F. - 1867 sells a mill property in Center Twp to David C. Hite, Jr. (4/30/68)

HITE, David O. - 1868 sells 2.5 ac in Center Twp to CC&IC RR (4/30/68)

HITE, Mary - sells 40 ac in Van Buren Twp (11/3/69)

HITE, William - Jul 1868 buys license to m E[mma] J. Conger (8/5/68)

HIX, J. [prob James] - SS tchr, Salem Ch (5/5/69)

HIX, Oliver H. - of Washington Twp; CW vet (1/19/70)

HIX, Oliver P. - of Washington Twp; is on a Co bd to assess property (1/5/70)

HIX, William - song leader, Salem Ch SS (5/5/69); sells 10 ac in Washington Twp to Samuel Secrist (12/28/70)

HOBAUGH, George - 1850 is Whig candidate for Grant Co Coroner (8/18/69); Jun 1870 att Old Settlers meeting (6/8/70)

HOCKETT, Gilean - 1867 buys Franklin Twp ac (1/8/68)

HOCKETT, Zimri - Liberty Twp landowner (1/6/69)

HODGE, John - of Center Twp; is on a Co bd to assess property (1/5/70); Center Twp Assessor (1/12/70)

HODGE, William - is att Marion Public Sch (11/6/67)

HODSON, David - sells 160 ac in Monroe Twp (12/25/67)

HODSON, Reuben - 1867 buys 40 ac in Monroe Twp (1/8/68); sells 40 ac in Monroe Twp to William Bright (1/26/70)

HODSON, Robert E. - sells Monroe Twp ac (2/26/68; 3/4/68)

HODUFF, Joseph - 1868 owns property in Jonesboro (1/12/70); mbr Jonesboro Masonic Lodge (5/18/70)

HOGAN, William - is att Marion Public Sch (11/6/67)

HOGIN, Benoni C. - Jun 1850 is Whig candidate for Grant Co delegate to State Constitutional Conv (8/18/69)

HOGIN, Charles - is att Marion Public Sch (1/12/70); is att Marion HS (12/23/70)

HOGIN, David S. - 1867 sells 1 ac in Center Twp (2/12/68); has a room in rear of office of Dr's. Williams & Cubberly where he paints portraits (3/3/69); & Cimon Goldthait are props, Hogin & Goldthait Drygoods Store (12/29/69)

HOGIN, Dr. W[illiam] E.L. - f of Peru; new partner in Marion group of Dr.'s Jay, Webster & Hogin (1/12/70); is an Eclectic Physician; office is on SW corner of Square (9/7/70)

HOLLAND, Lydia J. - 1869 Sims Twp landowner (12/21/70)

HOLLETT, Lucinda C. - buys ac in Van Buren Twp (1/29/68)

HOLLINGSWORTH, Henry - 22 Sep 1870 m Rachel A. Beatty (9/28/70)

HOLLINGSWORTH, Joseph - 1869 owns land in Mill Twp & Fairmount Twp (12/21/70)

HOLLINGSWORTH, Wesley B. - sells property near Fairmount to Jonathan P. Winslow (1/22/68)

HOLLOWAY, Abner - admin estate of James C. Fleming, dec (3/17/69; 7/20/70)

HOLLOWAY, Amos - 1869 buys ac in Monroe Twp (1/5/70)

HOLLOWAY, Isaac - sells 30 ac in Monroe Twp (5/14/68)

HOLLOWELL, Alexander - 1866 buys 25 ac in Washington Twp from William S. King (5/14/68)

HOLMAN, G.F. - dec; owned land in Center Twp (1/6/69)

HOLMAN, Nicholas D. - Coroner, Grant Co (10/1/67; 11/2/70)

HOLMAN, Thomas - Feb 1868 buys license to m M[ahala] A. Floyd (3/4/68)

HOLT, Benjamin - of Mill Twp; CW vet (1/19/70)

HOOVER, David Y. - sells land in Liberty Twp (1/29/68); sells 40 ac in Liberty Twp to John H. Colville (10/19/70)

HOPKINS, D. - a tailor (9/18/67)

HOPKINS, Daniel - & John Brownlee in Mar 1868 lay out Haws & Hopkins' Addn to Marion (4/16/68)

HOPPIS, Elizabeth - 1867 sells ac in Fairmount Twp (4/30/68)

HOPPIS, George W. - sells 80 ac in Fairmount Twp (12/21/70)

HORINE, Harrison - 1867 sells ac in Green Twp (1/8/68)

HORNE, Lewis S. - owns property in Fairmount (1/6/69)

HORNE, Dr. Samuel S. - physician & surgeon with office on Water St, Jonesboro (9/18/67); mbr/pres, Grant Co Medical Soc (11/20/67)

HORNE, Dr. Samuel S., Jr. - grad, Ohio Medical Coll; new mbr Grant Co Medical Soc (7/13/69); practice is in Fairmount (2/9/70); may have d recently on a steamboat that sank while going from Madison, IN to Louisville, KY (12/7/70)

HORNER, David H. - buys 1 lot in Upland (2/9/70)

HORNER, John - viewer for a rd between Jonesboro and Harrisburg (7/23/69); lived 3 mi N of Jonesboro; m; 1 Nov 1870 while cutting a tree with his brother, was killed by the falling tree (11/2/70; 11/16/70)

HORNER, M[oses] R. - Apr 1868 buys license to m N[ancy] M. Winters (5/14/68)

HORTON, David E. - buys a lot in Marion (9/28/70)

HORTON, David F. - buys a lot in Marion (6/29/70); Rep candidate for Co Comm (7/13/70); sells property near Marion to Rose Moore (11/2/70)

HORTON, Miss Icy - is att Marion Sch (11/6/67; 1/12/70)

HORTON, Joseph B. - Jun 1850 is on committee to help Marion citizens celebrate our 74th Independence Day (8/18/69); 1869 owns property in Marion (12/21/70)

HOSTETTER, Isaac - owns property in Marion (1/6/69)

HOUCK, Mary A. - 1867 buys 0.5 ac in Center Twp (1/15/68)

HOUCK, William - is att Marion Sch (11/6/67; 1/12/70)

HOWARD, John - buys 80 ac in Fairmount Twp (1/15/68)

HOWARD, John A. - of Washington Twp; CW vet (1/19/70)

HOWE, John T. - 1865 sells 3 lots in Fairmount (2/26/68)

HOWE, T.E. - Trustee for 1st Ward, Jonesboro (5/11/70)

HOWELL, Charles - buys 40 ac in Liberty Twp (2/9/70)

HOWELL, James - Jan 1869 buys license to m S[arah] A. Williams (2/3/69)

HOWELL, Jeremiah 'Jerry' - Trustee, Liberty Twp (9/18/67)

HUBART, John - Rep candidate, Grant Co Recorder (3/4/68)

HUDSON, Milton - owns land in Green Twp (1/8/68)

HUESTON, John - dec; owned land in Monroe Twp (1/8/68)

HUESTON, William H. - Mar 1869 buys a license to m Sarah E. Kinney (4/7/69)

HUFF, Susan E. - Washington Twp landowner (1/8/68)

HUFFMAN, Ambrose - sells 20 ac in Monroe Twp (3/30/70)

HUFFMAN, Mary E. - 1869 owns Marion property (12/21/70)

HUFFMAN, Miss Matie - is att Marion Public Sch (11/6/67)

HULLEY, Samuel - & J. Hulley, props, Marion Foundry (2/26/68); organizes support for the proposed GR,W&C RR (11/3/69)

HULLINGER, Abraham - 1869 Franklin Twp landowner (12/21/70)

HULLINGER, Alexander - Franklin Twp landowner (1/6/69)

HULLINGER, Ambrose - 1866 sells 80 ac in Franklin Twp to Lemuel Hullinger & 1867 sells 40 ac in Franklin Twp (1/15/68)

HULLINGER, E.B. - sells 40 ac in Franklin Twp (4/13/70)

HULLINGER, Reuben - sells 13 ac in Sims Twp (11/24/69)

HULLINGER, William - Franklin Twp landowner (1/6/69)

HULS, Julia A. - 1867 sells 80 ac in Richland Twp (1/8/68)

HULTZ, George W. - sells 40 ac in Monroe Twp (2/26/68); Monroe Twp dir, Grant Co Agric Soc Fair (7/29/68)

HULTZ, John B. - of Monroe Twp; is on a Co bd to assess property (1/5/70); is Monroe Twp Assessor (10/19/70); buys 74 ac in Monroe Twp from George W. Hultz, then sells that 74 ac to A.J. Hays (11/30/70)

HULTZ, James F. - sells 40 ac in Monroe Twp (11/10/69)

HUMMELL, Charles - att Old Settlers meeting (6/8/70)

HUMMEL, James - Washington Twp dir, Grant Co Agric Soc Fair (7/29/68); 1869 buys a lot in Marion (1/5/70)

HUMMEL, James - is att Marion Public Sch (11/6/67)

HUMMELL, John - buys an IOOF Cem lot from IOOF Trustees for $28 (11/3/69); Jun 1870 is a v pres, Old Settlers meeting; is one of oldest settlers of Grant Co (6/8/70)

HUMMELL, John L. - Union Party candidate for Grant Co Recorder (3/4/68); Mar 1868 buys license to m A[manda] M. Sherwood (4/2/68); serv 8th Ind Regt Inf during CW (4/2/68); Washington Twp dir, 1870 Grant Co Fair (8/3/70); buys 24 ac in Washington Twp from Michael Coon (10/5/70); 1869 Washington Twp landowner (12/21/70)

HUMPHREY(S), Charles W. - prop, Humphrey Hardware (9/7/70); lives on Adams St (9/28/70)

HUMPHREY, Mary L. - 1867 buys Center Twp ac (2/12/68)

HUNT, E.F. - assesses benefits/damages of a ditch in Franklin Twp (6/23/69)

HUNT, Eli T. - sells 40 ac in Franklin Twp (11/24/69); sells 80 ac in Franklin Twp to Boaz M. Pettay (10/5/70)

HUNT, Rachel - 1867 sells 40 ac in Liberty Twp to James Wright (4/16/68); Liberty Twp landowner (1/8/68)

HURLEY, Harrison - sells 36 ac in Franklin Twp (1/29/68)

HURLEY, J[ohn] W. - Mar 1870 buys license to m M[argaret] J. Beam (4/6/70)

HUSTON, J.M. - of NE Madison Co; Emily, wife of John Wells, on 5 Mar 1868 started to home of her son-in-law, James Dickey, from the home of Joseph Dickey; going through a 1.5 mi-long woods, she lost her way; searchers found her at 1 AM at the home of J.M. Huston where she had sought shelter (3/12/68)

HUTCHINS, Harvey A. - is Fairmount HS tchr (8/3/70)

HUTTON, John - sells 40 ac in Liberty Twp (5/14/68); Liberty Twp landowner (1/6/69); sells Liberty Twp ac (11/24/69)

IAMS, George - Jun 1870 att Old Settlers meeting (6/8/70); is elected Center Twp Constable (10/19/70)

IAMS, Jesse - buys interest of G.W. Eyestone in 'Stove Depot' (2/17/69); 3 Feb 1870 m Angeline Young, both of Marion (2/9/70)

ICE, Benjamin, Sr. - Fairmount Twp landowner (1/6/69); viewer for a rd in Jefferson Twp (7/23/69)

INDEPENDENCE, Town of - 5 Nov 1853, the part in Grant Co is laid out with 16 lots by Daniel Bayless, Sr.; 6 May 1858 Pryor Rigdon lays out 18 lots in Rigdon's Addn making a total of 34 lots in Grant Co (4/23/68); has fewer than 1,000 residents; is located in 2 counties, Grant on the N and Madison on the S; is also in 4 twps., Green & Liberty in Grant Co, and Duck Creek & Boone in Madison Co; has Methodist Ch, a Christian Ch, 1 grist mill, 1 sawmill, 1 pump factory (these 3 driven by steam), 2 dry goods stores & 1 drugstore, recently est by Dr. Hazzard who also practices medicine in connection with his drug store, 2 wagonmakers, 2 blacksmiths, 1 cooper shop, 1 shoe shop, & 2 boarding houses; 6 physicians are in town - Drs. P. Rigdon, Riggs, Mock, Lusby, Dr. Hazzard, Sr. & Dr. Hazzard, Jr. (3/31/69); at N end of town stands the Carver Mill, Lightfoot Blacksmith Shop, and the Jones, Brumfiel & Adair Steam Sawmill; nearby is the Calloway & Hacker Pump Factory; Dr. Riggs office is at Calloway & Parson's Store; at the W end of town, William Johns works at an anvil (6/16/69); John Bayless, lawyer here (4/6/70)
CALLOWAY STAVE FACTORY - William Calloway, prop (1/19/70)
'DOGLEG' - makes pumps, staves, and saws walnut tops into table legs (4/6/70)
HAZZARD DRYGOODS & DRUGSTORE - Dr. Hazzard, prop (4/6/70)
JOHNS BLACKSMITH SHOP - William Johns, prop, has built an addn to his shop (1/19/70); shop is at W end of town; makes wagons (4/6/70)
MURPHY WAGON SHOP - on Mud St; Boze Murphy, prop; makes wagons and carts (4/6/70)
PARSON & ROSS GENERAL STORE - is on corner of town square (4/6/70)

SAWMILL - Jonathan Adamson & Jasper F., props (4/6/70)

INK, Charles - 1868 Mill Twp landowner (1/12/70)

INK, Ezra C. - Jun 1850 is publ of the Marion newspaper 'Whig Thermometer' (8/18/69)

IRELAND, W.C. - sells 80 ac in Van Buren Twp (9/28/70)

IRWIN, Dr. Albert C. - mbr, Grant Co Medical Soc (11/20/67; 7/13/69); 1869 owns property in Jalapa (12/21/70)

IRVINE, John - buys 40 ac in Richland Twp (12/15/69)

JACKS, Hallet B. - Oct1870 buys a license to m Sarah Parks (11/2/70)

JACKS, Jeremiah - 1867 buys 1 lot in Jefferson Twp from John F. Price & 1868 buys 1 lot in Upland from Jacob Bugher (3/26/68); admin estate of John Jacks, dec (7/20/70)

JACKSON, Curtis - sells property on S side of Square in Marion to Elijah Stebbens (7/13/70)

JACKSON, Isaac - owns property in Jonesboro (1/8/68)

JACKSON, James M. - sells 80 ac in Franklin Twp (7/20/70)

JACKSON, Job - dec; owned land in Liberty Twp (1/8/68)

JACKSON, Dr. L.M. - of Upland; mbr, Grant Co Medical Soc (5/21/68)

JACKSON, Mrs. M. [prob Margaret (Bond)] - age 33; her husband [prob John] d in army in 1863; mother of 3 children; d 3 Aug 1869 (8/11/69)

JACKSON & LEVEL'S SAWMILL - is 8 mi W of Jonesboro; to be site of a 'spiritual meeting' this weekend (8/12/68)

JACOBS, Dorty - buys 13 ac in Sims Twp (11/24/69)

JACOBS, Hester A. - dec; James Sweetser is exor of her estate (7/8/68)

JADDEN, Town of - is in Monroe Twp; has a Post Office (11/30/70)

JALAPA, Town of - original plat of 27 lots is laid out 7 Apr 1849 by Jacob Sprecher, who later, 13 Nov 1850, laid out 13 lots of Sprecher's Addn for a total of 40 lots in Jalapa (4/23/68) FRANTZ DRUGSTORE - Michael Frantz, prop (9/25/67)

JAMES, David S. - of Van Buren Twp; s of Judge Henley James (7/6/70)

JAMES, [Judge] Henley - 1842 is Grant Co Sheriff (7/13/70); Union Party candidate for Grant Co Treas (3/4/68); Center Twp delegate to State Rep Conv (2/9/70)

JAMES, Mary - age 92y, 5m, 17da; 5 Mar 1869 d near Marion at home of her s, Judge Henley James (3/11/69)

JAMES, Mary 'Mollie' - dt Judge Henley James (3/30/70); - see Dr. D[avid] H. SNODGRASS

JAMES, Dr. Milton - of Muncie; 29 Oct 1867 m Mattie, dt the Honorable A. Kennedy (dec) of Muncie (11/6/67)

JANES, Harry - is att Marion HS (12/23/70)

JANES, James W. - agent for sales of Wheeler & Wilson's Sewing Machine (6/4/68); prop, City Shoe Store (3/24/69); buys a lot on Washington St, Marion (10/27/69)

JAY, Denny, Sr. - 1862 buys 3 ac in Mill Twp (3/12/68); buys 10 ac in Mill Twp (5/14/68); sells 153 ac in Liberty Twp to Isaac W. Carter (9/14/70); of near Jonesboro; age 61; mbr/Elder, Friends Ch; d 23 Nov 1870 (12/7/70)

JAY, Denny, Jr. - a dir of Jonesboro & Kokomo Gravel Rd Co (5/7/68); sells 85 ac in Liberty Twp (11/3/69); buys 182 ac in Mill & Franklin Twp's from Nathan Coggeshall (5/11/70); buys 85 ac in Liberty Twp from Isaac W. Carter (9/14/70)

JAY, Ezra - 1865 sells 120 ac in Liberty Twp to Willis Cammack (4/30/68); buys 1 lot in Harrisburg (2/2/70)

JAY, Isaac - lives on Jonesboro Rd; two of his horses strayed recently (11/6/67); Center Twp taxpayer (1/26/70)

JAY, Jesse - sells 42 ac in Mill Twp to Milton Winslow (10/27/69); buys ac in Mill Twp (7/20/70)

JAY, John - 1865 buys property in Jonesboro (1/15/68)

JAY, Lydia - sells/buys Mill Twp property (4/2/68)

JAY, Dr. M. - of Marion; was medical mentor of Dr. Steele (5/14/68); is eclectic physician & surgeon (5/19/69); partner in Dr.'s Jay, Webster & Hogin; is Prof. of Physiology & Pathology, Bennett Eclectic Medical Coll., Chicago, IL; to lecture there until Jun 1870 (1/12/70)

JAY, Samuel - sells property adjoining Jonesboro (4/9/68); Mill Twp landowner (1/6/69); buys 45 ac in Fairmount Twp from Aaron D. Bates; organizes Mill Twp support for the proposed GR,W&C RR (11/3/69); sells a lot in Harrisburg to Albert Jay (2/9/70); sells 1 ac lot in Jonesboro (4/27/70)

JAY, Thomas - 1865 sells Liberty Twp ac (5/14/68); Friends Minister; had charge of funeral of Thomas Harvey (2/26/68)

JAY, Thomas, Jr. - 1869 owns property in Jonesboro (12/21/70)

JAY, Walter D. - buys 12 ac in Center Twp (1/15/68)

JAY, William L. - buys 40 ac in Liberty Twp (3/12/68)

JEFFERSON TOWNSHIP - Solomon Duling, Trustee (9/18/67)

JEFFERSON TOWNSHIP, Schools of - 494 school children reside in Twp (11/17/69)

JEFFREY, Henry - Dec 1867 buys license to m Mary E. Parker (1/8/68)

JEFFREY, William C. - 1869 Liberty Twp landowner (12/21/70)

JELLISON, Dr. J.W. - 1851 is a phiso-medical physician practicing in Marion (8/17/70)

JENKINS, Belfield - Jun 1870 att Old Settlers meeting (6/8/70)

JENKINS, Israel - sells 160 ac in Mill Twp (4/16/68)

JENNINGS, James S. - buys 2 lots in Marion from Jacob M. Wells (1/22/68); CW vet (1/19/70)

JENNINGS, John Q. - 1867 buys a lot in Jonesboro (3/12/68)

JESSUP, Zenas - dec; owned property in Jonesboro (1/6/69)

JESTER, Emerson - 1867 sells 79 ac in Green Twp to Abraham Weimer (4/16/68); Green Twp landowner (1/6/69)

JOHNS, David - buys 7 ac in Green Twp (10/5/70)

JOHNS, William - a blacksmith at W end of Independence (6/16/69; 1/19/70)

JOHNSON, Rev. Alfred P. - of Paoli, KS; 3 Dec 1867 m Theresa E. Shively of Marion (12/11/67; 1/8/68)

JOHNSON, Enos - sells 30 ac in Monroe Twp (4/9/68)

JOHNSON, Enos, Jr. - 1867 sells Monroe Twp ac (3/12/68)

JOHNSON, Gen'l(?) G.W. - 1868 Mill Twp landowner (1/12/70)

JOHNSON, Gabriel - sells 203 ac in Mill Twp (1/26/70)

JOHNSON, James - buys 160 ac in Monroe Twp (12/25/67); Jefferson Twp delegate to State Rep Conv (2/9/70); is largest land holder in Grant Co, owning ca 1,200 ac (7/13/70)

JOHNSON, Jesse - Sims Twp landowner (1/6/69)

JOHNSON, John - Dec 1867 opened the 'Oyster Bar' in the 1st room above the City Drug Store (1/13/69)

JOHNSON, John F. - Monroe Twp landowner (1/6/69)

JOHNSON, Joseph - owns property in Jonesboro (1/6/69)

JOHNSON, Lewis - Van Buren Twp landowner (1/8/68); Oct 1870 buys a license to m Perlina E. Johnson (11/2/70)

JOHNSON, M[ahlon] - Jul 1868 buys license to m M[artha] J. Clester (8/5/68)

JOHNSON, Sol - is att Marion HS (12/23/70)

JOHNSON, William - is elected JP, Van Buren Twp (10/19/70)

JOLLY, Elijah - viewer for a rd in Sims Twp (6/23/69)

JOLLY, F[rancis] M. - May 1868 buys license to m Sarah E. Hulse (6/4/68)

JONES, Allie - mbr IOGT Lodge, Jonesboro (6/22/70)

JONES, Almeda - tchr, Jonesboro HS (3/11/69)

JONES, Mrs. Amanda (Wall) - see Milton C. POLK

JONES, Ann - dec; Enoch P. Jones admin estate (9/25/67)

JONES, Burtney R. - Dec 1869 buys license to m E[liza] J. Duling (1/5/70)

JONES, Byron H., Esquire - atty with office on W side of Square (9/18/67); is agent for Home Insurance Co of NY (11/27/67); Franklin Twp landowner (1/8/68); sells part of a lot in Marion (5/14/68); buys 'Bob,' the warhorse of the dec Col. David Shunk (see CIVIL WAR) (6/9/69); sells 40 ac in Green Twp (11/24/69), & sells 40 ac in Green Twp (12/29/69); sells 1 lot in Jonesboro (2/9/70), & sells/buys ac in Monroe Twp (11/2/70)

JONES, C.R. - 1869 buys a lot in Jonesboro (1/5/70)

JONES, Rev. D.W. - 1854 publishes the 'Mississinewa Gazette' (7/6/70); f of Marion; now of Ft. Wayne (9/8/69)

JONES, Dr. Enoch P. - admin estate of Ann Jones, dec (9/25/67); secy, Jonesboro & Kokomo Gravel Rd Co (5/7/68); admin estate of Mary Chamness, dec (3/3/69); of Jonesboro; is an eclectic physician (5/19/69); 1869 sells property in Jonesboro (1/5/70); buys property in Jonesboro (7/13/70)

JONES, Harry - is att Marion Sch (1/12/70)

JONES, Henry - buys 160 ac in Green Twp from Philip C. Jones & sells 80 ac in Green Twp to Philip Jones (12/25/67)

JONES, Horace Clinton - age 4; s Dr. Enoch P. and Lydia Ann [(Ellis)] Jones of Jonesboro; d 18 Aug 1868 (8/19/68)

JONES, James M. - [15 Oct 1867] m Margaret Small (10/23/67); is now dec (3/12/68)

JONES, James M. - Monroe Twp landowner (1/6/69)

JONES, John, Sr. - admin estate of William Mathis, dec (12/11/67)

JONES, Capt. John F. - of Fairmount; is a Rep candidate for Sheriff (2/17/69; 7/13/70); Sheriff, Grant Co; 6 Oct 1870 m Jennie Winslow in Kokomo (11/2/70)

JONES, John W. - admin estate of James M. Jones, dec (3/12/68)

JONES, Jonathan H. - 1862 sells 3 ac in Mill Twp (3/12/68); dec; 1869 owned property in Jonesboro (12/21/70)

JONES, Joseph N. - Jun 1868 buys license to m Caroline Craig (7/1/68)

JONES, Prof. Lewis H. - Principal, Jonesboro HS; grad, Oswego Normal & Training Sch, Oswego, NY (3/11/69)

JONES, Mattie E. - tchr, Jonesboro HS (3/11/69)

JONES, Nathan - Dec 1868 buys license to m Ellen Weaver (1/6/69); dec; 1869 owned land in Liberty Twp (12/21/70)

JONES, Obadiah - Dec 1837 lays out original plat of Jonesboro; & Ephraim C. Overman Dec 1846 lay out Overman & Jones' Addn, Jonesboro; Feb 1847 lays out Jones' Southern Addn, Jonesboro; & B.C. Hiatt Apr 1852 lay out Jones & Hiatt's Addn, Jonesboro (4/23/68); dec; owned Jonesboro property (1/8/68)

JONES, Philip C. - buys/sells ac in Green Twp (12/25/67)

JONES, Col. R[obert] B. - dec [25 Jul 1866]; 1869 his estate owns property in Marion (12/21/70)

JONES, Richard - 1868 owns property in Marion (1/12/70)

JONES, Ross C. - Green Twp landowner (1/6/69); sells 80 ac in Green Twp to Reuhama J. Hinton (11/10/69)

JONES, S.S. - Sims Twp landowner (1/8/68)

JONES, Starkie - Dec 1867 buys license to m [Susannah Johnson] (1/8/68)

JONES, Thomas - sells 16 ac in Liberty Twp (4/6/70)

JONES, Thomas C. - dec; owned land in Mill Twp (1/8/68)

JONES, W.R. - Washington Twp landowner (1/8/68)

JONES, William F., Jr. - s William Jones, Sr.; 30 Oct 1867 m Caroline Vertrice (11/6/67); 19 Aug 1870 m Anna C. Baugh; last Sunday his home, adjacent to his father's house, burned, leaving both families without a home (8/24/70)

JONES, William, Sr. - lives on his farm across the rd W of Co Infirmary; his home burned last Sunday (8/24/70)

JONESBORO, Town of - 8 Dec 1837 is laid out by Obadiah Jones, contains 43 lots; 22 Dec 1846 Obadiah Jones & Ephraim C. Overman lay out 20 lots in Overman & Jones Addn; 27 Feb 1847 Obadiah Jones lays out 16 lots in Jones' Southern Addn; 27

Apr 1852 Obadiah Jones & B.C. Hiatt lay out 20 lots in Jones & Hiatt's Addn; 5 Oct 1854 Jehu J. Ellis lays out 6 lots in Ellis Addn; Solomon Knight & Thomas Harvey lay out 11 lots in Knight & Harvey's Addn; 5 May 1855 Simon Kaufman, A. Kaufman, Moses Kaufman & G.H. Broyles lay out 24 lots in Kaufman & Broyles Addn; 6 May 1867 D.S. Hiatt lays out 36 lots in Hiatt's Addn; Jonesboro now contains 175 lots (4/23/68); S.T. Baldwin, Postmaster; town officers: Trustees - T.E. Howe, John Zeek, W.G. Wilson, T.P. Moore, L.D. Baldwin; J.H. Ford, clerk; J.W. Shideler, treas; William Dunkle, Marshal (5/11/70); population is ca 600; prior to bldg of Panhandle RR through Harrisburg, Jonesboro bought the region's grain sending it through Anderson; is across Mississinewa River from Harrisburg Station on RR; town has 1 hotel (9/14/70)
FREE LABOR STORE - f owned by Levi Coffin of Cincinnati, in 1847 is purchased by Small, Jones & Co (7/20/70)
GOODWIN & FANKBONER GENERAL STORE - is moved to Cottage Corner (6/16/69)
HAHN & JENNINGS DRUGSTORE - mentioned (9/25/67)
JORDON BARBER SHOP - mentioned (12/16/70)
MOORE HOTEL - Samuel Moore, prop; rents out his open buggy and horse, 'Bloomer', to his patrons (9/14/70)
PEMBERTON & BALDWIN MILL - recently burned; was insured for $6,700; insurance is now paid (9/29/69)
PFIEFFER BAKERY/GROCERY - recently opened; J.C. Pfieffer, prop (8/31/70)
SHIDELER'S STORE - mentioned (9/18/67)

JONESBORO, Schools of - 275 school children reside in Jonesboro (11/17/69)

JORDAN, Timothy - Sims Twp landowner (1/8/68)

JOSEPHY, Magnus - prop, Boston Store (10/26/70); buys a lot on South St, Marion from Noah Thomas (11/2/70)

JUMP, Amanda - 1869 owns Fairmount Twp land (12/21/70)

JUMP, G.W. - of Fairmount Twp; CW vet (1/19/70)

KABEL, Adam - sells 40 ac in Monroe Twp (5/18/70)

KAUFMAN, Simon - & A. Kaufman, Moses Kaufman & G.H. Broyles 5 May 1855 lay out Kaufman & Broyles' Addn to Jonesboro (4/23/68)

KEELER, Foster W. - Sims Twp landowner (1/8/68)

KEEVER, George - sells a lot in Upland (4/13/70)

KEEVER, Martin - Green Twp landowner (1/6/69)

KELLEY, Abraham - of Green Twp; CW vet (1/19/70)

KELLEY, D.B. - Green Twp landowner (1/8/68)

KELLEY, Elizabeth - asst chorister, Morris Chapel SS (5/26/69)

KELLEY, I.C. - sells his interest in Tripp & Kelley to Dr. M.S. Vail (3/3/69)

KELLEY, Jonathan - Green Twp landowner (1/8/68)

KELLEY, Lydia - tchr, Morris Chapel SS (5/26/69)

KELLEY, M[alachi] - May 1869 buys license to m Sarah Redford (6/2/69)

KELLEY, William - of Blackford Co; 16 Oct 1869 m Rebecca Haines of Grant Co (10/27/69)

KEM, Florence O. (Eyestone) - youngest dt of Jonathan and Nancy Eyestone; m Luther A. Kem 20 Jan 1870; d 11 Oct 1870 (10/26/70)

KEM(M), John - viewer for a rd in Center Twp (3/11/69); appraiser on route of Liberty Twp Pike (8/4/69)

KEM, Joseph T. - buys 60 ac in Pleasant Twp (5/14/68)

KEM, Samuel - 1866 buys 40 ac in Green Twp (1/8/68)

KENDELL, J. - sells 40 ac in Green Twp (1/26/70)

KENNEDAY, Samuel D. - 1 Jun 1854 he lays out Prosper Town with 53 lots (4/23/68)

KENNEDY, Michael - 1869 owns property in Jonesboro & in Harrisburg (12/21/70)

KENNEDY, Moses - Franklin Twp landowner (1/6/69); organizes Sims Twp support for proposed GR,W&C RR (11/3/69)

KERR, James - owns property in Jonesboro (1/8/68; 1/6/69)

KESTER, Mrs. Mary A. - see William A. DOLMAN

KIBBEY, Jonah - buys 125 ac in Jefferson Twp (4/27/70)

KIDNER, John W. - 4 Mar 1869 m Frances R. Candy at her home 2 mi E of Jonesboro (3/11/69)

KIDWELL, James - Green Twp landowner (1/6/69)

KILEY, John - is refused a license to sell liquor in Marion (3/11/69); buys the site of the old jail & intends to build a brick residence there (7/13/70)

KILGORE, James - Green Twp landowner (1/6/69)

KILGORE, Joseph - 1868 Pleasant Twp landowner (1/12/70)

KILGORE, Marcus M. - at the Spencer House, Marion, 14 Jul 1870 m Jennie Lane (7/20/70)

KIMBLE/KIMBALL, H.H. - Sims Twp landowner (1/8/68)

KIMBALL, Dr. Abner D. - mbr Grant Co Medical Soc (7/13/69)

KIMES, E.M. - a dir, Big Deer Creek Ditching Co (9/18/67)

KIMMER, Jacob - 1869 owns property in Upland (12/21/70)

KINE, Patrick - sells a lot in Jonesboro (4/9/68)

KING, George F. - Van Buren Twp landowner (1/8/68)

KING, John A. - sells 40 ac in Pleasant Twp to Amos Sisson (2/26/68); Pleasant Twp landowner (1/6/69)

KING, Thomas S. - Liberty Twp landowner (1/8/68)

KING, William J. - buys 40 ac in Franklin Twp (11/24/69)

KING, William S. - 1866 sells 25 ac in Washington Twp to Alexander Hollowell (5/14/68); sells 95 ac in Washington Twp to James Price (2/26/68), & owns property in Marion (1/12/70)

KINNEMAN, Malinda - 1869 owns Marion property (12/21/70)

KINNAMON, John - Mar 1868 buys license to m Sarah Lennet/Tennet (4/2/68)

KINNEER, Miss Maggie - & Miss Mary Allen, props, Millinery & Fancy Goods Shop now open in Pierce Bldg, N side of CH Square, Marion (4/9/68)

KINNEY, John - dec; owned land in Liberty Twp (1/6/69)

KINSEY, Joseph - 1867 sells 80 ac in Fairmount Twp (1/15/68)

KIRKWOOD, Jefferson - Liberty Twp landowner (1/6/69)

KIRKWOOD, John D. - 1867 sells 80 ac in Jefferson Twp (4/30/68); 1869 Jefferson Twp landowner (12/21/70)

KIRKWOOD, John R. - 19 Jul 1868 m Mrs. Mary C. (Barnard) Newcom in the Jonesboro M.E. Ch (8/5/68; 8/19/68); 1868 Franklin Twp landowner (1/12/70); is new Postmaster, Jonesboro (11/23/70)

KIRKWOOD, William M. - Liberty Twp landowner (1/6/69)

KISER, Daniel E. - sells 80 ac in Van Buren Twp (4/16/68)

KISER, William - 1868 Richland Twp landowner (1/12/70)

KITCH, Elijah - 1867 sells 40 ac in Monroe Twp to Jonathan C. Hays (2/12/68); owns property in Jalapa (1/6/69)

KITE, Henry - 1869 Sims Twp landowner (12/21/70)

KLING, Amos H. - & George H. Kling & David Laufman are props, New Hardware Store (1/13/69)

KNIGHT, John L. - sells 40 ac in Van Buren Twp (11/10/69)

KNIGHT, Lizzie - Marion HS student (12/23/70)

KNIGHT, S.M. - buys a lot in Upland (10/5/70)

KNIGHT, Samuel - Fairmount Twp landowner (1/8/68)

KNIGHT, Solomon - & Thomas Harvey laid out Knight & Harvey's Addn to Jonesboro (4/23/68)

KNIGHT, William - 1867 buys 1 lot in Marion (2/26/68)

KNOX, Martin - sells 80 ac in Green Twp (12/15/69); buys 73 ac in Liberty Twp (7/20/70); sells Green Twp ac (11/16/70)

KNOX, William - 1867 sells 40 ac in Green Twp to Albert G. Messmore (4/2/68); Feb 1869 buys license to m Lousena E. Phillips/Phelps (3/3/69)

KOB, John R. - sells 80 ac in Sims Twp (1/12/70)

KOONS, Margaret - Green Twp landowner (1/6/69)

KORPORAL, A[nthony] - sells Van Buren Twp ac (12/29/69)

KRETSINGER, David - att Old Settlers meeting (6/8/70)

KRETSINGER, H.R. - 1869 sells 80 ac in Center Twp (1/5/70)

KUHN, Catherine - Sims Twp landowner (1/8/68)

KUHN, Margaret - 1869 Green Twp landowner (12/21/70)

KUNTZELMAN, Moses M. - sells 60 ac in Monroe Twp to Martin Lucas (3/12/68)

LACY, G[eorge] W. - Jun 1869 buys license to m E[lizabeth] Fitzsimmons (7/7/69)

LACY/LACEY, James - is dec (6/6/72)

LaFRAGE, William - Sims Twp landowner (1/6/69)

LAKE GALATIA - contains ca 40 ac and is surrounded by woods, its water is clear and blue with no current, no outlet, and no apparent source of water supply; no bottom has been found, is said to be 'bottomless' (9/14/70)

LANCKTON, H.C. - Center Twp Constable (10/19/70); & Capt. Bigelow are putting up ice in the old wagon shop at the ft of Washington St, the ice is 6" thick and is clear (12/28/70)

LANDER, Noah M. - buys land in Green Twp (6/25/68)

LANE, Amanda J. - buys 160 ac in Liberty Twp (2/26/68)

LANE, S[tephen] R. - Dec 1869 buys license to m Anna Small (1/5/70)

LANGSDON/LANGSTON, Edgar - Mar 1869 buys a license to m Lucetta Hughes (4/7/69)

LANIER, Sampson - 1869 Washington Twp landowner (12/21/70)

LARIMORE, Elizabeth - b PA; age 81; came to IN ca 1838; d 12 May 1868 (5/28/68)

LARKIN, Moses - Fairmount Twp dir, Grant Co Agric Soc Fair (7/29/68); in Oct 1868 he fell from his horse, dislocating head of his humerus; 48 hours after the fall he called Dr. E.P. Jones, an eclectic physician of Jonesboro, who wanted to physically exam the shoulder but Larkin refused saying the Dr. should be able to diagnose the injury by looking at it and he requested some liniment to ease the swelling & pain; Dr. Jones complied;

later Larkin consulted other physicians who found the arm to be dislocated; Larkin sued Dr. Jones for malpractice and called Dr. Lomax, Dr. Jay & other local allopathic physicians to testify for him; none of his witnesses suggested that the dislocation should now be reduced (5/19/69); apparently lost his case since he is now asking for a new trial which is pending; is crippled for life (6/2/69)

LAUFMAN, David - & Amos H. Kling & George H. Kling are props, New Hardware Store (1/13/69)

LAUFMAN, Harry - age 15; of Marion; is in jail for breaking & entering (12/16/70)

LAWSON, Howard - buys 40 ac in Liberty Twp (5/14/68)

LAWSON, Lucinda - 1867 buys 2 lots in Marion (3/12/68)

LAWSON, Theodore C.P. - sells 160 ac in Richland Twp to Edward F. Lawson (2/26/68)

LAY, Columbus E. - Jefferson Twp landowner (1/8/68)

LEACH, Andrew - 1868 owns Independence property (1/12/70)

LEACH, Edmund - & Co own land in Fairmount Twp (1/8/68; 1/6/69); sells 10 ac in Fairmount Twp (4/27/70)

LEACH, Elam - Fairmount Twp taxpayer (1/26/70)

LEACH, Esau - 1867 sells land in Fairmount Twp (5/14/68)

LEACHBURG, Town - 24 Jul 1855 was laid out with 32 lots by John Leach; "the Leaches are there, but the Burg has gone" (4/23/68)

LEAS, Alpheus - of Van Buren Twp; CW vet (1/19/70)

LEAS, Dan - 1850 is in tanning & harness business in Marion; he advertised in the 'Whig Thermometer' seeking to buy 103 cords of tan bark; in later yr he moved to Van Buren (8/18/69); Jun 1870 att Old Settlers meeting (6/8/70)

LEAS, F.J. - v pres, Grant Co Live Stock Assn (8/5/68)

LEAVITT, Boardman - 7 Apr 1869 m Bernice James (4/14/69; 5/5/69)

LEDFORD, Buis - Liberty Twp landowner (1/8/68)

LEE, Milton - dec; Daniel Ridgeway admin his estate (12/11/67)

LEER, Charles - of NE of Independence; argued with Samuel Hazzard during a card game in Liberty Twp near Antioch Sch; Leer threatened to hit him with a club and Hazzard shot him in the hand with a revolver; Hazzard mounted his horse and fled, supposedly for Elwood; the ball is not yet extracted from Leer's hand (5/18/70); files charges against Hazzard (5/25/70)

LEER, David W. - buys 20 ac in Green Twp from William Hamilton & sells 40 ac in Green Twp to A. Wimmer (2/2/70)

LEESON, Bell - is att Marion HS (12/23/70)

LeFEVER, H.H. - officer, Rebekah Lodge, Jonesboro (4/28/69)

LeFEVER, Mrs. Lydia - officer, Rebekah Lodge, Jonesboro (4/28/69)

LEFEVRE'S BLACKSMITH SHOP - is 6 mi from Marion near E line of Washington Twp (12/28/70)

LEISURE, B[enjamin] N. - Trustee, Sims Twp (9/18/67)

LEISURE, Nathan J. - buys 40 ac in Green Twp (12/7/70)

LEISURE, W[illiam] R. - Apr 1869 buys license to m Mary Page (5/5/69); losing candidate for JP, Green Twp (10/19/70)

LEMING, Gabriel - Nov 1867 buys license to m Mildred Corner (12/11/67)

LEMMINGTON, William - Green Twp landowner (1/6/69)

LENFESTY, Capt. Edward S., Esq - an atty in Judge Brownlee's law office (9/18/67); Nov 1867 buys license to m Laura Brownlee (12/11/67); owns property in Marion (1/6/69); CW vet (1/19/70); sells 73 ac in Liberty Twp (7/20/70)

LENFESTY, Emma - buys part of a lot in Marion (5/14/68)

LENFESTY, Joseph F. - sells property in Marion (11/10/69)

LENFESTY, Robert F. - secy, Salem Ch SS (5/5/69); 27 Dec 1870 m Cerelda A. Nelson (12/28/70)

LENFESTY, Robert D. - buys 1 lot in Marion (4/30/68)

LENFESTY, William - m; mbr IOOF; d recently (11/24/69)

LENOX, Adda 'Addie' - is att Marion Public Sch (1/12/70)

LENOX, Frank - is att Marion Public Sch (11/6/67)

LENOX, William - 1867 buys 1 ac near Marion (1/22/68)

LEVELL, Eliza J. - buys ac in Liberty Twp (11/10/69)

LEVERTON, Thomas - Mar 1870 buys license to m M[ariah] Modlin (4/6/70)

LEWELLEN/LEWALLEN, W.G. - 1868 Green Twp landowner (1/12/70)

LEWIS, [James Oliver] - only s of William G. Lewis; last wk fell from a moving wagon while holding an ax, the ax cut into the [liver of the] boy's right side; he may [did] survive (7/13/70)

LEWIS, John R. - sells a lot in Mier to L.P. Hilton (5/18/70)

LEWIS, John S.D. - Jefferson Twp landowner (1/8/68); Mar 1870 buys license to m H[annah] E. McCoy (4/6/70)

LEWIS, Morgan O. - Fairmount Twp Trustee; was recently injured when thrown by a horse (6/29/70)

LEWIS, Nimrod - dec; owned property in Marion (1/6/69)

LEWIS, William G. - a Rep of Fairmount Twp (6/8/70)

LIBERTY TOWNSHIP - a little more than half of the township is in the Indian Reserve, the rest is in the Old Purchase; 20 yr ago, 'D.C.S.' hunted wolf, deer & turkey here; now during winter, people are principally engaged in cutting & hauling logs to the six circular sawmills in the township; most of the sawmills are portable; the timber cut for lumber includes poplar [i.e. tulip-tree], walnut, sycamore & ash; the logs are sawn into lumber during spring & summer and are ready for market in fall; lumber from the township is hauled to railroads at Jonesboro, Anderson, Quincy & Windfall; 9 sch houses are in the twp, and since there are only 5 ch houses, most of schs are also used for worship; 6 SS meet during the summer (4/2/68); J. Howell, Trustee (9/18/67); 5 Feb 1867 buys 0.5 ac from Jacob Galbreath for $1.00 (4/2/68); A.F. 'Jack' Seward, Trustee (4/7/69; 8/3/70); Goodwin's Store is 1 mi W of Center Sch; Jay's Store is 6 mi from Marion on Strawtown Rd (12/7/70)

LIBERTY TOWNSHIP, Schools of - 852 school children, including colored children, reside in Twp (11/17/69)
ANTIOCH SCH - mentioned (5/18/70)
DISTRICT NO. 9 - site of a meeting to plan a rd from W end of Little Ridge Pike to Independence, a distance of 5 mi (3/31/69)
CENTER SCH - is 10 mi from S end of Washington St in Marion (4/14/69); new sch is being built (11/16/70)

LIGHTFOOT, Christopher C. - of Green Twp; recently found a stray mare (1/15/68)

LIGHTFOOT, Eli B. - Green Twp landowner (1/8/68)

LIGHTFOOT, Newton - 1869 owns property in Independence (12/21/70)

LILLARD, Darius - 1867 buys property adjoining Mier from Hamden & Rowland (1/29/68); sells a lot in Mier (2/2/70)

LIMES, George - buys a lot in Marion (1/22/68)

LINDER, Jacob G. - Jefferson Twp landowner (1/8/68)

LINDER, J[ohn] W. - of Jefferson Twp; CW vet (1/19/70)

LINE, Jacob - 1842 admin estate of Isaac Norman, dec (7/13/70); 1869 Washington Twp landowner (12/21/70); dec (8/3/70)

LIPSEY, Oliver G. - is att Marion Public Sch (1/12/70)

LIPSEY, Rachel - is att Marion Public Sch (1/12/70)

LIPSEY, W.B. - has the Grant Co agency for the Elias Howe Sewing Machine (10/12/70)

LITTLE RIDGE MILLS - see FINLEY & ALLEN STEAM MILL

LITTLE, Alexander - Mar 1868 buys license to m Mary F. Johnson (4/2/68); buys 2 lots in Fairmount (11/10/69)

LITTLE, John - buys 21 ac in Fairmount Twp (12/15/69)

LITTLE, Joseph M. - during CW serv in 89th Ind Vol Regt; recently m Millie P. Brooks in the Fairmount W.M. Ch (1/20/69); buys 40 ac in Mill Twp (10/5/70)

LITTLER, Joel - dec; 1869 owned Jefferson Twp land (12/21/70)

LITTLER, John - sells 45 ac in Jefferson Twp (4/27/70)

LIVINGOOD, William - 20 Oct 1869 m Angelina Moore (10/27/69)

LLOYD, Levi T. - owns property in Marion (1/6/69)

LLOYD, Hardin - Jun 1869 buys license to m Mahala Willis (7/7/69)

LLOYD, Thomas - Dec 1867 buys license to m Fanny Bradfield (1/8/68)

LOBDELL, A.T. - buys 30 ac in Washington Twp (8/17/70)

LOCK(E), John - owns property in Marion (1/6/69); sells 0.5 ac in Franklin Twp to Peter Michael (7/20/70)

LODGES
AMANA LODGE No. 82, IOOF - has hall over Shideler's Store in Jonesboro (9/18/67); Charter Mbr Thomas C. Beall is dec; Rev. William E. Pierce, James H. Bates & A.L. Barnard are mbrs (3/24/69); mbr Allen Winslow is dec (3/31/69); mbrs who live in Franklin Twp and often come to meetings on horseback, purchased a lot and erected on it a stable to shelter their horses while they are att meetings; each mbr has a lock for his stall where he keeps feed for his horse (2/9/70; 3/30/70)
BEACON LODGE No. 320, IOOF - 4 Mar 1869 will be organized/est in Zenia (3/3/69)
GOOD TEMPLAR'S, IOGT, Fairmount Lodge No. 46 - meets in Fairmount (9/18/67)
GOOD TEMPLAR'S, IOGT, Vienna Lodge No. 539, Jonesboro - Charter Mbr Elijah Lucas is dec; mbrs include Allie Jones, Susie Clark, Adelia Zeek (6/22/70)
GOOD TEMPLAR'S, IOGT, Marion Lodge No. 303 - has a hall over A.C. Swayzee & Co Store (9/18/67)
GOOD TEMPLAR'S, IOGT, Marion District - their Conv will be held in Fairmount for 3 da in Apr 1868 (3/26/68)
GRANT ENCAMPMENT No. 66, IOOF - has a meeting hall on Washington St (9/18/67)
GRANT LODGE No. 105, F&AM - mentioned (8/18/65; 9/18/67); mbrs include R.V. Speelman (dec), A.W. Tripp, D.H. Sanders, A. Patterson (4/30/68)
JONESBORO LODGE No. 109, F&AM - mbr Leander Ward is dec (8/19/68); mbrs include J.H. Ford, M. Fankboner, J. Hoduff (5/18/70)
MISSISSINEWA LODGE No. 96, IOOF - has a meeting room on Washington St (9/18/67)
Mt. ETNA LODGE No. 333, F&AM - mbrs include Nathan R. Fleming (dec), J.R. Alpaugh, A.R. Large & R.S. Reed (11/13/67)
R.A.M., Marion Chapter No. 55 - meets in Masonic Hall (9/18/67)
REBEKAH LODGE, Jonesboro No. 16 - recently est; officers are F.J.F. Clark, Mrs. Sallie J. Shideler, Mrs. Eliza A. Bates, Mrs. Lydia Lefever, Mrs. Avis Nelson, Elijah Carter, Mrs. Susie D.

Clark, John Ruley, H.H. Lefever, Mrs. Caroline Moore, Mrs. Keziah Wilson, Mrs. E.A. Simons & Mrs. S.E. Eviston (4/28/69)

LOER, David E. - Apr 1868 buys license to m Mariah Glasgow (5/14/68)

LOER, Sarah - is Green Twp landowner (1/6/69)

LOER, Thomas B. - sells 9 ac in Green Twp (11/2/70)

LOGAN/LAGAN, Samuel K. - dec; owned land in Richland Twp (4/6/70)

LOMAX, Miss Addie - is att Marion Public Sch (11/13/67)

LOMAX, Dr. Constantine - brother of W. Lomax; mbr, Grant Co Medical Soc (11/20/67); & wife celebrated their 25th wedding anniv 5 Mar 1868 (3/12/68); is an allopathic physician (5/19/69); and Dr. Hess recently cut a cancer from the side of a horse's head (6/2/69)

LOMAX, Joseph - 1851 is Marion storekeeper; 1870 lives in Kalamazoo, MI (8/17/70)

LOMAX, Dr. William - brother of C. Lomax; mbr, Grant Co Medical Soc (11/20/67; 7/13/69); 1867 buys 160 ac in Franklin Twp (1/15/68); buys part of a lot in Marion (4/30/68); is an allopathic physician (5/19/69); office is in White's Bldg, E side of Square (9/7/70)

LONG, A.R. - dec; owned land in Sims Twp (1/6/69)

LONGFELLOW, William B. - 23 Oct 1867 m Ann M. Connelly (10/30/67)

LORD, John A. - gives 40 ac in Green Twp to Mary J. Lord (2/2/70)

LOVE, Elizabeth - b PA; age 84; came to Marion ca 1834; mbr M.E. Ch; d 29 Apr 1868 (5/28/68)

LOVE, Frame, Jr. - 1867 buys property in Marion from John M. Ammons & 1868 buys more property in Marion (1/29/68)

LOVE, Frederick - is elderly and blind; moves to IA from Marion (8/18/69)

LOVE, Henry - 1867 buys Fairmount Twp property (1/15/68)

LOVE, Lemon - yg. man of Marion; is in jail for breaking and entering (12/16/70)

LOVE, Lydia A. - owns property in Marion (1/6/69)

LOVE, Nancy M. - sells N half of a lot in Marion (11/2/70)

LOVE, William - prop of an omnibus that takes passengers & baggage from RR depot to hotels, sometimes has to use a four-horse hitch due to deep mud holes in streets around CH (4/23/68)

LOVELAND, A.B. - of Richland Twp; is on a Co bd to assess property (1/5/70)

LOWRY, John - buys 40 ac in Fairmount Twp (5/11/70)

LOY, Jacob - Mar 1870 buys license to m Mary E. Said (4/6/70)

LUCAS, Albert - Apr 1868 buys license to m Amanda Kidner (5/14/68)

LUCAS, Benedict - buys 40 ac in Green Twp (12/29/69)

LUCAS, David C. - 1867 sells a lot in Jonesboro to Jacob M. Barnard (1/29/68); buys 54 ac in Fairmount Twp (11/2/70)

LUCAS, Elijah - age 74; mbr M.E. Ch; Charter Mbr, Vienna Lodge, IOGT, Jonesboro; d 27 May 1870 (6/22/70)

LUCAS, Israel - buys 45 ac in Center Twp (12/28/70)

LUCAS, Martin - sells 40 ac in Washington Twp to Ezra Conn (2/12/68); buys 60 ac in Monroe Twp (3/12/68); 1869 Monroe Twp landowner (12/21/70)

LUCAS, T[heophilus] F. - Oct1870 buys a license to m M[argaret] Bechtel (11/2/70)

LUCAS, Theresa (Dolman) - mentioned 1/15/68)

LUCAS, Thompson A. - 1867 buys property in Jonesboro (1/15/68); buys/sells Jonesboro lots (4/2/68; 1/29/68)

LUGAR, J. - Pleasant Twp dir, Grant Co Agric Soc Fair (7/29/68)

LUGAR, Joseph - of Van Buren Twp; CW vet (1/19/70)

LUGAR, William G. - sells 116 ac in Van Buren Twp (1/15/68)

LYNCH, A[ndrew] J. - Feb. 1868 buys license to m M[ary] J. Hardacre (3/4/68)

LYON, John - buys 50 ac in Sims Twp (1/12/70)

LYON, Richard M. - Van Buren Twp landowner (1/8/68)

McALPIN, George W. - Sims Twp landowner (1/6/69)

McARTHUR, Charles H. - 1869 Van Buren Twp landowner (12/21/70)

McARTHUR, John B. - Nov 1867 buys license to m Drucilla Isenhour (12/11/67)

McCAN, Samuel - asst secy, Morris Chapel SS (5/26/69)

McCARTY, Sallie - a girl living with M/M __ St. John; she is charged with manslaughter in the death by exposure of her illegitimate newborn son; the infant is bur in the 'old graveyard' by the Center Twp Trustee (11/23/70); she has left the county (12/16/70)

McCAUSLAN, John - an Irishman; lived in Jefferson Twp for past 3 yr; 1 Nov 1870 was found dead of natural causes in that Twp (11/2/70)

McCLAIN, J.F. - sells 20 ac in Green Twp (1/12/70)

McCLAIN/McLAIN, Miss Olive - is att Marion Sch (11/6/67)

McCLAIN, Mrs. Sarah - 1867-68 tchr, Marion Sch (9/25/67)

McCLURE, David R. - of Pleasant Twp; recently found a stray horse (10/30/67)

McCLURE, Erastus P. - 28 Oct 1867 m Celia Carey (12/4/67; 12/11/67)

McCLURE, Robert - sells 36 ac in Pleasant Twp (3/30/70); almost 50 yr ago settled on Mississinewa River near Marion & cleared his farm there; a sporting man, he had a 'race course' on his farm that was heavily used; recently he sold out and with his family left for the West with 6 families in a train of wagons (7/6/70); his carriage is sold to Dr. L.P. Hess (7/13/70)

McCLURE, Samuel - exor of will of Col. David Shunk, dec [21 Feb 1865] (6/9/69); Center Twp taxpayer (1/26/70); att Old Settlers meeting (6/8/70)

McCOMBS, William N. - buys 20 ac in Green Twp (4/30/68)

McCONNELL, James W. - sells 100 ac in Liberty Twp (2/2/70)

McCORMICK, Jacob - sells 200 ac in Mill Twp (4/27/70)

McCORMICK, John M. - admin estate of Dianna [(Lee)] McCormick, dec (10/12/70)

McCOY, Ezekiel - owns property in Jonesboro (1/6/69)

McCOY, N[athan] H. - May 1868 buys license to m Achsah T. Arnett (6/4/68)

McCRATE, Robert - Dec 1867 buys license to m Mary E. Troxell (1/8/68)

McCRAY, Milton - 1869 buys 40 ac in Van Buren Twp (1/5/70)

McCRORY, William S. - sells 160 ac in Liberty Twp (4/27/70)

McDONALD, B[ernard] W. - Dec 1868 buys license to m R[achel] Beauchamp (1/6/69)

McDONALD, T.B. - f of Fairmount; now of Nebraska (12/1/69)

McDONNELL, Bernard - raises hogs (1/26/70); Fairmount Twp farmer living on Little Ridge Gravel Rd, he has "well-repaired fences with good buildings" (2/9/70)

McDOWELL, George L. - is att Marion Public Sch (11/6/67)

McDOWELL, James F. - 1851 he & T.J. McDowell publishes the 'Marion Journal' (8/17/70); & __ VanDevanter are attys with offices in the Spencer House (9/18/67); organizes Center Twp support for the proposed GR,W&C RR (11/3/69); buys 45 ac in Franklin Twp (6/8/70)

McDOWELL, Miss Linnie - is att Marion Public Sch (11/6/67; 1/12/70); is att Marion HS (12/23/70)

McELDOWNEY, Robert - sells a lot in Marion (9/28/70)

McFARLAND, Enoch - Sims Twp landowner (1/6/69); sells 40 ac in Sims Twp to Cimon Clevenger (10/26/70)

McGREGORY, __ - engineer on CC&IC RR freight train that was derailed 11 Apr 1869, he was killed instantly (4/14/69)

McGREW, William - is att Marion Sch (11/6/67)

McGUIRE, Jones - dec; owned property in Mier (1/13/69)

McILWAIN, Mary J. - buys a lot in Marion (1/12/70)

McINTIRE, William - is att Marion Public Sch (1/12/70), & now the Marion HS (12/23/70)

McKAHN, Israel - Sims Twp landowner (1/6/69)

McKAY, O[liver] H.P. - Liberty Twp landowner (1/6/69)

McKEEVER, John - buys 406 ac in Mill Twp (1/26/70)

McKINLEY, George H. - Green Twp landowner (1/6/69); dec (12/21/70)

McKINNEY, D.R. - is att Marion Public Sch (1/12/70)

McKINNEY, David R. - Apr 1855 lays out McKinney's Addn to Marion (4/16/68); & son left for Washington, D.C. this wk to att inauguration of pres Grant (3/3/69); Center Twp dir, 1870 Grant Co Fair (8/3/70)

McKINNEY, Elias W. - sells 60 ac in Pleasant Twp (5/14/68); lives on Peru rd 3 mi out of Marion (6/9/69); sells his 120- ac farm near Marion in Pleasant Twp; he intends to move to CA (12/15/69); buys 200 ac in Washington Twp (4/6/70)

McKINNEY, E[mily E. (Hogin)] - age 41; wife of David R. McKinney; d 13 Jun 1870 (6/29/70)

McKINNEY, F.S. - Jun 1867 lays out McKinney's Addn of Out-Lots, Marion (4/16/68); is an old & well-known Marion builder (9/8/69); sells a lot in Marion to James Fann (11/10/69); buys a Marion planing mill (7/6/70)

McKINNEY, P[atterson] - Jun 1868 buys license to m A[lcha] A. Marine (7/1/68)

McKINNEY, Robert - is att Marion Sch (12/18/67)

McKINNEY, William - left for Washington, D.C. this wk to att inauguration of pres Grant (3/3/69)

McLAIN, J.J. - is dec; John R. Hannah is exor of his estate (10/27/69)

McLAIN, James - losing candidate for JP, Sims Twp (10/19/70)

McLAIN, Olive - is att Marion Public Sch (1/12/70)

McLAIN, Mrs. Sarah - is on faculty of Academic Institute, Marion (3/4/68)

McLAIN, Thomas O. - 1866 buys 10 ac in Green Twp (2/2/70)

McMAHAN, Joel W. - is Marion agent for John Hancock Life Insurance Co (4/6/70)

McMASTERS, J[ohn] C. - Oct1870 buys a license to m N[ancy] S. Wood (11/2/70)

McMILLEN, Irish - 1869 Van Buren Twp landowner (12/21/70)

McNARY, Samuel - dec, his estate is settled by the Court (3/12/68)

McNEAL, John - dec; 1868 his heirs own land in Franklin Twp (1/12/70)

McNEAL, William - of Monroe Twp; CW vet (1/19/70)

McPATTERSON, John - 1867 sells Center Twp ac (3/12/68)

McQUISTON, Robert - buys 20 ac in Green Twp (1/12/70)

McRAE, Calvin B. - owns land in Fairmount Twp (1/8/68; 1/6/69), & in Washington Twp (1/6/69)

McREA, Harrison C. - Union Party candidate for Grant Co Recorder (3/4/68)

McREA, Leander - is att Marion Public Sch (1/12/70)

McREA, Miss Permelia - is att Marion Public Sch (11/6/67)

McWHINNERY, William - sells 80 ac in Van Buren Twp to Samuel Davis (9/14/70)

McWILSON - see WILSON

MACK, Mary - is att Marion Public Sch (11/6/67)

MACON, Jesse - buys 80 ac in Fairmount Twp (8/17/70)

MACON, John - 1868 Fairmount Twp landowner (1/8/68)

MACY, John C. - 1867 sells 3 ac in Mill Twp to Elijah Thomas (3/26/68); 1868 Mill Twp landowner (1/12/70)

MACY, Joseph - 1865 buys 3 lots in Fairmount from John T. Howe (2/26/68); sells 3 lots in Fairmount (3/4/68)

MADDOCK, Walter J. - 1867 sells Monroe Twp ac (4/30/68)

MADDOX, Thomas - dec; 1869 owned land in Monroe Twp (12/21/70)

MADDUX, Mr. __ - last wk rescued the baby s of M/M J.L. Custer; the child had fallen into a well (8/4/69)

MAFFIT(T), William N. - owns property in Marion (1/6/69); Dec 1869 buys license to m C[harlotte] J. Hamilton (1/5/70)

MAGEE, James - 1869 buys 89 ac in Richland Twp (11/10/69)

MAGGART, James H. - owns land in Franklin Twp (1/6/69)

MAGGERT, Julia A. - buys 4 ac in Franklin Twp (2/26/68)

MAKEPEACE, Allen - Liberty Twp landowner (1/6/69)

MALCOM, Isaac - May 1868 buys license to m S[arah] A. Randolph (6/4/68)

MALCOM, Morgan V. - Van Buren Twp landowner (1/8/68)

MALCOM, Samuel - sells 80 ac in Mill Twp (6/25/68)

MALOTT, Daniel - owns property in Mier (1/6/69)

MALOTT(E), Lucy - tchr, Morris Chapel SS (5/26/69)

MALOTT, Robert - owns land in Franklin Twp (1/8/68)

MANGIN, Rev. Charles - 26 May 1868 m Thomas F. Dolan to Julia Ann Dillon (6/11/68)

MANN, A[ndrew] J. - Fairmount Twp landowner (1/8/68); buys 5 ac in Fairmount Twp from James E. Fear (12/29/69)

MANN, Isham - sells 40 ac in Jefferson Twp (12/21/70)

MANN, James - Dec 1868 buys license to m Hannah Bevard (1/6/69)

MANNING, R[obert] A. - Mar 1870 buys license to m H[arriet] Walker/Welker (4/6/70)

MANTAGUE, Orson - May 1868 buys license to m Eliza Dove (6/4/68)

MANUEL, Levi - 1867 sells 40 ac in Liberty Twp (5/14/68)

MAPLE, Adda 'Addie' - is att Marion Public Sch (11/6/67)

MAPLE, E.G. - 1869 Sims Twp landowner (12/21/70)

MAPLE, James - pastor/Elder, Marion Christian Ch (9/18/67); wife is Sarah A. Maple (1/8/68); his Ch recently gave him his house which is worth $1,190 (1/27/69)

MAPLE, Sarah - 1869 Sims Twp landowner (12/21/70)

MARINE, Daniel - Dec 1867 buys license to m Mary E. Wright (1/8/68); is on a Co bd to assess property (1/5/70); is elected Jefferson Twp Assessor (10/19/70)

MARION, Public Schools - 1867-68 tchrs are Prof. A.H. Harritt, Principal, and Lindley M. Overman, Mrs. Sarah McClain, Mrs. M.E. Adams (9/25/67); 250 students are enrolled (10/23/67); H.H. Hall of Peru is penmanship tchr at the Academy bldg on Adams St (2/12/68); 15 Mar 1869 begins spring term at Marion

Academy (3/3/69); 534 sch children live in Marion (11/17/69); sch begins 19 Sep 1870 with William Russell, Principal; Miss Emma Harter, HS tchr; Miss M. Cleaveland, grammar sch tchr; Jennie Snorf & Ella Snorf, intermediate dept. tchrs; & __ Cherry, primary tchr (9/14/70)

MARION, Town of - original plat, now contains 179 lots, laid out 10 Feb 1832 by David Branson & Martin Boots; Oppy's Addn of 12 double lots is laid out 4 Jan 1838 by Abraham Oppy; 12 Apr 1838 Nelson Conner lays out Conner's Addn of six double & 2 single lots; 6 May 1838 Martin Boots lays out Boots' Addn of 6 double lots; 1838 Ezra S. Trask lays out 28 large lots of Trask's Addn of Out-Lots; 18 Jan 1840 Nathan Branson lays out 24 double lots of Branson's Addn; 13 Jan 1842 James Turner lays out the 16 lots of Turner's Addn; 6 Nov 1849 Clark Wilcutts lays out 48 lots of Willcuts' Addn; 16 Oct 1854 the RR Co lays out 24 lots in the M&MV RR Addn; 14 Dec 1854 Elihu & Gideon Small lay out 12 lots of Small's Addn; 12 Apr 1855 David R. McKinney lays out 8 lots of McKinney's Addn; 20 Aug 1855 Thomas J. Neal lays out 7 lots of Neal's Addn; 23 Apr 1860 Enoch Thomas lays out 16 lots of Thomas' Addn; 28 Jun 1867 F.S. McKinney lays out 10 lots (5 to 8.5 ac each) of McKinney's Addn Out-Lots; 10 Oct 1867 the heirs of Clark Willcuts (dec) lay out 38 lots of Willcuts' 2nd Addn; 19 Oct 1867 Charles S. Tibbits lays out 36 lots of Tibbits' Addn; 4 Mar 1868 John Brownlee & Daniel Hopkins lay out 10 lots of Haws & Hopkins' Addn; Marion now contains 400 single lots, 34 double lots & 38 out-lots (4/16/68); James R. Noland, Postmaster (9/18/67); Horse Fair to be held here next wk (10/23/67); Horse Fair has 50 entries including 12 stallions (10/30/67); Monroe St between Washington St & Boots St is being graded (11/20/67); William Love, prop of an omnibus that takes passengers & baggage from RR depot to hotels, sometimes has to use a four-horse hitch due to deep mud holes in Adams St & other St around CH; the alley between Washington & Adams Streets is almost impassable on account of mud, trash & manure piles; the east-west alley between Jackson & Madison St is full of lumber, wood & old wagons; the alley between Clay & Monroe St is full of wood & manure piles; Monroe St from Washington over to Branson has sidewalks so full of manure piles that citizens must walk in the middle of the St (4/23/68); John Kiley is refused a liquor license (3/11/69); Harrison St is opened between

Washington St & Branson St (12/15/69); of the 17 Marion lawyers, 2 are Democrats (2/2/70); S of river, Marion has 14 cross streets (6/1/70); new bridge over river is being built on E 3rd St; stone for the bridge abutments & piers are obtained from the Sanders Quarry on the E side of the river ca 1 mi N of Marion (7/6/70); the Pierce Bldg, on NE corner of Square, is being roofed with slate (8/3/70); Capt. Reuss is pres, bd of Town Trustees (12/28/70)

ARNOLD & GUNDER DRY GOODS - buys wool from farmers (6/2/69); located on Adams St (4/13/70)

ATLANTIC & PACIFIC TELEGRAPH - lines extend down Adams St to room over Post Office as telegraph office in business district (1/20/69); F.T. Colver, telegrapher (12/15/69); has agreement with RR telegraph office to send messages on both lines through either office (8/24/70)

BARTLETT JEWELRY STORE - W.K. Bartlett, prop (3/30/70)

BESHORE & BRO. - on S side of Square; L.C. Beshore, prop; sells stoves (11/2/70)

BIGELOW BOARDING HOUSE - on Boots St opposite M.E. Ch parsonage; Capt. __ Bigelow, prop (3/30/70); can accommodate 6 to 8 da boarders (4/13/70)

BIRDEYE'S HAT STORE - sells men's hats on N side of Square (11/3/69)

BIRELEY & CLUNK BOOTS & SHOES - on N side of Square; dealers & manu of boots & shoes (6/4/68); will occupy Sweetser's new room, 2nd door from the back (6/2/69); are in new quarters 2nd door from Sweetser's Bank (7/13/69)

BLUMENTHAL & JOSEPHY - M. Blumenthal & M. Josephy, props; now dissolve their firm (1/13/69)

BOOK, STATIONARY & NOTION STORE - on W side of Square; A.H. Harritt, prop (10/23/67)

BOOT & SHOE SHOP - on S side of Square next to City Drugstore; Reef & Creviston, props (10/30/67)

BOSTON DRY GOODS & CLOTHING STORE - M. Josephy, prop (10/26/70)

BUCHANAN & HATHAWAY MARBLE WORKS - on Washington St (10/27/69)

BUTLER HOTEL - 1842, at 'sign of the green tree' (7/13/70); was on Adams St, it burned down several yr ago (7/6/70)

CAMPBELL & STOUT - sash, door & blind factory; is operated by steam (1/27/69; 5/5/69)

CAREY PHOTOGRAPHY - S.B. Carey, prop & photographer; on second floor, above Mark & Carey's Book Store (4/2/68)
CASE & HICKMAN CHAIR CO - uses new machinery in the Case & Lawton Mill to make 12 dozen chairs per da (1/5/70)
CASE & LAWTON SAWMILL & PLANING MACHINE WORKS - is now in operation (8/12/68); is operated by steam (1/27/69; 5/5/69)
P. & W. CHARLES FLOURING MILL - below town on river (1/27/69); is run by water (5/5/69)
CHRONICLE (f JOURNAL & MONITOR) - Tingley & Joel Reece, prop; office is on NW corner of CH Square (9/18/67); Joel Reece leaves Chronicle (3/4/68)
CITY BAKERY - next door to the Post Office (6/16/69)
CITY BOOK STORE - SW of Square; sells wall & window paper (11/3/69); A.H. Harritt, prop (11/10/69)
CITY DRUGSTORE - on N side of Square; J.H. Clark & John Davis, props (9/18/67); John Davis is now sole prop; A.B. Springer fills drug prescriptions (8/18/69); property now has a 'plank pavement' (9/14/70)
CITY SHOE STORE - on Washington St opposite City Drug Store; J.W. Janes, prop (3/24/69)
COMPTON FURNITURE STORE - located in Pierce Bldg, NE corner of Square; J.W. Compton, prop (8/24/70)
CUSTER & HARVEY LAW OFFICE - in White's Bldg; J.L. Custer & G.W. Harvey, partners (6/9/69)
DAVIS WAGON SHOP - on Front St between Washington St & Boots St; D.F. Davis, prop (11/23/70)
DAVIS & STARRETT - 8 Aug 1868 buys ca 1,000 bushels of flaxseed which is now being harvested (8/12/68); stock flax seed for sale to farmers (3/3/69); partnership is dissolved; Davis carries on the business (8/18/69)
DeLONG STORE - W.C. DeLong, prop; on E side of Square; sells clothing, buys butter, eggs, beeswax, feathers and hides (10/30/67); located 1st door N of Post Office (11/10/69); sells oysters (11/16/70)
DEER CREEK VALLEY MILLS - Hollingsworth & Small, props; grind meal & flour for bread (12/29/69)
DOTY MILLINERY STORE - above Neal & Lenox; Mrs. M. Doty, prop (5/11/70)
EAGLE DRUGSTORE - on E side of Square; L.J. Starritt, prop (11/17/69)

EAGLE SHOE STORE - L.D. Carey & Bro., props (12/25/67); their new business room is being built on Washington St (1/1/68)
EXCHANGE BANK - Jason Willson & Co, props (9/7/70)
FARMERS GROCERY - on Adams St, 1st blk above Square (6/25/68); Daniel Gunder, prop (1/13/69)
GORDON & JONES - have an office in their new bldg on S side of Square (5/5/69)
GUNDER GROCERY - Daniel Gunder, prop; opens on Adams St on corner of 1st blk above Square, next door to Marion Marble Works (6/4/68)
HAYS & MASON - planing mill; is operated by steam (1/27/69; 5/5/69); is constructing an extensive bldg on Adams St beyond [S of ?] the RR (6/16/69)
HIATT FEED & LIVERY STABLE -1 blk S of Spencer House; Lee M. Hiatt, prop (1/12/70)
HICKMAN, CASE & Co - chair factory; has a new bldg adjoining their mill for finishing and storing chairs (5/18/70)
HITE & HARMON FLOURING MILL - above town on river (1/27/69); is run by water (5/5/69)
HITE & HARMON SAWMILL - is operated by water (1/27/69)
HOGIN & GOLDTHAIT DRYGOODS - located in White Bldg; D.S. Hogin & Cimon Goldthait, props (12/29/69)
HUMPHREY'S HARDWARE - mentioned (8/12/68); on SE corner of Square; C.W. Humphrey, prop (9/7/70)
INDIANA HOUSE - existed in 1851 with Dr. __ Williams, prop (8/17/70)
JAY & MOORE DRUG STORE - was robbed of a small amount of cash last night (8/12/68)
JOHNSON'S ICE CREAM PARLOR - is above/over City Drug Store (6/2/69); sells ice cream, strawberries & lemonade (6/9/69)
JOSEPHY'S CLOTHING STORE - on N side of Square beside Pierce Hardware (10/30/67); see BOSTON DRY GOODS & CLOTHING STORE
McLANE & BROS. - a branch of the Somerset Woolen Mills; is on SW corner of the Square; buys wool & sells woolen goods (5/25/70)
MARION CHRONICLE - began publication in 1867 succeeding a newspaper called the 'Journal and Monitor'; 'Chronicle' was 1st located in Neal & Lenox's Bldg on NW corner of Square; in

Dec 1868 it was moved to J.C. Nottingham's Bldg 2 blks further up Washington St (9/1/69)

MARION DEMOCRATIC HERALD - began publication in 1842 with Jeremiah Harry, publ, and John Gilbert, ed; its office was on Adams St opposite Henry Pierce's Store (7/6/70)

MARION FOUNDRY - S. Hulley & J. Hulley, props; manuf Hackley Breaking Plows (2/26/68); is run by steam (5/5/69); has new steam engine (11/16/70)

MARION JOURNAL - 1851 was edited & publ by J.F. & T.J. McDowell; was only publ for 14 weeks (7/6/70)

MARION MARBLE WORKS - is on site of f Butler Hotel that burned several yr ago (7/6/70); on S Adams St; Adams & McDowell, props (12/11/67); is in 2nd blk above [north of] CH (3/26/68); Shook & McDowell, props (5/5/69)

MARION NURSERY - 0.5 mi SW of Marion RR depot; W.B. Lipsey, prop; sells Elias Howe sewing machines (11/30/70)

MARION OMNIBUS LINE - f owned by Reece & King; now A. Bigelow is prop; will meet all trains (1/5/70); on NE corner of Square (9/7/70)

MARION TELEGRAPH - 1847 is publ by J.A. Stretch, eds are Benjamin Woolman & James Brownlee; office is in Carey's brick bldg on N side of Square; it is Whig in politics (7/6/70)

MARION WESTERN UNION - 1849, E.C. Overman, ed & J.D. Cook, publ; is Whig in politics (7/6/70)

MARION WOOLEN MILLS - W.D. & N. Mowrer, props; is at mouth of Boots Creek; is run by water (5/5/69)

MARKS & CAREY'S JEWELRY & BOOKSTORE - on N side of CH Square (9/18/67); S. Carey, prop (11/2/70)

MILLER GROCERY STORE - on S Washington St; C.C. Miller, prop (11/10/69)

MILLINERY & FANCY GOODS SHOP - now open in Pierce Bldg, N side of CH Square; Mary Allen & Maggie Kinneer, props (4/9/68)

MISSISSINEWA GAZETTE - 1854, publ by D.W. Jones; office on Adams St opposite the Marion Hotel (7/6/70)

MOORE & EYESTONE STOVE DEPOT - T.C. Moore is a prop (12/11/67); is now MOORE & IAMS; is located next door to Sweetser's Bank (6/16/69)

NEW CASH STORE - William E. Doyle, prop (8/12/68)

NEW HARDWARE - on corner of Washington & Clay Streets; props are David Laufman, Amos H. Kling & George H. Kling (1/13/69)

NEW TOBACCO STORE - 1st door N of Doyle's Drygoods Store; G.B. Rowan, prop (1/6/69)
NEW YORK CASH CLOTHING STORE - mentioned (9/18/67)
OYSTER BAR - 23 Dec 1867 opens in the 1st room above the City Drug Store; John Johnson, prop (1/13/69)
PEGDEN PAINT SHOP - located over Zahn & Barley's Wagon Shop; William Pegden, prop; house & ornamental painting (9/7/70)
PEOPLE'S DRUG STORE - on N side of Square; C. Reece, prop (2/26/68)
PIERCE HARDWARE - 1842 is on Adams St (7/6/70); on N side of Square (10/30/67); Henry Pierce, prop (7/23/69)
REECE KILN - 1 mi N of Marion; J. Reece, prop; makes & sells brick (8/24/70)
J. REECE & SISTERS MILLINERY STORE - mentioned (9/18/67; 10/27/69)
REED, BUTLER & CO - hub, spoke & bending factory; is steam operated (1/27/69)
D.H. & J.W. SANDERS - brick layers & builders; residence is on S Branson St (1/5/70)
J. & J. SECRIST FLOURING MILL - below town on river (1/27/69); is run by water (5/5/69)
SECRIST & FISHELL ARCHITECTS - advertisement (9/7/70)
SHAW SADDLE SHOP - existed in 1847; Francis A. Shaw, prop (7/20/70)
SIZEMORE BARBERSHOP - James A. Sizemore, prop/barber in renovated barbershop under the Spencer House (7/1/68)
SOHN's GROCERY - is on N side of Square (1/13/69); sells white fish, catfish & mackerel by the half barrel (6/16/69); on NE corner of Square in bldg next to H. Pierce's Hardware Store; John Sohn, prop (7/23/69)
SPENCER HOUSE - Jacob W. Spencer, prop; is constructing a bldg adjoining his hotel (5/5/69)
STEBBENS MILLINERY SHOP - Mrs. M. Stebbens, prop; on Washington St SW of Webster's New York Cash Store (10/1/67); is located next door to City Drug Store (7/8/68)
STOVE DEPOT - on Washington St, sells eave troughs & spouting (3/12/68); prop G.W. Eyestone sells his interest to Jesse Iams; Moore & Iams are now props (2/17/69); is next door to Sweetser's Bank (8/17/70)

SWAYZEE & CO STORE - A.C. Swayzee, prop; store is on W side of CH Square (9/18/67); sells dry goods, groceries & notions (6/4/68)

SWOPE BLACKSMITH & HORSE SHOEING SHOP - is on Adams St S of Spencer House; William J. Swope, prop (9/18/67)

TAILOR SHOP - D. Hopkins, tailor; located 1 door S of Sweetser & Co (9/18/67)

THARP & NEAL GROCERY - on E side of Square; T.D. Tharp & William Neal, props (6/2/69)

THOMAS & BESHORE GROCERY - on SW corner of Square (7/23/69)

TIBBITTS & Co HUB & SPOKE FACTORY - C.S. Tibbitts, prop; is run by steam (5/5/69); the factory burned last wk causing a loss of $25,000, it may be re-built next yr (11/3/69)

TRIPP & VAIL - replaces Tripp & Kelley because 16 Jan 1869 Dr. M.S. Vail buys out the interest of I.C. Kelley (3/3/69)

TURNER BLACKSMITH SHOP - James P. Turner, prop; is located on Adams St 1 blk above Spencer House (4/7/69)

UNION HOUSE - Houck & Kennedy, props; is 1 blk SE of Square at corner of Clay St & Branson St (9/18/67); is closed; furnishings are being sold by Mr. Houck (1/15/68); is reopened with C.S. Barley, prop (4/2/68)

WATERBURY & KELLER TAILOR SHOP - located next to City Drug Store on N side of Square; do tailoring and sell hats, capes & gent's clothing (4/9/68)

WINCHEL & CO DRYGOODS - props are G.N. Winchel and Miles Murphy (8/18/69)

SAMUEL WOOD & CO STAVE FACTORY - a distance E of the RR Depot is Barley's Bldg, intended for a sash, door & blind factory; it was purchased and transformed into a stave factory; up to 40 employees will make 5,000 staves per da; staves will be kiln dried and shipped to Pittsburg, PA, to make coal oil barrels (8/12/68); near RR in SE part of Marion; uses steam power (1/27/69; 5/5/69)

YOUNG ICE CREAM SALOON - Benjamin Young, prop; located over/above Eshelman & Reuss Grocery; sells ice cream & lemonades (6/2/69)

YOUNG TAILOR SHOP - in Flinn's Bldg below G.N. Winchel & Co; H. Young, prop (7/13/70)

E.S. ZAHN & Co - on Adams St 2nd blk above Square; they manuf wagons, carriages & buggies to order (7/8/68); are constructing their new business bldg at corner of Adams St & Monroe St (5/5/69)

MARION, Schools of - Marion has 3 sch houses for ca 450 [potential?] scholars between the ages of 6 and 21 (7/23/69); William M. Russell, Principal (1/12/70); now has 540 potential students (8/31/70)

MARION LITERARY SOCIETY - is organized; to have declamations, essays & debates; meets each Monday evening in the sch bldg on Adams St; officers: G.W. Harvey, pres; J.W. Beshore, v pres; M.F. Tingley, secy; J.L. Custer, treas; L.M. Overman, doorkeeper (1/15/68)

MARION SILVER BAND - 25 Apr 1868 will play at 49th Anniv of IOOF in America (4/23/68); has its headquarters in the City Drug Store Bldg (7/8/68)

MARKS, Commodore P. - finds a stray steer calf (1/13/69)

MARKS, George O. - 1867 sells Jalapa lots to Isaiah Conner (1/22/68); sells 1 lot in Mier to Noah Minnick (1/29/68)

MARK(S), James B. - Sims Twp taxpayer (1/26/70); buys 120 ac in Sims Twp from Benjamin Moore (11/2/70)

MARKS, John - owns property in Jalapa (1/6/69)

MARK(S), Joseph B. - viewer for a rd in Sims Twp (6/23/69); 1869 buys/sells Sims Twp ac (1/5/70); contractor; was bldg an M.P. Ch in Sims Twp when it burned (11/2/70)

MARKS, M.J. - Pleasant Twp landowner (1/6/69)

MARONEY, John - 1867 buys 80 ac in Fairmount Twp from Joseph Kinsey & 1868 sells 80 ac in Fairmount Twp (1/15/68)

MARSH, Ann - b PA; age 73; mbr M.E. Ch for 45 yrs; d 18 May 1868 (5/28/68)

MARSH, B.W. - buys/sells Marion lots (3/4/68; 4/2/68)

MARSH, Benjamin - 1867 buys Washington Twp ac (4/30/68)

MARSH, Daisy - age 2y, 6m, 12da; dt Marcus L. and M[artha] E. Marsh; d recently (2/12/68)

MARSH, Rev. E. - pastor, Marion Wesleyan Ch (3/26/68)

MARSH, Enoch - sells 100 ac in Washington Twp (10/5/70)

MARSH, John - Feb 1869 buys license to m Sarah P. Evans (3/3/69)

MARSH, Joseph - one of Marion's oldest citizens; d 4 May 1869 (5/5/69)

MARSH, J[oseph] L. - buys a lot in Marion (7/13/70)

MARSH, M.D. - admin estate of Sarah Calentine, dec (12/11/67)

MARSH, Marcus L. - sells 40 ac in Green Twp (5/14/68); left for Washington, D.C. this wk to att inauguration of pres Grant (3/3/69); organizes support for the proposed GR,W&C RR (11/3/69); Rep candidate for Co Clerk (7/13/70); admin estate of Jacob Line, dec (8/3/70)

MARSHALL, E[li] B. - losing candidate for JP, Franklin Twp (10/19/70)

MARSHALL, Jane - Monroe Twp landowner (1/8/68)

MARSHALL, John D. - sells 80 ac in Van Buren Twp (7/13/70)

MARSHALL, Joshua - appraises the benefits/damages of Wild Cat Prairie Ditch; sells 40 ac in Franklin Twp (3/12/68)

MARSHALL, Lindsey - 1869 Mill Twp landowner (12/21/70)

MARSHALL, Linneus - Dec 1867 buys license to m Harriett Jeffries (1/8/68)

MARSHALL, M.A. - 1868 Pleasant Twp landowner (1/12/70)

MARSHALL, Rebecca - dec; John Cantwell admin her estate (12/11/67)

MARSHALL, Samuel - 21 May 1869 m Mary A. Roberts (5/26/69; 6/2/69)

MARSHALL, Sol R. - 1869 Jefferson Twp landowner (1/6/69)

MARSHALL, Z[imri] N. - Jan 1869 buys license to m Lydia A. Price (2/3/69)

MART, James J. - sells 40 ac in Liberty Twp (12/29/69)

MART, J[ohn] W. - Apr 1868 buys license to m S[arah] J[ane] Achor (5/14/68)

MARTAL, Stephen - Franklin Twp landowner (1/6/69)

MASON, Anna [(Coleman)]- 1869 owns 37.89 ac of land in Franklin Twp, part of NE 1/4 of NW 1/4, Sec. 22 & part of E half of SW 1/4 of Sec. 15, T24, R7 (12/21/70)

MASON, David B. - sells a Marion ac (2/12/68); sells a planing mill in Marion to C.W. Hill & F.S. McKinney (7/6/70)

MASON, Frederick - 1867 buys 14 ac in Fairmount Twp (4/30/68); buys 80 ac in Fairmount Twp (12/21/70)

MASON, George - dec; owned Fairmount Twp land (1/6/69)

MASON, Mahala [(Coleman)] - 1868 Franklin Twp landowner (1/12/70)

MASON, Michael S. - of Franklin Twp; May 1868 found a stray sorrel mare (6/25/68)

MASON, S.J. - 1869 Fairmount Twp landowner (12/21/70)

MASON, Samuel S. - 1868 Liberty Twp landowner (1/12/70)

MASON, Samuel W. - Dec 1867 buys license to m Eliza R. Evans (1/8/68)

MASON, Sarah A. - 1869 Fairmount Twp landowner (12/21/70)

MASON, Susannah - sells land in Fairmount Twp (5/14/68)

MASSER, Bartley - sells 1 lot in Marion (4/30/68)

MASSEY, Enos B. - Van Buren Twp landowner (1/6/69)

MASSEY, Evan E. - buys Pleasant Twp land (4/30/68; 5/14/68)

MASSEY, Lewis A. - buys 40 ac in Pleasant Twp (4/30/68)

MASSEY, P.J. - 1869 buys 80 ac in Washington Twp(1/5/70)

MASSEY, Rebecca L. - buys ac in Washington Twp (5/18/70)

MASSEY, Robert - Washington Twp landowner (1/8/68)

MASSEY, R[obert] C. - Mar 1868 buys license to m M[ary] E. Endsley (4/2/68)

MASTERS, William Z. - buys 8 ac in Center Twp from William M. Evans (11/30/70); sells 8 ac in Green Twp (12/21/70)

MATCHETT(E), Daniel - buys 40 ac in Green Twp (5/14/68)

MATHENY, Benjamin - 1866 sells 62 ac in Van Buren Twp to Dr. Lavanner Corey (4/2/68)

MATHER, Miss Addie - is att Marion Sch (11/13/67)

MATHES, William - Liberty Twp landowner (1/6/69)

MATHIS, William - recently dec (12/11/67)

MAY, Amos - Van Buren Twp landowner (1/8/68)

MAY, H[enry] F. - Dec 1869 buys license to m Lucinda Carriens (1/5/70)

MAYNARD, William - 1867 sells 80 Fairmount Twp ac (3/4/68)

MAYNE, [William] - of Tipton; 23 Nov 1870 m Louise Seward, dt Frederick Seward, Esq (11/23/70)

MEEK, Dr. J[ohn] A. - mbr, Grant Co Medical Soc (11/20/67)

MELDRUM, Henry - buys 37 ac in Liberty Twp (11/3/69)

MELLETT, Joshua F. - Rep candidate, Circuit Judge (7/13/70)

MENDENHALL, Aaron - sells 20 ac in Green Twp (4/30/68)

MENDENHALL, Isaac - is att Marion Public Sch (12/18/67)

MENDENHALL, John - Franklin Twp landowner (1/8/68)

MENDENHALL, William K. - 1866 sells 10 ac in Liberty Twp to Mary A. Haisley (1/22/68)

ME-SHIN-GO-ME-SIA 'SHINGLEMACY' - his father was killed in 1812 near Jalapa in battle with Col. Campbell's troops (10/27/69); Chief of the Miamis; and wife were in town last wk walking about town in Indian file; they left on horseback still in Indian file (5/25/70)

MESSMORE, Albert G. - 1867 buys 40 ac in Green Twp from William Knox (4/2/68); buys 80 ac in Green Twp (12/15/69)

MICHAEL, Peter - and wife, Eveline, separated in 1842 (7/13/70); buys 0.5 ac in Franklin Twp (7/20/70)

MICHAEL(S), William - Feb 1869 buys license to m Jemima J. Meeks (3/3/69); buys 40 ac in Franklin Twp (6/8/70)

MIDDLETON, William - sells 40 ac in Center Twp to A.C. Swayzee & buys 2 lots in Marion (12/16/70)

MIER, Town of - original plat of 30 lots is laid out 11 & 12 Sep 1848 by Charles Parker & John P. Sinclair; 29 Mar 1849 John P. Sinclair lays out the 12 lots of Sinclair's Addn; 26 Mar 1864 Benjamin Hamden lays out the 38 lots of Hamden's Addn making a total of 80 lots in Mier (4/23/68)

MILES, Adda - is att Marion Public Sch (1/12/70), & now att Marion HS (12/23/70)

MILES, David F. - admin estate of Lorenzo Miles, dec (4/2/68)

MILES, Lorenzo - dec; owned land in Jefferson Twp (1/6/69)

MILES, Luther - petitioned bd of County Comm for a new rd in Pleasant Twp, petition granted (3/11/69)

MILES, William C. - 1850 is Whig candidate for Grant Co Comm (8/18/69)

MILL TOWNSHIP - sometime after 1847 Mill Twp was formed from the S part of Center Twp & the NE part of Liberty Twp (7/20/70); T.C. Beall, Trustee (9/18/67); bd of County Commissioners gave the Mill Twp Trustee $75.00 to aid in bldg a bridge over Walnut Creek on the Mill Twp & Monroe Twp line; Morris Fankboner is a Constable for Mill Twp (3/11/69)

MILL TOWNSHIP, Schools of - 294 school children reside in Twp, not including Jonesboro (11/17/69)
JONESBORO HIGH SCHOOL - Sch Trustees are Dr. _ Wright, Morris Fankboner & Elijah Carter; 29 Mar 1869 will open for a term of 12 wk; this is the 3rd term of its 4th yr [having been est in 1864]; L.H. Jones, Principal; tchrs are Almeda Jones, Addie Evans & Mattie E. Jones (3/11/69)

MILLER, Aaron - dec; Isaac Rybolt admin his estate (1/1/68)

MILLER, Andrew - sells 0.25 ac in Green Twp to Green Twp [for sch site?] for $25 (4/2/68)

MILLER, Ann - dec; 1868 her heirs owned land in Sims Twp (1/12/70)

MILLER, Archibald - Green Twp landowner (1/6/69)

MILLER, D.C. - Sims Twp landowner (1/8/68)

MILLER, Ephraim - buys 73 ac in Liberty Twp (4/16/68)

MILLER, George - Jan 1869 buys license to m Margaret Corey (2/3/69)

MILLER, George W. - Dec 1867 buys license to m Anna M. Stebbins (1/8/68); 1867 buys 1 ac in Richland Twp (3/12/68)

MILLER, Henry - buys 30.97 ac in Pleasant Twp (1/29/68)

MILLER, Henry C. - 1868 Van Buren Twp landowner (1/12/70)

MILLER, Isaac - buys 80 ac in Sims Twp (9/7/70)

MILLER, Isaiah - is dec (8/18/65)

MILLER, Jeremiah - Apr 1869 buys license to m Salina Patterson (5/5/69)

MILLER, Samuel - Mar 1868 buys license to m Eliza Millhollen (4/2/68)

MILLER, William - dec; 1869 owned Liberty Twp land (12/21/70)

MILLS, Isaac N. - 1867 buys land in Fairmount Twp (5/14/68)

MILLS, Job S. - 1866 buys 10 ac in Franklin Twp (4/9/68); sells 1 Marion lot (2/12/68); sells 160 ac in Franklin Twp (11/2/70)

MILLS, Jonathan - sells 145 ac in Franklin Twp (8/17/70)

MILLS, Joseph - 1869 buys 80 ac in Monroe Twp & buys 80 ac in Center Twp & buys 2 ac in Monroe Twp (1/5/70)

MILLS, Naomi - is att Marion Public Sch (11/6/67)

MILTON, William - buys 2 ac in Liberty Twp (1/22/68)

MINER/MINOR, John H. - Dec 1868 buys license to m Anabell Holliday (1/6/69)

MINNICK, Jacob - a Grant Co Comm (10/1/67); lives near M.H. Crist in Richland Twp (9/1/69)

MINNICK, Noah - buys 1 lot in Mier (1/29/68)

MINTON, John R. - 1869 Fairmount Twp landowner (1/6/69)

MISER, Nancy - buys a lot in Marion from C.S. Tibbits (2/9/70)

MISSISSINEWA RIVER - Charles Mill mentioned (10/9/67); Heffner's Wharf is at ft of Adams St, Marion (4/23/68); a new bridge is to be built over the river at Somerset (8/3/70)

MITCHELL, Osborn - Apr 1869 buys license to m Patience Green (5/5/69); is colored; his house, 2 mi from Marion near the Jonesboro Rd, burned last wk; C.S. Ratliff furnished another house & the Friends Meeting is helping family (12/28/70)

MITTANK, Christopher - 1867 sells 58.33 ac in Jefferson Twp (4/16/68); att Old Settlers meeting (6/8/70)

MITTANK, John - sells property in Jefferson Twp (10/5/70)

MITTANK, Michael - 1867 buys a Washington Twp property from Zimri S. Richardson (1/8/68)

MODLIN, G.W. - of Sims Twp; CW vet (1/19/70)

MONROE, William - Van Buren Twp landowner (1/8/68)

MONROE TOWNSHIP - George Strange, Trustee (9/18/67); 8 Sep 1866 buys 24 rods(?) in Monroe Twp from John Finney, Sr. for $10 [for schoolyard (?)] (5/14/68)

MONROE TOWNSHIP, Schools of - 404 school children reside in Twp (11/17/69)

MONTGOMERY, James S. - Van Buren Twp landowner (1/8/68)

MONTGOMERY, John J. - of Center Twp recently found a stray cow (2/9/70)

MOON, Elkanah - 1869 sells 20 ac in Monroe Twp (1/5/70)

MOON, James - 1868 Liberty Twp landowner (1/12/70)

MOON, Martin H. - 1869 Franklin Twp landowner (12/21/70)

MOORE, Benjamin - sells 120 ac in Sims Twp (11/2/70)

MOORE, Mrs. Caroline - officer, Rebekah Lodge, Jonesboro (4/28/69)

MOORE, Effa Ann [(Williams)] - 1868 Sims Twp landowner (1/12/70)

MOORE, Henry - 1869 Jefferson Twp landowner (12/21/70)

MOORE, Henry C. - 1869 Monroe Twp landowner (1/6/69)

MOORE, I[saac] E. - April 1868 buys license to m M[argaret] J. Wilson (5/14/68)

MOORE, Isaac - f of 2 mi NE of Marion for over 30 yr; recently moved to IA to live with a dt; d IA 27 Jun 1869 (7/13/69)

MOORE, Jabez - att recent Old Settlers meeting (6/15/71)

MOORE, James A. - 1867(?) sells 1 lot in Jonesboro (6/25/68)

MOORE, John - 1869 owns property in Fairmount (12/21/70)

MOORE, Maggie - is att Marion Public Sch (1/12/70)

MOORE, Miss Mollie - is att Marion Public Sch (11/6/67)

MOORE, Nathan - 1867 buys 80 ac in Fairmount Twp from Isaac Carey (1/22/68); sells 10 ac in Liberty Twp (4/9/68)

MOORE, Patterson - 1867 sells Gabriel Prickett 5 ac in Washington Twp (1/8/68)

MOORE, Mrs. Rose - 1869 owns Marion property (12/21/70); buys property near Marion (11/2/70)

MOORE, Samuel - Mill Twp dir, 1870 Grant Co Fair (8/3/70); prop, Moore Hotel, Jonesboro; owns driving horse named 'Bloomer' (9/14/70); buys property in Jefferson Twp (10/5/70); losing candidate for JP, Mill Twp (10/19/70)

MOORE, Stephen W. - serv 4 yr as soldier during CW; is a Rep candidate for Sheriff (2/17/69)

MOORE, T[homas] C. - a prop, Moore & Eyestone Stove Depot (12/11/67); Union Party candidate for Grant Co Recorder (3/4/68), withdraws his candidacy (3/26/68)

MOORE, Thomas P. - 1863 buys 1 lot in Jonesboro (2/12/68); Trustee for 4th Ward, Jonesboro (5/11/70)

MOORE, W[illiam] H. - Dec 1869 buys license to m M[ahala] Jordon (1/5/70)

MOORMAN, Levi - 1869 Jefferson Twp landowner (1/6/69)

MOREHEAD, Silas G. - buys Jalapa lots (12/16/70)

MOREHEAD, William - buys 30 ac in Center Twp (12/29/69)

MORELAND, David - is dec (8/18/65)

MORGAN, James - buys 40 ac in Liberty Twp (11/3/69)

MORGAN, John T. - Sims Twp landowner (1/6/69)

MORGAN, Lewis F.R. - Sims Twp landowner (1/8/68); sells 1 ac to Pleasant View Christian Ch (2/26/68)

MORGAN, Patrick - sells 20 ac in Sims Twp to Sarah A. Floyd (3/4/68), & buys 1 ac in Center Twp (4/2/68)

MORRIS, Benjamin F. - buys 4 ac in Center Twp (11/2/70)

MORRIS, Caleb - dec farmer; Cornelius Romaine admin his estate (9/18/67)

MORRIS, G[eorge M.] - Dec 1869 buys license to m M[artha J.] Lackey (1/5/70)

MORRIS, George W. - sells 40 ac in Liberty Twp (4/13/70)

MORRIS, Leander W. - 1867 sells land in Center Twp & 1868 buys 1 lot in Marion & 1868 buys 36 ac in Franklin Twp from Harrison Hurley (1/29/68); sells 1 lot in Marion (3/4/68)

MORRIS, Thomas E. - Dec 1867 buys license to m Martha E. Knight (1/8/68)

MORROW, Rev. Joseph, Jr. - Clerk, Grant Co (10/1/67); 1867 sells property in Jonesboro (1/15/68;1/29/68), & sells part of a lot in Jonesboro (5/14/68); buys 2 lots in Marion (11/10/69), & buys property in Jonesboro & sells Marion property (1/5/70)

MORROW, Joseph, Sr. - 1850 is Whig candidate for State Representative (8/18/69); dec; 1868 his heirs owned property in Jonesboro (1/12/70)

MORSEMAN, Abel - Sims Twp landowner (1/8/68)

MOWRER, Daniel - of Marion; declares bankruptcy (10/23/67); is collecting funds for erection of new Marion Presbyterian Ch (8/17/70)

MOWRER, Hattie - is att Marion Public Sch (11/6/67)

MOWRER, W.D. - 1869 owns property in Marion (12/21/70)

MOXENBARGER, Samuel - buys ac in Green Twp (1/26/70)

MULLEN, Amos - 1866 sells 160 ac in Van Buren Twp to G.K. Thompson (2/26/68)

MULLEN, Catherine - 1868 owns property in New Cumberland (1/12/70)

MULLEN, Wilson - buys 2 lots in Marion (7/13/70)

MULLER, John - of Liberty Twp; recently found a stray yearling calf (12/8/69)

MURPHY, Boaz - buys 1 lot in Independence (3/4/68); prop of a wagon shop in Independence (4/6/70)

MURPHY, C. - SS tchr, Salem Ch (5/5/69)

MURPHY, Laura - buys 2 lots in Marion (2/2/70)

MURPHY, Miles - f of Wabash; new partner with G.N. Winchel in drygoods business (8/18/69)

MURPHY, Patrick - buys 2 lots in Marion (10/26/70)

MURRAY, Andrew - of Liberty Twp; recently found a stray steer (2/12/68)

MURRAY/MURRY, Caroline - 1869 buys a lot in Marion from Cimon Goldthait (1/5/70)

MURRAY, E. Constantine - is att Marion Public Sch (11/6/67)

MURRAY/MURRY, Elias C. - 1869 buys a Marion lot (1/5/70)

MURRAY, Henry - Mar 1869 buys a license to m Hannah Price (4/7/69)

MURRAY, John - sells 152 ac in Sims Twp to William Wood (4/13/70); 30 Aug 1870 m Mary A. Mullen (8/31/70)

MYERS, David - Mar 1869 buys a license to m Mary McCoy (4/7/69)

MYERS, Evan - buys 40 ac in Sims Twp (4/27/70)

MYERS/MYRES, Jacob - 1869 owns property in Jonesboro (12/21/70)

MYERS, John - owns property in Mier & in Jonesboro (1/6/69)

MYERS, M. - Sexton, Salem Ch SS (5/5/69)

MYERS, M.J. - Washington Twp landowner (1/6/69)

MYERS, Thomas - sells 40 ac in Monroe Twp (9/21/70)

MYRES, H.J. - Washington Twp landowner (1/8/68)

MYRES, Jonathan - Oct 1870 buys a license to m M[ary] A. McDaniel (11/2/70)

NEAL, Charles E. - 19 May 1870 m Abbie E. Patterson (5/25/70)

NEAL, Eli - sells property in Fairmount (11/10/69)

NEAL, H.M. - owns property in Jalapa (1/6/69)

NEAL, James - is att Marion Public Sch (11/6/67)

NEAL, James B. - 3 Jun 1869 m Mary E. Knight (6/2/69; 6/9/69)

NEAL, Dr. James C.M. - Union Party candidate for Grant Co Recorder (3/4/68); mbr, Grant Co Medical Soc (5/21/68)

NEAL, Jane - is att Marion Public Sch (11/6/67; 1/12/70); Marion HS student (12/23/70)

NEAL, Oliver - is att Marion Public Sch (11/6/67)

NEAL, Rachel - sells two lots in Fairmount (12/25/67)

NEAL, Thomas C. - is att Marion Public Sch (11/6/67; 1/12/70); Marion HS student (12/23/70); tchr, Sch No. 9, Washington Twp (12/16/70)

NEAL, Thomas J. - Aug 1849 offers clocks for sale (8/3/70); 1850 is a Marion grocer (8/18/69); Aug 1855 lays out Neal's Addn, Marion (4/16/68); 1867 sells 2 Marion lots to U&L RR (6/25/68); owns property in Jonesboro (1/6/69; 12/21/70); buys 40 ac in Center Twp from Mary E. Adams (10/27/69)

NEAL, William - Grant Co Auditor (2/26/68); left for Washington, D.C. this wk to att inauguration of pres Grant (3/3/69); while in D.C., his home here burned due to a faulty flue (3/11/69); partner in new Tharp & Neal Grocery on E side of Square (6/2/69); organizes support for the proposed GR,W&C RR (11/3/69); sells a lot in Marion (5/11/70)

NEEDLER, David M. - JP, Jefferson Twp (10/19/70)

NEEDLER, John - Jefferson Twp landowner (1/6/69)

NEFF, Joseph - of Pleasant Twp; is on a Co bd to assess property (1/5/70); Pleasant Twp Assessor (10/19/70)

NELSON, Avis (Harvey) - officer, Rebekah Lodge, Jonesboro (4/28/69)

NELSON, Benoni - 24 Jul 1869 m Rebecca Connelly (7/28/69)

NELSON, Jesse H. - 22 Dec 1867 m Avis Harvey of near Jonesboro (1/8/68; 1/15/68); Jonesboro merchant, sells Elias Howe sewing machines (11/30/70)

NELSON, [John] C. - Feb 1868 buys license to m [Sarah] H. Entzminger (3/4/68)

NELSON, John W. - buys 88 ac in Center Twp (10/27/69)

NELSON, Johnson - Jun 1868 buys license to m Sarah Thrasher (7/1/68)

NELSON, Martin, Jr. - buys 40 ac in Monroe Twp (9/21/70)

NELSON, Martin, Sr. - buys 40 ac in Monroe Twp from Robert E. Hodson (3/4/68); recently found a stray red cow (1/5/70)

NELSON, Micah - Dec 1867 buys license to m Mariah W. Williams (1/8/68)

NELSON, William - buys property adjoining Jonesboro from Samuel Jay & buys a lot in Jonesboro (4/9/68); sells 80 ac in Jefferson Twp to Henderson Nelson (5/25/70)

NEW CUMBERLAND, Town of - Sep 1853 its 38 lots were laid out by Robert Sanders (4/23/68); is on W bank of Mississinewa River 18 mi from Marion; has 3 general stores, 1 MD, 1 blacksmith shop, 1 flouring mill, and a Presbyterian Ch is being built (2/3/69); is 12 mi SE of Jonesboro; has 11 houses, 1 store, & a bridge crossing the river (9/14/70)

NEWBERGER, Jacob - 1866 sells 40 ac in Jefferson Twp (4/30/68); buys a lot in New Cumberland (1/26/70)

NEWBY, Harvey W. - 1868 Richland Twp landowner (1/12/70)

NEWCOMB, Mrs. Mary C. - see John R. KIRKWOOD

NEWELL, James P. - Jan 1869 buys license to m Louisa Frantz (2/3/69)

NEWKIRK, A[braham] - Dec 1867 buys license to m Rebecca J. Gray (1/8/68)

NEWKIRK, Cassie A. - Green Twp landowner (1/8/68)

NEWPORT, David - Monroe Twp landowner (1/8/68)

NEWTON, Nathaniel - 1868 Liberty Twp landowner (1/12/70)

NICHOLS, Martha A. - 1869 Van Buren Twp landowner (12/21/70)

NIXON, J.H. - 1868 Monroe Twp landowner (1/12/70)

NOFTSKER, Jacob - Green Twp landowner (1/6/69)

NOLAND, Mr. F.F. - age 18y, 10m; d 28 Apr 1868 (4/30/68)

NOLAND, James R. - Marion Postmaster (9/18/67)

NOLAND, Miss Susan Ann - age 22; mbr Marion Christian Ch; d 22 Oct 1869 (10/27/69)

NORMAN, Benjamin R. - buys a lot in Marion (11/2/70)

NORMAN, Isaac - dec 1842 or before (7/13/70)

NORRIS, Edward B. - sells 60 ac in Sims Twp (9/21/70)

NORTON, A[lfred] F. - Aug 1869 buys license to m M[ary] E. Crowell (9/8/69)

NORTON, Arthur - 1869 Liberty Twp landowner (12/21/70)

NORTON, Eugene - 1850 is Democrat candidate for Grant Co delegate to the State Constitutional Conv (8/18/69)

NORTON, James - Center Twp landowner (1/6/69)

NORTON, Lester L. - is att Marion Public Sch (11/6/67)

NORTON, Mary (Booth) - age 80; b Newton, CT; dt Jonathan Booth; widow for 30 yr; mbr Episcopal Ch; d 6 Dec 1867 (12/11/67)

NORTON, Mollie - is att Marion Public Sch (11/6/67)

NORTON, Pierce - is att Marion Public Sch (11/6/67)

NOSE, John - Dec 1869 buys license to m E[mma] W. Douglass (1/5/70); 1869 Fairmount Twp landowner (12/21/70)

NOTE, Benjamin F. - 25 Sep 1869 m Tabitha Morgan, both of Grant Co (9/29/69)

NOTTINGHAM, James - organizes Jefferson Twp support for proposed GR,W&C RR (11/3/69)

NOTTINGHAM, John C. - treas, Grant Co (10/1/67); buys 0.52 ac lot in S end of Marion & buys 1 lot in S end of Marion (2/12/68); Union Party candidate for Grant Co treas (3/4/68); his Bldg is on Washington St 2 blk N of Square (9/1/69); sells a lot on Washington St, Marion (10/27/69), & buys 40 ac in Green Twp (11/24/69); of Center Twp; CW vet (1/19/70)

NOTTINGHAM, O.P. - buys 45 ac in Jefferson Twp (4/27/70)

NOTTINGHAM, P[eter] P. - Feb 1868 buys license to m S[arah] F. Fankboner (3/4/68)

OAKLEY, Ezra N. - May 1868 buys license to m Nancy Thomas (6/4/68)

OATESS, George A. - sells 80 ac in Washington Twp (9/14/70)

OATES(S), J[ohn] A. - 4 Nov 1869 m A[nna] E. Shuff in Morris Chapel (11/10/69)

O'BRIEN, John - Monroe Twp landowner (1/6/69)

OLIVER, Henderson - 1867 buys Harrisburg ac (1/15/68)

OLIVER, Jeremiah - 1868 Monroe Twp landowner (1/12/70)

OLIVER, Martha A. - sells a lot in Harrisburg (12/29/69)

OLIVER, Samuel - buys 80 ac in Monroe Twp (9/21/70)

OLIVER, William H. - Monroe Twp landowner (1/8/68)

OLIVER, Winborn - buys land in Monroe Twp (4/30/68)

O'NEAL, Dr. L. - mbr, Grant Co Medical Soc (2/1/71)

OPPY, Abraham - Jan 1838 lays out Oppy's Addn to Marion (4/16/68); dec (8/17/70)

OPPY, David - owns property in Marion (1/6/69)

OSBORN, E. - Liberty Twp landowner (1/8/68); sells 120 ac in Liberty Twp to J.C. Fink (12/15/69)

OSBORN, John - 1869 Green Twp landowner (12/21/70)

OSBORN, Samuel - buys 40 ac in Franklin Twp (4/13/70)

OSBORN, Samuel L. - dec, his estate is settled by the Court (3/12/68)

OSBORN, William - 1866 buys 10 ac in Fairmount Twp from Spencer Reeder (2/26/68)

OSBORN, William P. - 1867 buys 80 ac in Fairmount Twp from William Maynard (3/4/68)

OSBORNE, John - age 14y, 1da; s Mahlon and Polly Osborne; d 25 Mar 1870 in Fairmount (4/6/70)

OSBORNE, Jonathan - 11 Jan 1868 m Lucinda Carpenter (1/29/68)

OTIS, James - tchr, Morris Chapel SS (5/26/69)

OTIS, John - tchr, Morris Chapel SS (5/26/69); is Constable for Washington Twp (7/23/69)

OVERHALTS, Eli - Dec 1867 buys license to m Mary J. Strain (1/8/68)

OVERLY, David - Jul 1868 buys license to m Mary Small (8/5/68)

OVERMAN, Anderson - Surveyor, Grant Co (10/16/67)

OVERMAN, Ephraim C. - & Obadiah Jones in Dec 1846 lay out Overman & Jones' Addn, Jonesboro (4/23/68); 1849 is ed of 'Marion Western Union' (7/6/70); now lives in Indianapolis (8/3/70)

OVERMAN, Joel - a proposed rd will go through his land (7/23/69)

OVERMAN, John - sells 1 ac in Center Twp to Patrick Morgan (4/2/68); a proposed rd will go through his land (7/23/69); sells 35 ac in Center Twp to Joel Overman (11/16/70)

OVERMAN, Joseph H. - of W of Jonesboro; last Sunday while returning from Meeting [at Deer Creek Friends(?)] upset his carriage on Deer Creek Hill; his family had slight injuries but he was severely hurt (7/13/70); buys 70 ac in Mill Twp from Elam T. Harris (8/17/70)

OVERMAN, Lindley M., Esq - 1867-68 tchr, Marion Sch (9/25/67); Doorkeeper, Marion Literary Soc (1/15/68); 11 Mar 1869 m Emily A. Baldwin (3/17/69; 4/7/69); Grant Co Surveyor; is ill (8/24/70)

OVERMAN, Milton - 28 Apr 1868 was m to Miss Mary Powell by Elder James Maple (4/30/68; 5/14/68)

OVERMAN, N. - Richland Twp dir, Grant Co Agric Soc Fair (7/29/68)

OVERMAN, Reuben - dec; owned property in Marion (1/6/69)

OVERMAN, S.C. - is att Marion Public Sch (12/18/67)

OVERMAN, Silas - erected a sawmill on Deer Creek in early da of Grant Co (3/8/71)

OVERMAN, Willis - 1869 Franklin Twp landowner (12/21/70)

OWINGS, Elizabeth A. - sells 2 lots in Upland (2/9/70)

OXLEY, Jesse - 1867 sells 40 ac in Monroe Twp (1/8/68)

OXLEY, William J. - sells 50 ac in Green Twp (1/26/70)

PAGE, Lewis M. - Green Twp landowner (1/6/69)

PALMER, Allen - Nov 1867 buys license to m Harriett L. Livingood (12/11/67)

PALMER, Dr. David - mbr, Grant Co Medical Soc (11/20/67); March 1868 buys license to m Jane Burson (4/2/68)

PALMER, George - Monroe Twp landowner (1/8/68; 1/6/69)

PALMER, James - buys 80 ac in Monroe Twp (12/29/69)

PALMER, John - buys an Upland lot (10/27/69)

PALMER, Samuel - buys lots in Harrisburg (11/24/69)

PARKER, Charles - & John P. Sinclair lay out the original plat of 30 lots in Mier in Sep 1848 (4/23/68)

PARKER, Thomas J. - 1867 buys 1 Fairmount lot (1/8/68; 4/2/68)

PARKS, E.J. - Mill Twp landowner (1/6/69)

PARKS, Felix - Jul 1868 buys license to m Margaret Griffin (8/5/68); 1868 Jefferson Twp landowner (1/12/70)

PARKS, Isaac - owns property in Jonesboro & in Mill Twp (1/8/68; 1/6/69); Mar 1869 buys license to m H[annah] A. Hamilton (4/7/69); sells 120 ac in Franklin Twp to Silas Parks (11/3/69); buys 20 ac in Monroe Twp (3/30/70)

PARKS, Silas - dec; owned land in Mill Twp (1/8/68)

PARKS, William F. - Jefferson Twp landowner (1/6/69)

PARLETT(E), Rev. John Y. - pres, Marion & Warren Gravel Rd Co (6/25/68); is visiting relatives in VA (2/3/69); organizes a SS at Salem Ch (5/5/69); lives in Washington Twp (11/24/69); is elected JP, Washington Twp (10/19/70)

PARSHALL, William F. - landowner in Monroe Twp (1/6/69), & in Jefferson Twp (12/21/70)

PARSON(S), 'Jot' - a businessman in Independence (6/16/69)

PATTERSON, Andrew - 1869 Washington Twp landowner (12/21/70)

PATTERSON, Andrew, Sr. - mbr Grant Lodge, F&AM (4/30/68)

PATTERSON, Jerusha - owns property in Jonesboro (1/6/69)

PATTERSON, John - sells property in Marion (1/29/68); dec; 1868 his heirs owned land in Monroe Twp (1/12/70)

PATTERSON, M.E. - Liberty Twp landowner (1/8/68)

PATTERSON, Robert - Fairmount Twp landowner (1/6/69)

PATTERSON, Robert H. - sells 80 ac in Jefferson Twp to L.L. Bond (7/13/70); losing candidate for JP, Mill Twp (10/19/70)

PATTERSON, Samuel - owns property in Farmington (1/6/69); 1868 Jefferson Twp landowner (1/12/70); dec; 1869 owned land in Jefferson Twp (12/21/70)

PATTERSON, William H. - 1870 owns property in Harrisburg (12/21/71)

PAULUS, William - Richland Twp landowner (1/6/69); organizes support in Richland Twp for the proposed GR,W&C RR (11/3/69); buys 80 ac in Richland Twp (1/12/70); Richland Twp delegate to State Rep Conv (2/9/70)

PAXTON, [Dr.] James - dec; [Rev.] William Paxton admin his estate (7/20/70)

PAXTON/PAXTEN, James S. - sells 40 ac in Van Buren Twp to Palmer Sinclair (4/9/68)

PAYNE, A[llen] W. - Dec 1869 buys license to m Bathsheba Nose (1/5/70)

PAYNE, E[phraim] L. - Feb 1868 buys license to m R[achel] M. Bookout (3/4/68)

PAYNE, George W. - 1869 Fairmount Twp landowner (1/6/69)

PAYNE, Wesley E. - 1867 buys 58.33 ac in Jefferson Twp from Christopher Mittank (4/16/68)

PAYNE, William - of 2 to 3 mi SE of Fairmount; recently found a small stone, that may be a diamond, ca 15' below the surface while digging a well (8/24/70)

PEARSON, John C. - Apr 1868 buys license to m Martha J. Bone (5/14/68)

PEARSON, Josephine B. - buys 40 ac in Washington Twp from James Phillips (1/15/68)

PEARSON, Lemuel - Dec 1869 buys license to m A[ngelina] Harvey (1/5/70)

PEEBLES, Sarah A. - sells 10 ac in Center Twp (4/6/70)

PEGDEN, William - house & ornamental painter (9/7/70)

PEMBERTON, Elihu W. - buys 200 ac in Mill Twp from Jacob McCormick (4/27/70)

PEMBERTON, Harmon - owns Fairmount property (1/8/68); 1865 sells 1 lot near Fairmount to Alexander Richard (4/30/68)

PEMBERTON, John - dec; owned Jonesboro property (1/6/69)

PEMBERTON, Lemuel - & Co owns Jonesboro property (1/6/69)

PENCE, David - organizes Sims Twp support for the proposed GR,W&C RR (11/3/69)

PENCE, John S. - Feb 1868 buys license to m Elizabeth A. Eakins (3/4/68)

PENCE, Lewis - buys 60 ac in Sims Twp (9/21/70)

PENCE, Lewis J. - of Richland Twp, recently found a stray dry cow (12/22/69)

PENCE, Solomon - petitions Co Comm for a new rd in Richland Twp; petition granted (3/11/69); organizes Richland Twp support for proposed GR,W&C RR (11/3/69)

PENNINGTON, Isaac - 1868 Sims Twp landowner (1/12/70)

PERKINS, Eliza - 1868 owns property in Marion (1/12/70)

PERRY, Allen - Liberty Twp landowner (1/6/69)

PERRY, John W. - Franklin Twp landowner (1/8/68)

PERSINGER, Zachariah - Jul 1868 buys license to m E[lizabeth] Oliver (8/5/68)

PETERS, Leona - Sims Twp landowner (1/8/68)

PETERS, P[ernel] - Sims Twp delegate to State Rep Conv (2/9/70)

PETERS, Samuel - 1868 Liberty Twp landowner (1/12/70)

PETTAY/PETTY, Boaz W. - sells 40 ac in Franklin Twp to Caleb B. Davis (12/25/67); buys 80 ac in Franklin Twp (10/5/70)

PETTAY/PETTEY, John W. - dec; Nathan Small admin his estate (9/18/67); owned land in Sims Twp (1/8/68)

PETTIFORD, Edmund - 1867 sells a Liberty Twp property to Fountain Evans (1/8/68)

PFIEFFER, J.C. - prop, Pfieffer Bakery/Grocery, Jonesboro (8/31/70)

PHILLIPS, James - Trustee, Washington Twp (9/18/67); sells 40 ac in Washington Twp to Josephine B. Pearson (1/15/68)

PHILLIPS, Orton - buys land in Sims Twp (2/12/68)

PHILLIPS, William - 1864 sells 2 ac in Mill Twp to Lorenzo Bole (4/9/68); Mill Twp landowner (1/6/69)

PICKARD, Alex - 1867 buys 1 lot in Fairmount (6/25/68)

PICKARD, John L. - Nov 1867 buys license to m Sarah Hiatt (12/11/67)

PIERCE/PEIRCE, Addie - is att Marion Public Sch (11/6/67)

PIERCE, D. Birman - 1867 buys land in Monroe Twp (4/30/68); buys part of 160 ac in Monroe Twp (6/1/70)

PIERCE, George M. - 1869 Liberty Twp landowner (12/21/70)

PIERCE, George W. - sells 40 ac in Fairmount Twp (10/27/69)

PIERCE, Henry - 1842 his store is on Adams St (7/6/70); prop, Pierce Hardware Store (7/23/69); sells property in Marion & 166 ac to Telitha Pierce (3/30/70)

PIERCE, L.M. - sells a lot in Jonesboro (3/30/70)

PIERCE, Rev. William E. - pastor, Jonesboro M.E. Ch (1/15/68); mbr IOOF, Jonesboro (3/24/69)

PILCHER, A. - Jun 1850 is on committee to help Marion citizens celebrate our 74th Independence Day (8/18/69); sells 2 lots in Marion to Chamberlain & Co (10/27/69)

PILCHER, George A. - Rep Party candidate for Grant Co Recorder (3/4/68); sells 4 lots in Marion (1/26/70)

PILCHER, James - is att Marion Public Sch (11/6/67)

PILCHER, James R. - sells a lot in Marion to Hiram Brownlee (11/3/69); sells 2 lots in Marion to John F. Furnish (11/10/69)

PILCHER, Jane R. - buys 95 ac in Franklin Twp & sells 10 ac in Center Twp to C.S. Tibbits & sells 8 lots in Marion to C.S. Tibbits (1/26/70); 1869 Center Twp landowner (12/21/70)

PINKERTON, James - 1857 sells 44 ac in Liberty Twp (1/15/68)

PIXLER, Margaret - 1867 sells 1 ac in Richland Twp (3/12/68)

PLASTER, John - sells 17.5 ac in Fairmount Twp (4/30/68)

PLEASANT TOWNSHIP - John Renaker, Trustee (9/18/67); Luther Miles petitioned Co Comm for a new Pleasant Twp rd; petition granted, Wesley Simmons, A.Y. York & George White are viewers for the new rd; Co Comm gave $150 to Pleasant Twp Trustee to aid in constructing a bridge over Pipe Creek & also over Taylor's Creek, both on Delphi State Rd (3/11/69)

PLEASANT TOWNSHIP, Schools of - 571 school children are in Twp (11/17/69)

POLK, Amanda (Wall) - sells 2 lots in Marion (2/2/70)

POLK, Milton C. - recently m Mrs. Amanda (Wall) Jones (2/12/68; 3/4/68)

POOLE, William - buys 1 lot in Marion (3/4/68)

POPE, William A. - Sims Twp landowner (1/6/69)

PORTER, A.G. - losing candidate for JP, Pleasant Twp (10/19/70)

PORTER, William H. - sells 80 ac in Washington Twp (2/26/68)

POTTER, H[enry] - Mar 1870 buys license to m Mary M. Marsh (4/6/70)

POWELL, Caroline - 1869 owns Independence property (12/21/70)

POWELL, H. - dec; owned land in Liberty Twp (1/8/68)

POWELL, John - dec; John Bayless admin his estate (8/18/65; 12/11/67)

POWELL, J[ohn] H. - April 1868 buys license to m Minerva Brandon (5/14/68)

POWELL, Lewis A. - 1867 sells 0.5 ac in Center Twp to Mary A. Houck (1/15/68); Center Twp landowner (1/6/69)

POWELL, Thomas H. - Liberty Twp landowner (1/8/68)

POWER, John Hull - age 26; m, father of 2 children; WIA at Chickamauga while serv 36th Regt Ind Vol Inf, laid on battlefield for 7 da with no medical attention, brought home in Jun 1864; was an invalid until his death at Fairmount 29 Feb 1868, bur by GAR Post No. 3 (4/2/68)

PRICE, Abraham - owns property in Farmington (1/8/68)

PRICE, James - buys 95 ac in Washington Twp (2/26/68)

PRICE, John F. - 1867 sells 1 lot in Jefferson Twp (3/26/68)

PRICE, Levi G. - owns property in Jonesboro (1/6/69)

PRICE, W.H. - recently dec (11/20/67)

PRICKETT, Gabriel - 1867 buys 5 ac in Washington Twp from Patterson Moore & buys 42.11 ac in Washington Twp (1/8/68)

PRICKETT, Milton - owns property in Jalapa (1/6/69); Pleasant Twp landowner (1/13/69)

PRICKETT, Presley - Jun 1868 buys license to m C[atharine] Brocht (7/1/68)

PRIOR, Nicholas - buys 160 ac in Monroe Twp (11/16/70)

PROCTOR, Sarah A. - 1869 owns Marion property (12/21/70)

PROPS, James M. - buys 30 ac in Pleasant Twp (2/26/68)

PROSPER TOWN, Town of - 1 Jun 1854 is laid out with 53 lots by Samuel D. Kenneday; this town "died an unnatural death" (4/23/68)

PUGH, Jefferson - Pleasant Twp taxpayer (1/26/70)

PUGH, Mahlon - 1869 owns property in Mier & in Upland (12/21/70)

PULLEY, Marion - Mar 1868 buys license to m [Katurah] E. Lansberry (4/2/68)

PULLEY, Reuben - buys 71 ac in Van Buren Twp (1/22/68)

PULLEY, W[illiam] - Mar 1870 buys license to m [Margaret] Camblin (4/6/70)

PULSON, John - 1869 Sims Twp landowner (12/21/70)

PURDUM, Jonah - Sims Twp landowner (1/8/68)

PYEATTE, Catherine - 1869 owns Marion property (12/21/70)

PYEATTE, John - dec; owned property in Marion (1/6/69)

QUICK, D[avid] - Oct1870 buys a license to m Mary A. McCann (11/2/70)

RAILROADS (RR)
COLUMBUS & INDIANA CENTRAL (C&IC) - has a train arriving daily in Jonesboro, the end of the line (9/25/67); rails are being laid on way to Marion, crossed the river 14 Oct 1867, will reach Marion 17 Oct 1867 (10/16/67); is completed to Marion 21 Oct 1867 and is now being extended westward (10/23/67); two trains come to Marion daily; first RR accident in Marion occurred last wk when a s of David Hogin fell under wheels of a handcar(?), he will recover (10/30/67); a very large water tank on a high frame was put up on the RR; as track is completed, trains run from Marion W to Mier & Xenia (11/6/67); track now passes through Xenia 12 mi W of Marion and in 15 da will be in Bunker Hill where it will cross the P&I RR (11/13/67); track is laid to 2 mi of Bunker Hill (11/27/67); 5 Dec 1867 buys 2 lots in RR Addn, Marion from Orvin Free for $200 (1/29/68); Philip Cole of near Jonesboro is arrested & jailed on suspicion of attempting to derail a train 10 Dec 1867 (2/12/68); may now be called COLUMBUS, CHICAGO & INDIANA CENTRAL RR (CC&IC); 11 Apr 1868 buys 2.5 ac in Center Twp from David O. Hite for $505 (4/30/68); 26 Nov 1867 C&IC RR buys 2 ac in Richland Twp from Benjamin Harnden for $1; 26 Jan 1868 buys 1 lot & parts of 2 lots in Mier from Jonathan Harnden (6/25/68); new passenger & freight depot is completed in Marion with 2 passenger rooms, one for ladies & one for gentlemen, a ticket/telegraph office & lunch room; a room 40' square for freight & grain; a track to be laid on N side of bldg for freight trains & on S, a platform 200' long for passenger trains; Major W.C. Emerson is depot agent/manager (7/1/68); Express & Telegraph Office is moved to new depot (7/8/68); 11 Apr 1869 a freight train was derailed by a plank placed on the track by a vandal; the engineer, __ Mc-Gregory, was killed

instantly; damage to RR is estimated to be over $20,000 (4/14/69); on this branch of the RR, 16 regular trains now run in addn to 'wild' ones (4/28/69); - see PENNSYLVANIA CENTRAL RR

LAKE MICHIGAN, WABASH & CINCINNATI - James Brownlee & Charles S. Tibbits were elected to bd of dir last wk with Tibbits elected v pres; $55,000 is subscribed to build this RR from Elkhart Co to Delaware Co (3/3/69); now called the GRAND RAPIDS, WABASH & CINCINNATI RR - meeting is held to organize citizens in favor of this N-S RR Line with M.L. Marsh, chairman & J.A. Stretch, secy; a committee including William Neal, S. Hulley, John Secrist, A.R. Barley & Dr. L. Williams selects canvassers in each Twp; canvassers are: Van Buren Twp - Isaac Anderson & J.F. Swan; Washington Twp - Franklin Thompson, Isaac Bradford & Asbury Steele; Pleasant Twp - Jonathan Seegar & Nelson Conner; Richland Twp - Solomon Pence, William Paulus & William Wood; Center Twp - James A. Stretch & James F. McDowell; Mill Twp - Nathan Coggshall, D.B. Shideler, S.R. Spence & Samuel Jay; Monroe Twp - S.R. Thompson & Absolem Thomason; Jefferson Twp - James Nottingham & Otho Hardy; Fairmount Twp - J.P. Winslow, Jonathan Baldwin & Micajah Wilson; Liberty Twp - Train Caldwell & Willis Cammack; Green Twp - Isaac Rybolt & Virgil Hale; Sims Twp - David Pence & Moses Kennedy; Franklin Twp - Jacob Drukemiller, John Ratliff & Henry Shugart (11/3/69) PENNSYLVANIA CENTRAL - recently consolidated with [took over?] the CC&IC RR (2/3/69)

U&L RR - Aug 6, 1867 buys 7 ac in Jefferson Twp from Jacob Bugher for $1, buys 6 ac in Jefferson Twp from James L. Williams for $1, buys 6 ac in Jefferson Twp from Jacob Brumfiel for $1, buys 1.25 ac in Jefferson Twp from Isaac Ballinger for $1; 28 Aug 1868 buys 2 lots in RR Addn, Marion from T.J. Neal for $225, buys 2 lots in RR Addn, Marion from Isaac Vandeventer for $225 (6/25/68)

RAPER, Ansel E./M. - of Anderson; 21 Apr 1868 is m to Mrs. Margaret E. (Rush) Smithson in Liberty Twp by J.N. Rush, JP (4/23/68; 5/14/68)

RASSNER, Charles - b Dayton, OH 20 May 1849; s William Rassner, druggist in Peru; f Marion businessman; d Peru 11 Dec 1870 (12/21/70)

RATCLIFFE, John - pres, Jonesboro & Kokomo Gravel Rd Co (5/7/68)

RATLIFF, C.S. - organized help from the Friends Meeting & supplied a house for the family of Osborn Mitchell, colored, whose home burned last wk (12/28/70)

RATLIFF, John - admin estate of W.H. Price, dec (11/20/67), & estate of Thomas Baldwin, dec (1/13/69); Rep candidate for State Representative (3/26/68); assesses benefits/damages of a ditch in Franklin Twp (6/23/69); organizes Franklin Twp support for the proposed GR,W&C RR (11/3/69)

RATLIFF, Joseph - Marion HS student (12/23/70)

RATLIFF, Levi - Marion HS student (12/23/70)

RAUGH, Mills - 1867 buys 80 ac in Jefferson Twp (4/30/68)

RAY/KAY, J[oseph] B. - Oct 1870 buys a license to m M[ary] C. Stewart/Stuart (11/2/70)

RAYPHOLTZ, E[phraim] - Aug 1869 buys license to m M[ary] A. Palmer (9/18/69)

REASONER, Dr. H.D. - mbr Grant Co Medical Soc (7/13/69)

REASONER, Hanna D. - 1867 buys 1 lot in New Cumberland & 1868 buys 1 lot in New Cumberland from Grant Co Auditor (2/12/68); sells a lot in New Cumberland (1/26/70)

REASONER, John - dec; 1869 owned land in Jefferson Twp (12/21/70)

REASONER, Noah - dec; 1869 owned land in Jefferson Twp (12/21/70)

REASONER, Richard - Monroe Twp landowner (1/6/69)

REASONER, Solomon - dec; owned land in Jefferson Twp (1/6/69)

RECK, Daniel - Jun 1869 buys license to m Rachel Harris (7/7/69), & is now sued for divorce by Rachel (12/22/69)

RECKER, Clara - 1869 Pleasant Twp landowner (12/21/70)

RECTOR, John M. - of Howard Co; 7 Aug 1869 m Nancy Godfrey of Grant Co (8/11/69; 9/8/69)

REDDEN, James - dec, was insolvent; Nixon Winslow admin his estate (6/2/69)

REDDING, James - Fairmount Twp landowner (1/6/69)

REECE, Charles - prop, People's Drug Store, Washington St, Marion (2/26/68)

REECE, Evan - buys a lot in Mier from Darius Lillard (2/2/70), & buys 1 ac near Mier from Benjamin Harnden (4/6/70)

REECE, George W. - 13 Jan 1869 m Sarah E. Day (1/27/69; 2/3/69)

REECE, Miss J. - a Marion milliner (3/22/71)

REECE/REES, Jesse - sells Fairmount Twp property (12/25/67; 8/17/70; 11/30/70); Fairmount Twp landowner (1/6/69)

REECE, Joel - leaves Marion Chronicle; Union Party candidate for Grant Co Recorder (3/4/68); sells a blacksmith shop in Marion to William Weller (5/11/70)

REECE, Reuben - Nov 1867 buys license to m Cynthia A. Horner (12/11/67); buys lots in Fairmount (11/24/69)

REED, Allen - Jefferson Twp landowner (1/8/68)

REED, Henry C. - a yg man in Jun 1851 when drowned in river 0.5 mi below Marion (8/17/70)

REED, Owen - May 1871 buys a license to m Mary Standish (6/1/71)

REED, Richard J. - buys 100 ac in Van Buren Twp (1/29/68)

REEDER, John J. - 1869 owns property in Fairmount (12/21/70)

REEDER, Spencer - 1866 sells Fairmount Twp ac (2/26/68)

REEDER, William H. - owns Independence property (1/6/69)

REEVES, Dr. A.B. - admin estate of Saloma Bruss, dec (8/18/65); now of Fairview, Fayette Co (6/2/69)

REEVES, John K. - 1869 Liberty Twp landowner (12/21/70)

RENAKER, Elizabeth - Pleasant Twp landowner (1/6/69)

RENAKER, Jacob C. - Feb 1868 buys license to m [Martha] Arthurhultz (3/4/68)

RENAKER, John - Trustee, Pleasant Twp (9/18/67); buys 80 ac in Pleasant Twp from the Sheriff (11/24/69)

RENBARGER, Edward - sells 5 ac in Pleasant Twp (3/30/70)

RENBARGER, G.W.T. - buys 100 ac in Pleasant Twp (4/2/68)

RENBARGER, Henry A. - sells 91 ac in Pleasant Twp (4/2/68)

RENBARGER, John E. - sells 65.87 ac in Pleasant Twp (4/2/68); sells a sawmill in Pleasant Twp to John Snyder (5/11/70)

RENNAKER, Hiram - 18 Apr 1869 m Susannah Wise (4/21/69; 5/5/69)

REUSS, Capt. John - pres, bd of Marion Town Trustees (12/28/70)

REYNOLDS, Cyrus - 1868 Van Buren Twp landowner (1/12/70)

REYNOLDS, Green - buys 40 ac in Richland Twp (4/27/70)

REYNOLDS, Isaac - Liberty Twp landowner (1/8/68)

REYNOLDS, John H. - Nov 1867 buys license to m Caroline Millhollin (12/11/67)

REYNOLDS, Thomas - age 77; 7 Nov 1867 in Jonesboro m 'Grandma' Sarah Fisher, age ca 70 (11/13/67; 12/11/67)

REYNOLDS, Zimri - 1849 is elected Co Sheriff (8/3/70); now lives in Rantoul, IL (8/17/70)

RHEA, Archibold - losing candidate for JP, Franklin Twp (10/19/70)

RHONEMUS, George - Feb 1868 buys license to m Martha J. Anderson (3/4/68)

RICH, Alexander - sells 160 ac in Liberty Twp (2/26/68)

RICH, Daniel - 1869 Liberty Twp landowner (12/21/70)

RICH, Isaac - 1867 buys 32 ac in Fairmount Twp (1/29/68)

RICH, Jesse G. - buys 160 ac in Mill Twp from Israel Jenkins (4/16/68); 1868 Liberty Twp landowner (1/12/70)

RICH, Phebe - 1869 Liberty Twp landowner (12/21/70)

RICHARD, Alexander - 1865 buys 1 lot near Fairmount & 1866 sells 1 lot near Fairmount to Joel O. White (4/30/68)

RICHARDS, Jacob - exor for estate of John Richards, dec (12/11/67)

RICHARDS, John - recently dec; exor for his estate is Jacob Richards (12/11/67); 1868 his heirs owned land in Jefferson Twp (1/12/70)

RICHARDS, L.G. - buys 80 ac in Jefferson Twp (12/16/70)

RICHARDS, Samuel L. - buys 50 ac in Pleasant Twp (12/25/67)

RICHARDSON, Hogan - buys land in Liberty Twp (1/29/68)

RICHARDSON, Hopkin - buys/sells Fairmount lots (3/4/68; 4/30/68); Aug 1869 buys license to m P[oebe] Gossett (9/8/69)

RICHARDSON, Jonathan - mbr, Grand Jury (6/8/71)

RICHARDSON, Zimri S. - 1867 sells a Washington Twp property (1/8/68); 1867 sells 60 ac in Fairmount Twp to Nixon Winslow (2/26/68); sells 160 ac in Fairmount Twp (4/27/70)

RICHLAND TOWNSHIP - M[orris] H. Crist, Trustee (9/18/67; 10/19/70); Solomon Pence petitions County Comm for a new Richland Twp rd, petition granted; Alfred Drook, G. Hays & Sylvester Harndon are viewers for new rd (3/11/69)

RICHLAND TOWNSHIP, Schools of - 410 school children reside in Twp (11/17/69)
DROOK SCH - had an exhibition (i.e. singing, etc.) last wk (4/2/68)

RICKMAN, William - Dec 1869 buys license to m E[mma] Maberry (1/5/70)

RIDGEWAY, Capt. _ - see CIVIL WAR

RIDGEWAY, Daniel - admin estate of Milton Lee, dec (12/11/67); 1867 sells 80 ac in Fairmount Twp (4/30/68)

RIFE, Jacob - buys 91.59 ac in Pleasant Twp (4/2/68)

RIFFLE, John - of Fairmount Twp; CW vet (1/19/70)

RIGDON, Dr. Pryor - 6 May 1858 lays out the 18 lots of Rigdon's Addn to Independence (4/23/68); owns property in Independence (1/6/69); of near Independence; he and all of his family are having the smallpox, one of his family has d of it (2/2/70)

RIGDON, R[obert] M./W. - May 1869 buys license to m Rachel Barrett (6/2/69; 7/7/69)

RIGGS, Dr. C.E. - mbr Grant Co Medical Soc (7/13/69)

RIGGS, Samuel - 4 Oct 1867 m Sarah Herron (10/9/67)

RING, George W. - buys/sells Center Twp & Marion property (4/2/68; 6/29/70)

RIX, John - sells 88 ac in Center Twp (10/27/69)

ROACH, William - Sims Twp landowner (1/6/69)

ROADS
JONESBORO & KOKOMO GRAVEL ROAD CO - John Ratcliffe, pres; Dr. E.P. Jones, secy; dir are A.L. Barnard, Willis Cammack, and Denny Jay, Jr. (5/7/68)
JONESBORO & FAIRMOUNT RD - is re-graveled (8/24/70)
LIBERTY TOWNSHIP PIKE CO - pike will extend to Center Sch, Liberty Twp; 24 Apr 1869 stockholders meet and choose the following dir: Jacob W. Spencer, Nathan Coggeshall, Willis Cammack, William H. Ayers & Eli Thomas (4/28/69); work starts 2 mi out of Marion and proceeds in both directions; it is hoped to have 4 mi completed this season (9/1/69)
LITTLE RIDGE TURNPIKE - starting on the Fairmount-Alexandria Pike 1 mi S of Fairmount, it is being constructed W for 4 mi (10/23/67); also called LITTLE RIDGE GRAVEL ROAD - at W end of graveled part is the Finley & Allen Steam Mill, this is 1 mi E of Big Deer Creek (2/9/70)
MARION & LIBERTY GRAVEL ROAD CO - Articles of Assoc are drawn up with James Brownlee, chairman & M.F. Tingley, secy; proposed rd to begin at S end of Washington St, Marion and run on or near Strawtown State Rd for 6 mi or, perhaps, for 10 mi to Center Sch in Liberty Twp (4/14/69); now is
MARION & LIBERTY TWP TURNPIKE - Mahlon Harvey, Jacob Wright & Joseph Bond assess lands for its construction (7/23/69); John Kem & Nathan Haines, appraisers for this pike, are examining area 13 mi long & 3 mi wide; pike to be graveled (8/4/69); 4 mi is now graded, 3 mi is graveled (11/10/69)
MARION & WARREN GRAVEL ROAD CO - John Y. Parlett, pres (6/25/68)
WABASH & MARION GRAVEL ROAD CO - D.R. Seegar, secy (9/18/67)

ROBBINS, H.C. - sells 20 ac in Franklin Twp (5/11/70)

ROBERTS, B.F. - 1869 Pleasant Twp landowner (12/21/70)

ROBERTS, Elijah - 1867 buys 40 ac in Center Twp (3/12/68)

ROBERTS, James H. - Liberty Twp landowner (1/8/68)

ROBINSON, C[olumbus] - Dec 1869 buys license to m Mary J. Bryant (1/5/70)

RODGERS, G. - buys 40 ac in Liberty Twp (12/29/69)

RODGERS, John R. - Liberty Twp dir, Grant Co Fair (8/3/70)

RODGERS, J[oseph] H. - Jun 1869 buys license to m Amanda Kimes (7/7/69)

ROGERS, Elizabeth - 1867 sells 40 ac in Franklin Twp to Francis M. Simmons (4/30/68); Franklin Twp landowner (1/8/68)

ROGERS, John - of Liberty Twp; 4 of his horses were injured, two fatally, by a large boar sharing their pasture (12/18/67)

ROMAINE, Cornelius - admin estate of Caleb Morris, dec (9/18/67)

ROSEBURG, Town of - the plat, if it exists, has not been recorded (4/23/68)
STEAM SAWMILL - __ Drukemiller, owner; 11 Nov 1870 its boiler exploded killing the engineer, Samuel Tyser, a horse & a dog (11/16/70)

ROSS, John - Mar 1869 buys license to m Jane Stuart (4/7/69)

ROUSH, Isaac - viewer for a new Jefferson Twp rd (3/11/69)

ROUSH, W[illiam] P. - April 1868 buys license to m Anna M. Lucas; 1864 buys 197.73 ac in Mill Twp from John W. Bates (5/14/68)

ROWAN, George B. - prop, New Tobacco Store (1/6/69); 2 Jan 1869 m Mary E. Hite, m by Rev. Henry L. Brown (1/20/69; 2/3/69)

ROWLAND, Joseph - buys 40 ac in Van Buren Twp (11/10/69)

ROWLAND, Reuben - owns land in Sims Twp (1/6/69), 1868 in Franklin Twp (1/12/70), 1869 in Green Twp (12/21/70)

ROWLETT, E[dwin] - of Jay Co 11 Jul 1870 m Mary Sherwood of Marion (7/20/70)

ROYE, Henry - Dec 1868 buys license to m Catherine Jolly (1/6/69)

RUE, Richard - sells 80 ac in Jefferson Twp (10/27/69)

RUESS, John - buys a lot in Marion (5/11/70)

RUFF, John - buys 80 ac in Pleasant Twp from Moses Baldwin (12/29/69); buys 40 ac in Franklin Twp (12/7/70)

RULEY, B.W. - now of Jonesboro; 1847 was Grant Co Treas; sells 150 ac in Mill Twp to Henry Wise (7/20/70)

RULEY, John C. - officer, Rebekah Lodge, Jonesboro (4/28/69); is on a Co bd to assess property (1/5/70); is elected Mill Twp Assessor (10/19/70)

RULEY, Joseph J. - is dec (8/18/65); owned land in Mill Twp (1/6/69)

RUMINUS, George - of Sims Twp; CW vet (1/19/70)

RUSH, Azel - dec; 1869 owned land in Liberty Twp (12/21/70)

RUSH, Elizabeth - 1867 buys 63 ac in Fairmount Twp (3/4/68)

RUSH, I.B. - f of Marion where he owned a velocipede; now of Columbia City (1/5/70); 9 Jun 1870 m Nancy Elliott in Beaver, PA (6/22/70)

RUSH, J.N. - JP; in Liberty Twp 21 Apr 1868 m Mrs. Margaret E. (Rush) Smithson to Ansel M. Raper (4/23/68)

RUSH, Nixon, Jr. - 1867 sells 63 ac in Fairmount Twp (3/4/68)

RUSH, Thomas E. - dir, Big Deer Creek Ditching Co (9/18/67)

RUSSELL, Lizzie - Marion HS student (11/23/70)

RUSSELL, Maggie - is att Marion Public Sch (1/12/70); Marion HS student (12/23/70)

RUSSELL, William M. - Principal, Marion Public Schs (1/12/70; 9/14/70)

RUSSELL, William B. - of Jefferson Twp; CW vet (1/19/70)

RUST, A.L. - dec; 1868 his heirs owned land in Pleasant Twp (1/12/70)

RYBOLT, Isaac - admin estate of Aaron Miller, dec (1/1/68); Nov 1869 organizes Green Twp support for the proposed GR,W&C RR (11/3/69); Green Twp delegate to State Rep Conv (2/9/70); buys 40 ac in Green Twp from Abraham Downs & sells that 40 ac to Samuel W. Titus (10/19/70)

RYBOLT, Jarret - sells 7 ac in Green Twp (10/5/70)

SAFFORD, John P. - 1866 sells 5 lots in Independence (3/4/68)

SAID, William - sells 48 ac in Liberty Twp (4/30/68)

SAID, William H. - Liberty Twp landowner (1/6/69)

St. JOHN, Lizzy - is att Marion Public Sch (11/13/67)

St. JOHN, Margaret - sells a lot in Marion (10/19/70)

St. JOHN, Robert T. 'Tom' - & Asbury Steele are attys with offices on NW corner of CH Square (9/18/67); left for Washington, D.C. to att inauguration of pres Grant (3/3/69); Jun 1870 att Old Settlers meeting (6/8/70); Rep candidate for State Representative (7/13/70), & is elected (12/28/70)

SALE, Rev. F.A. - pastor, Marion M.E. Ch (9/18/67), is now replaced as pastor (4/30/68)

SALSBERRY, Samuel P. - 4 Jul 1868 m Sarah Welch (7/8/68; 8/5/68)

SAMPLE, Joseph - of near Marion; husband of __ (Briley) Sample (8/12/68)

SANDERMAN, Fred - buys 40 ac in Van Buren Twp from A. Korporal (12/29/69)

SANDERS, D.H. - mbr Grant Lodge, F&AM (4/30/68); lives on Branson St; & J.W. Sanders are bricklayers & builders (9/7/70)

SANDERS, David S. - buys 1 lot in Marion (2/26/68)

SANDERS, Robert - Sep 1853 lays out the 38 lots in New Cumberland (4/23/68)

SANFORD, Rev. A.W. - 1868 Center Twp landowner (1/12/70); f of Marion, is now visiting here (2/9/70)

SANGER(S), James M. - of Van Buren Twp; 16 Sep 1869 m Nancy Gardner (9/29/69)

SANGER, William L. - of Huntington Co; at Spencer House 19 Jun 1869 m Josephine Gardner of Grant Co (7/7/69; 7/23/69)

SATER, Noah W. - May 1868 buys a license to m Ruth A. Thomas (6/4/68)

SATTERTHWAITE, Samuel - 1868 owns property in Marion (1/12/70)

SAUNDERS/SANDERS, John - 13 Aug 1870 m Eva Wyant (8/17/70)

SAWYER, Rev. Samuel C. - f of Marion; lives in Chillicothe, MO (4/7/69); is Presbyterian minister (4/28/69)

SAWYER, Susan - age ca 47; wife of Samuel Sawyer; mbr Presbyterian Ch; d Chillicothe, MO 11 May 1869 (5/26/69)

SAXON, William - Van Buren Twp delegate to State Rep Conv (2/9/70)

SAYLOR, R.Y. - tailor with shop on Washington St, E side of Square (9/7/70)

SCHMUCK, Eli J. - Liberty Twp landowner (1/6/69)

SCHOCKEY, Daniel - Apr 1869 buys license to m Jane Berry (5/5/69)

SCHOOLEY, Benjamin - dec; 1869 owned land in Monroe Twp (12/21/70)

SCHOOLEY, Cam T. - buys Fairmount Twp ac (3/4/68)

SCHOOLEY, Daniel - sells 23 ac in Franklin Twp (1/26/70)

SCHOOLEY, Ira - admin estate of John Schooley, dec (12/11/67); sells 12 ac in Center Twp (1/15/68); 16 Jul 1870 m [Minerva] Lugar (7/20/70); 1870 sells 12 ac in Center Twp to William M. Evans (8/17/70)

SCHOOLEY, John - recently dec (12/11/67)

SCHOOLEY, Selah - 1868 Mill Twp landowner (1/8/68)

SCHOOLEY, William L. - buys/sells Monroe Twp ac (10/26/70)

SCOTT, Conrad - sells 50 ac in Pleasant Twp (12/25/67)

SCOTT, James - a dir, Big Deer Creek Ditching Co (9/18/67); is on a Co bd to assess property (1/5/70); Liberty Twp delegate to State Rep Conv (2/9/70); Liberty Twp Assessor (10/19/70)

SCOTT, Smith - 1868 Washington Twp landowner (1/12/70)

SCOTT, Thomas F. - sells 40 ac in Jefferson Twp (4/16/68)

SCOTT, Dr. W[illiam] - of Kokomo; 26 Oct 1870 m Jennie Snorf (10/26/70; 11/2/70)

SEABRELL/SEBRELL, Owen - dec; owned land in Liberty Twp (1/8/68)

SEARS, John - asst librarian, Morris Chapel SS (5/26/69)

SEARS, J[ohn] C. - Aug 1869 buys a license to m M. V[ictoria] Paxton (9/8/69)

SECRIST, John - Grant Co Comm (10/1/67); organizes support for the proposed GR,W&C RR (11/3/69); buys 2 lots in Marion (6/29/70)

SECRIST, M. - of Grant Co; 18 Jun 1869 m Martha Carmine in Wheeling, Delaware Co (7/13/69)

SECRIST, Samuel - Librarian, Salem Ch SS (5/5/69); buys 10 ac in Washington Twp (12/28/70)

SEEGAR/SEGAR, D.R. - secy, Wabash & Marion Gravel Rd Co (9/18/67); viewer for a rd in Center Twp (3/11/69); v pres, 1870 Grant Co Fair (8/3/70)

SEEGAR, Jonathan - 1864 buys land in Pleasant Twp (3/26/68); organizes Pleasant Twp support for proposed GR,W&C RR (11/3/69)

SEWARD, Andrew F. 'Jack' - Trustee, Liberty Twp (4/7/69; 8/3/70)

SEWARD, Andrew T. - of Liberty Twp recently found a stray bay mare (6/22/70)

SEWARD, Dudley - is att Marion Public Sch (11/6/67)

SEWARD, Frederick, Esq - of Marion (11/23/70)

SEWARD, Louise - is att Marion Public Sch (11/6/67); - see William MAYNE

SEXTON, E[dmund] G. - Aug 1869 buys a license to m Mary Lyon (9/8/69)

SHACKLEFORD, N.D. - Sims Twp landowner (1/8/68)

SHACKLEFORD, S.M. - Oct 1870 buys license to m R[osella] A. Stephens (11/2/70)

SHAMBAUGH, Frank H.- is att Marion Sch (11/6/67); Marion HS student (12/23/70)

SHANE, Thomas J. - Green Twp landowner (1/6/69)

SHANK, Abraham - of Delaware Co; buys 120 ac in Pleasant Twp from Elias W. McKinney (12/15/69)

SHANK, Thomas D. - Jun 1869 buys license to m D[elila] Skillman (7/7/69)

SHARK, Alexander - buys 40 ac in Franklin Twp (1/26/70)

SHARP, J.K. - 1869 sells property in Jonesboro (1/5/70)

SHARP, William - sells 20 ac in Franklin Twp to Lewis Williams (4/27/70); buys 20 ac in Franklin Twp (5/11/70)

SHARPE, George - Richland Twp landowner (1/6/69)

SHAW, Chalmer - 1869 Jefferson Twp landowner (12/21/70)

SHAW, Francis A. - 1847 is prop of a Marion saddle shop (7/20/70)

SHAW, Hugh - dec; 1868 his heirs owned land in Jefferson Twp (1/12/70)

SHAW, Mrs. R[ebecca] L. - see Rev. O[wen] C. GARRETSON

SHELTON, __ - engineer for Ward & Bond Sawmill, located 3 mi N of New Cumberland; killed 7 Aug 1868 when the sawmill boiler exploded (8/12/68)

SHENHOLSTER, Henry - of Van Buren Twp; recently found a stray heifer (1/15/68)

SHERMAN, Stephen M. - Pleasant Twp Trustee (10/19/70); sells part of a lot in Jalapa to S.G. Morehead (12/16/70)

SHERON, Henry - 1869 Pleasant Twp landowner (12/21/70)

SHERWOOD, Joseph - sells 2 lots in Marion (2/26/68); buys a lot in Marion from B.W. Marsh & sells a lot in Marion (4/2/68); buys 1.65 ac near Marion from C.W. Hill (11/16/70)

SHERWOOD, Mattie - is att Marion Public Sch (11/6/67; 1/12/70); Marion HS student (12/23/70)

SHIDELER, Aaron - 1867 buys 2 lots in Jonesboro (1/29/68); buys 3 ac in Mill Twp (3/26/68)

SHIDELER, D.B. - organizes Mill Twp support for the proposed GR,W&C RR (11/3/69); Mill Twp delegate to State Rep Conv (2/9/70); Mill Twp Trustee (10/19/70)

SHIDELER, John W. - buys 1 lot in Jonesboro from George W. Fankboner (4/30/68); Jonesboro Town Treas (5/11/70)

SHIDELER, Mrs. Sallie J. - officer, Rebekah Lodge, Jonesboro (4/28/69)

SHIELDS, John - of Franklin Twp; CW vet (1/19/70)

SHIELDS, John M. - buys 20 ac in Fairmount Twp (6/8/70)

SHIPLEY, Joseph - 1869 sells 40 ac in Van Buren Twp (1/5/70)

SHIPLEY, Samuel - of Van Buren Twp is a Rep candidate for Sheriff (2/17/69)

SHIVELY, Dr. James S. - physician & surgeon with offices on Washington St S of CH Square (9/18/67); mbr Grant Co Medical Soc (7/13/69; 6/29/70)

SHIVELY/SHIVELEY, Marshall - is att Marion Sch (11/6/67)

SHIVELY, Marshall T. - buys a lot in Marion (10/19/70)

157

SHOCKEY, Anthony - 1867 buys Franklin Twp ac (3/4/68)

SHOCKEY, Daniel - Franklin Twp landowner (1/8/68)

SHOEMAKER, William L. - buys a lot in Jonesboro (3/30/70)

SHORES, Walter E. - Jan 1869 buys license to m S[arah] E. Lawson (2/3/69)

SHORT, Marion T. - 1869 Washington Twp landowner (12/21/70)

SHOWALTER, A. - sells 40 ac in Green Twp (10/19/70)

SHOWALTER, Anderson - owns property in Independence (1/6/69); a businessman in Independence (6/16/69)

SHOWALTER, Andrew -- sells 37 ac in Liberty Twp (11/3/69)

SHUGART, Cornelius - buys 84 ac in Mill Twp (10/19/70)

SHUGART, George - sells property in Fairmount (4/27/70)

SHUGART, Henry - allows his grove [grassy area of shade trees] to be used as site of a union religious meeting by the Rev.'s James Maple, H.L. Brown & A. Greenman (6/25/68), the Friends took an active part in the union meeting (7/1/68), ca 1,000 people att (7/8/68); v pres, Grant Co Agric Soc Fair (7/29/68); organizes Franklin Twp support for the proposed GR,W&C RR (11/3/69); pres, Old Settlers meeting (6/8/70); pres, 1870 Grant Co Fair (8/3/70)

SHUMAKER, Mary S. - buys property in Jonesboro (10/26/70)

SHUNK, Col. David - serv in 8th Regt during CW; his warhorse 'Bob' (see Civil War) was returned to Marion (6/9/69)

SHUPE/SHOPE, Tunis A. - sells Pleasant Twp ac (1/22/68)

SIMMONS, Francis M. - 1867 sells 0.4 ac in Franklin Twp to Thomas Burson (1/15/68), & buys Franklin Twp ac (4/30/68)

SIMMONS, Joel W. - Pleasant Twp delegate to State Rep Conv (2/9/70)

SIMMONS, Wesley - viewer, new Pleasant Twp rd (3/11/69)

SIMONS, Mrs. E.A. - officer, Rebekah Lodge, Jonesboro (4/28/69)

SIMONS, Hiram S. - sells property in Jonesboro (4/30/68)

SIMONS, Mary F. - owns property in Marion (1/6/69)

SIMONS, Morris T. - Van Buren Twp landowner (1/6/69)

SIMONS, William - Monroe Twp landowner (1/6/69); sells 80 ac in Monroe Twp to Jacob Carroll (4/27/70)

SIMPSON, John T. - dec; 1869 owned land in Pleasant Twp (12/21/70)

SIMS TOWNSHIP - B.N. Leisure, Trustee (9/18/67; 10/19/70)

SIMS TOWNSHIP, Schools of - 350 school children reside in Twp (11/17/69)

SINCLAIR, Hiram - 1869 Jefferson Twp landowner (1/6/69)

SINCLAIR, James - dec; 1868 his heirs owned property in Mier (1/12/70)

SINCLAIR, John P. - & Charles Parker lay out the original plat of 30 lots in Mier 11 & 12 Sep 1848; Sinclair's Addn of 12 lots is laid out in Mar 1849 (4/23/68)

SINCLAIR, Palmer - buys 40 ac in Van Buren Twp (4/9/68)

SISSON, Amos - buys 40 ac in Pleasant Twp (2/26/68)

SIZELOVE, Andrew - sells 40 ac in Green Twp (12/25/67)

SIZEMORE, James A. - prop/barber in renovated barbershop under the Spencer House (7/1/68); shaves, cuts hair, dyes hair & beards (10/27/69)

SIZEMORE, James A. - sells Marion lots (4/2/68; 1/26/70)

SIZEMORE, W.J. - buys Marion lots (4/2/68)

SKINNER, Phineas - admin estate of Amanda Harlan, dec (7/20/70)

SLAGLE, Conrad - dec; owned property in Mier (1/6/69)

SLAGLE, Joseph T. - owns property in Marion (1/6/69); of Franklin Twp, recently found a stray bay mare (12/8/69)

SLATER, William - buys 80 ac in Jefferson Twp (12/7/70)

SLEETH, [Isaac] N. - Jun 1868 buys license to m Harriett Benoy (7/1/68)

SLODERBECK, Daniel - 1866 sells 10 ac in Franklin Twp to Job S. Mills (4/9/68); Franklin Twp landowner (1/8/68)

SLODERBECK, Jacob - Oct 1870 buys a license to m Asenath McCracken (11/2/70)

SLOVER, Anna - sells 1 ac in Washington Twp (12/21/70)

SLOVER, John A. - is re-appointed supt, Grant County Infirmary/Poor Farm (3/11/69)

SMALL, Elihu - & Gideon Small in Dec 1854 lay out Small's Addn to Marion (4/16/68)

SMALL, Enoch P. - 1862 buys Jonesboro property from Nathan Wright & 1865 sells Jonesboro property (1/15/68)

SMALL, Jesse - sells 30 ac in Center Twp (1/12/70)

SMALL, Jonathan - April 1868 buys license to m J[ane] B. Jenkins (5/14/68)

SMALL, Leander - Nov 1867 buys license to m Elizabeth J. Dinart (12/11/67); sells 40 ac in Franklin Twp (1/29/68)

SMALL, Nathan - admin the estate of John W. Pettey, dec (9/18/67; 7/20/70)

SMALL, Noah W. - 1865 buys/sells Jonesboro property (1/15/68); is a Jonesboro businessman (9/29/69)

SMALL, Reuben - owns property in Jonesboro (1/6/69)

SMALL, [Samuel] H. - Dec 1868 buys license to m Amanda Fleming (1/6/69)

SMALL, Sarah A. - buys 10 ac in Center Twp (4/2/68)

SMALLEY, Joseph W. - buys 160 ac in Liberty Twp (3/30/70)

SMILEY, George - buys 63 ac in Jefferson Twp (3/4/68)

SMILEY, Henry - sells 63 ac in Jefferson Twp (3/4/68)

SMILEY, John - of Jefferson Twp; CW vet (1/19/70)

SMITH, __ - age ca 16; dt Mrs. __ Smith, a Washington Twp widow of 5 mi N of Marion; disappeared while looking for cows last Sunday evening; was found 8 mi from home relating that she had been kidnapped, then released (5/12/69)

SMITH, Andrew - sells 40 ac in Sims Twp (9/28/70)

SMITH, Bethuel W. - tchr, Morris Chapel SS (5/26/69)

SMITH, Calvin J. - of Pleasant Twp recently found a stray heifer (1/5/70)

SMITH, Charles W.M. - exor for estate of Solomon Harter, dec (3/24/69); sells 49 ac in Pleasant Twp to Charles Campbell (12/16/70); moves to IA from Pleasant Twp (12/21/70)

SMITH, David - 5 May 1868 was m to Arrelia/Arrela Harris by Elder James Maple (5/7/68; 6/4/68)

SMITH, Deacon - f Marion sch tchr; serv/d in CW (1/5/69)

SMITH, Frances - 1869 owns property in Independence (12/21/70); - see Erastus WAITS

SMITH, Hugh R. - Center Twp landowner (1/6/69)

SMITH, Ichabod - of Fairmount Twp; is on a Co bd to assess property (1/5/70); sells 40 ac in Fairmount Twp (5/11/70)

SMITH, Isaac R. - losing candidate for JP, Center Twp (10/19/70)

SMITH, Jacob - 1867 sells a Marion lot (1/8/68); sells 1 lot in Marion (6/25/68); Center Twp dir, Grant Co Agric Soc Fair (7/29/68); 1869 sells 5 ac near Marion to Joseph Smith (1/5/70); sells 81 ac(?) in Franklin Twp to Joseph Clouse (9/14/70)

SMITH, James R. - 1868 owns property in Fairmount (1/12/70); sells property in Fairmount to William Thomas (2/2/70)

SMITH, John - 1865 buys 30.6 ac in Fairmount Twp (2/12/68)

SMITH, John A. - of Pleasant Twp; CW vet (1/26/70)

SMITH, John M. - of Sims Twp; is on Co bd to assess property (1/5/70)

SMITH, Joseph - is att Marion Sch (12/18/67)

SMITH. Lewis M. - 1869 buys Washington Twp ac (1/5/70)

SMITH, Mahlon - 9 Aug 1869 m Josephine Pulley, both of Grant Co (8/11/69; 9/8/69)

SMITH, Mary - sells a lot in Marion to George Limes (1/22/68)

SMITH, Noah - buys 16 ac in Liberty Twp (4/6/70)

SMITH, Robert - is att Marion HS (12/23/70)

SMITH, Robert - buys 40 ac in Liberty Twp (4/16/68)

SMITH, Thomas B. - Washington Twp landowner (1/8/68)

SMITH, Washington - Sims Twp dir, Grant Co Agric Soc Fair (7/29/68)

SMITH, Wells - Monroe Twp landowner (1/8/68)

SMITH, Wesley - sells 40 ac in Monroe Twp (10/27/69)

SMITH, William - Apr 1869 buys license to m Rebecca A. Burden, a colored person (5/5/69)

SMITH, William - sells 20 ac in Fairmount Twp (6/8/70)

SMITHSON, David - Fairmount Twp landowner (1/8/68)

SMITHSON, Isaac - 1867 sells 5 ac in Fairmount Twp (1/15/68); 1869 buys 2 Fairmount lots (1/5/70); of Fairmount; CW vet (1/19/70); Fairmount Twp Assessor (10/19/70)

SMITHSON, Judiah B. - buys 2 Fairmount lots (12/15/69)

SMITHSON, Mrs. Margaret E. - see Ansel E. RAPER

SNODGRASS, Dr. D[avid] B. - of Xenia; 29 Feb 1870 m Mary 'Mollie' James (3/30/70; 4/6/70); is an Eclectic Physician; now lives on Branson St N of Catholic Ch, Marion; office is on N side of Square (9/7/70)

SNORF, Miss Ella - Marion Sch tchr (9/14/70)

SNORF, Miss Jennie - Marion Sch tchr (9/14/70); see Dr. William SCOTT

SNORF, Milton - is att Marion Public Sch (1/12/70); Marion HS student (12/23/70)

SNYDER, John - Jun 1868 buys license to m A[senath] Conner (7/1/68); buys a sawmill in Pleasant Twp from J.E. Renbarger (5/11/70)

SNYDER, Stephen - buys 41 ac in Pleasant Twp (3/30/70)

SOHN, John - buys part of a Marion lot from Milton G. Harter (4/2/68); prop, Sohn Grocery (7/23/69)

SPAULDING, Ira B. - sells Monroe Twp ac (6/1/70)

SPEARS, Anderson/Andrew C. - 9 Aug 1868 m Sarah E. Ruley in Jonesboro (8/19/68)

SPEARS, Clark - of Mill Twp; CW vet (1/19/70)

SPEARS, John - 1864 is a Grant Co Comm (6/9/69)

SPEELMAN, Richard V. - sells 100 ac in Pleasant Twp (4/2/68); mbr Grant Lodge of F&AM; d 7 Apr 1868 (4/30/68)

SPENCE, S.R. - organizes Mill Twp support for the proposed GR,W&C RR (11/3/69)

SPENCE, Sarah A. - b 25 Jan 1800; widow of Dr. W.F. Spence; mbr M.E. Ch; d 10 Sep 1870 in Jonesboro home of her son-in-law, [William] Wilson (10/12/70)

SPENCE, Dr. W.F. - dec; owned Jonesboro property (1/6/69)

SPENCER, D[avid] - Aug 1869 buys a license to m M[atilda] E. Bole (9/8/69)

SPENCER, Jacob W. - a dir, Liberty Twp Pike Co (4/28/69); prop, Spencer House (5/5/69)

SPENCER, Mrs. Jacob W. - 2 Aug 1869 fell from the 2nd story rear porch of the Spencer House, is recovering (8/4/69)

SPENCER, J[ohn] F. - Aug 1869 buys a license to m B[eauley] Knight (9/8/69)

SPENCER, Mark - Apr 1869 buys license to m Milly Galbreath (5/5/69)

SPENCER, S[amuel] - Dec 1869 buys license to m M[artha] J. Lewellen (1/5/70)

SPERBECK, J[anetta (Thomas) - wife of John Sperbeck]; age 29y, 8m, 4da; mbr U.B. Ch; d 29 May 1868 (6/4/68)

SPRECHER, Jacob - 7 Apr 1849 lays out the original plat of 27 lots in Mier; in Nov 1850 he lays out the 13 lots of Sprecher's Addn to Mier (4/23/68)

SPRINGER, A.B. - fills prescriptions at City Drugstore (8/18/69)

SPRINGER, Jesse M. - 1847-1850 was Deputy, Grant Co Clerk (8/18/69; 7/20/70)

SPRINGER, O.D. - is att Marion Public Sch (11/6/67)

SPURGEON, Joseph - Sims Twp dir, 1870 Grant Co Fair (8/3/70)

STACKHOUSE, James - 1869 owns Marion property (12/21/70)

STAFFORD, Levina - sells 80 ac in Monroe Twp (9/21/70)

STALLINGS, James C. - sells 40 ac in Washington Twp to Thomas & James Willcuts (12/29/69)

STANFIELD, David - 28 Dec 1850 lays out the original plat of 45 lots in Fairmount; 2 Aug 1859(?) lays out the 8 lots in Stanfield's Addn to Fairmount (4/23/68); is dec; Nathan D. Wilson is exor of his estate (1/13/69)

STANFIELD, Isaac - 1867 sells 40 ac in Fairmount Twp to Enos Willcuts (4/2/68); sells 60 ac in Fairmount Twp (11/10/69)

STANLEY, Capt. J. - of near Jonesboro; f of Howard Co; m (1/15/68)

STARRETT, L.J. - prop, Eagle Drugstore; has 13 yr experience in drug business (11/17/69)

STEBBENS, Catharine - sells 119 ac in Center Twp (6/25/68)

STEBBENS, Elijah - buys property on S side of Square in Marion from Curtis Jackson (7/13/70)

STEBBENS, Mrs. M. - prop, Stebbens Millinery Shop (10/1/67)

STEBBINS, Phebe - 1869 Center Twp landowner (12/21/70)

STEBBINS, Sarah - 1869 Center Twp landowner (12/21/70)

STEELE, Dr. __ - now has medical practice in Farmington; studied medicine in the office of Dr. Jay of Marion (5/14/68)

STEELE, Col. Asbury - 1847 was Grant Co Clerk (7/20/70); and Robert T. St. John are attys with offices on NW corner of CH Square (9/18/67); organizes Washington Twp support for the proposed GR,W&C RR (11/3/69); is elected State Senator (12/28/70)

STEELE, Lieut. George W. - of the 14th US Regt; is on duty at Camp Grant, AZ (11/27/67; 8/12/68); his regt soon to return to Louisville, KY from where it is stationed in southern CA; his regt to be consolidated with 45th Regt; he will return by way of the Pacific RR (3/24/69); serv 3 yr in AZ and southern CA; is now visiting in Grant Co (6/16/69; 7/6/70)

STEELE, Richard G. - sells Washington Twp ac (11/2/70)

STEELMAN, Hezekiah - buys Pleasant Twp ac (11/10/69)

STEPHENS, Allen N. - Richland Twp Assessor (10/19/70)

STEPHENS, James H. - 1869 buys 120 ac in Franklin Twp from Jesse B. Harris (1/5/70)

STEPHENS, James E. - 1865 sells 80 ac in Van Buren Twp to William Evans (1/8/68)

STEPHENS, J[ohn] E.A. - Dec 1869 buys license to m Mary Farr (1/5/70)

STEPHENS, William T. - Liberty Twp landowner (1/6/69)

STEPHENSON, Elsa - sells 40 ac in Jefferson Twp (6/8/70)

STEPHENSON, George W. - 1869 owns land in Jefferson Twp & in Cumberland (12/21/70)

STEPHENSON, James A. - buys Liberty Twp ac (12/28/70)

STEVENS, Alma - Liberty Twp landowner (1/8/68)

STEVENS, Thomas - buys/sells Jefferson Twp ac (3/26/68)

STEVENS, William F. - 1869 Liberty Twp landowner (12/21/70)

STEWART, David - Sims Twp landowner (1/8/68)

STEWART, Hudson - sells part of a Jonesboro lot (4/16/68)

STEWART, James - 1868 Green Twp landowner (1/12/70)

STEWART, M.J. - buys 40 ac in Liberty Twp (2/2/70)

STEWART, Samuel W. - sells 40 ac in Liberty Twp (11/10/69)

STEWART, William - Liberty Twp landowner (1/6/69)

STEWART, William F. - Liberty Twp landowner (1/6/69)

STILES, Jacob - Washington Twp landowner (1/8/68)

STILLWELL, Thomas N. - Monroe Twp landowner (1/8/68)

STINEBRUNER, Detrick - Van Buren Twp landowner (1/8/68)

STOKES, John - 1869 owns property in Jonesboro (12/21/70)

STOTLAR, Isaac - Sims Twp landowner (1/8/68)

STOUT, Frances - 1866 sells a Marion lot (1/22/68)

STOUT, J.D. - 1868 owns property in Jonesboro (1/12/70)

STOUT, Joseph W. - Dec 1868 buys license to m Laura J. Horton (1/6/69)

STOUT, L.N. - SS tchr, Salem Ch (5/5/69)

STOUT, R[ufus] - SS tchr, Salem Ch (5/5/69)

STOUT, Warren J. - asst secy, Salem Ch SS (5/5/69)

STRAIN, Lucius M. - Jun 1868 buys license to m N[ancy] M. Maxwell (7/1/68)

STRANGE, George - Trustee, Monroe Twp (9/18/67; 10/19/70); 1867 buys 40 ac in Monroe Twp from Enos Johnson, Jr. (3/12/68); owns ca 1,000 ac (7/13/70); Monroe Twp dir, 1870 Grant Co Fair (8/3/70)

STRETCH, Capt. James A., Esq - 1847 publ of 'Marion Telegraph' (7/6/70); 1849 sells drygoods in Marion (8/3/70); 1850 sells cook stoves in Marion (8/18/69); an auctioneer with office over the Post Office since 23 Oct 1866 (9/18/67); 1866 buys a Marion lot from Frances Stout (1/22/68); is Special Prosecutor for Grant Co (3/12/68); owns Marion property (1/8/68; 1/6/69); organizes support for the proposed GR,W&C RR (11/3/69); CW vet (1/19/70); att Old Settlers meeting (6/8/70)

STRETCH, James Q. 'Quince' - is att Marion Public Sch (12/18/67); night operator, RR Telegraph Office (1/19/70)

STRETCH, Lieut. [John F.] - of the 10th Regt, US regular army; is visiting relatives in/near Marion (7/6/70)

STRETCH, Vicca - is att Marion Sch (11/6/67; 1/12/70)

STRICKLER, Jeremiah - of Richland Twp; CW vet (1/19/70); JP, Richland Twp (10/19/70)

STRIEB/STREIB, Jacob - 1842 is a Marion merchant who advertises 'whisky and salt' for sale, wholesale & retail (7/13/70); 1869 buys 40 Washington Twp ac from Daniel Gray (1/5/70); sells 30 ac in Washington Twp (8/17/70)

STUART, Doidamia J. - buys lot in Jonesboro (5/14/68)

STUCKEY, John A. - buys 80 ac in Liberty Twp (12/25/67)

SULLIVAN, Margaret - owns property in Marion (1/6/69)

SULLIVAN, Michael - buys half of a lot in Marion (11/2/70)

SULT, George - Mar 1869 buys a license to m Nancy Joslin (4/7/69)

SUMMERS, Daniel - 1868 Richland Twp landowner (1/12/70); sells 40 ac in Richland Twp to Lewis Summers (10/19/70)

SWAFFORD, C[hristian] L. - owns property in Jalapa (1/8/68; 1/6/69)

SWAFFORD, John P. - owns Independence property (1/6/69)

SWAFFORD, W[illiam] H. - May 1869 buys license to m Mary A. Ellis (6/2/69)

SWAN, Cyrus A. - Green Twp landowner (1/6/69)

SWAN(N), John F. - Trustee, VanBuren Twp (9/18/67); organizes support in Van Buren Twp for the proposed GR,W&C RR (11/3/69)

SWAN, L.D. - of Green Twp; CW vet (1/19/70)

SWAYZEE, A.C. - Jun 1850 is on committee to help Marion citizens celebrate our 74th Independence Day (8/18/69); mbr, Marion M.E. Ch (7/23/69); sells Marion lots (9/7/70; 10/26/70); buys 40 ac in Center Twp from William Middleton & sells 2 lots in Marion to William Middleton (12/16/70); att recent Old Settlers meeting (6/15/71)

SWAYZEE, Watson - is att Marion Public Sch (11/6/67)

SWEETSER, David Burr - dir, Grant Co Live Stock Assn (8/5/68); 5 Oct 1870 m Mary 'Mollie' L. Wood in Marion Christian Ch (10/5/70; 10/12/70; 11/2/70)

SWEETSER, James - 1867 & 1868 buys Marion lots (2/12/68; 11/8/68); buys 160 ac in Sims Twp (4/2/68); sells 2 lots in Marion to George Sweetser (6/25/68); exor of estate of Hester A. Jacobs, dec (7/8/68); pres, Grant Co Agric Soc Fair (7/29/68); buys 42 ac in Pleasant Twp (11/10/69)

SWEETSER, Lizzie (Carey) - age 20y, 10m, 29da; dt S.B. and L. Carey; wife of George B. Sweetser; d 7(?) Aug 1868 (8/12/68)

SWIFT, Stephen A. - owns property in Marion (1/8/68)

SWISHER, John - sells 40 ac in Jefferson Twp to Henry A. Swisher & buys 40 ac in Mill Twp (4/27/70)

SWOPE, George L. - of Center Twp; CW vet (1/19/70)

SWOPE, Mary C. - 1867 sells Washington Twp ac (1/8/68)

SWOPE, William J. - blacksmith, does horse shoeing; his shop is on Adams St S of Spencer House (9/18/67)

TACKETT, M.V. - Fairmount Twp landowner (1/8/68)

TAYLOR, Benjamin - Liberty Twp landowner (1/8/68)

TAYLOR, George W. - Richland Twp landowner (1/6/69)

TAYLOR, Lydia A. - 1867 sells Fairmount Twp ac (1/29/68)

TAYLOR, Martha - sells 45 ac in Center Twp (12/28/70)

TAYLOR, Matthew - of W of Marion; 2 of his horses were stolen last night, 1 was recovered (5/25/70)

TAYLOR, Rebecca - dec; owned land in Sims Twp (1/6/69)

TAYLOR'S CREEK - bd of County Comm gave $150 to the Pleasant Twp Trustee to aid in constructing a bridge over Taylor's Creek on the Delphi State Rd (3/11/69)

TERRELL, Mrs. Nancy - see Reuben BOOKOUT

TERRELL, Permelia - Fairmount Twp landowner (1/8/68)

THALLS, John - dec; owned land in Liberty Twp (1/6/69)

THARP, Capt. & Rev. Thomas D. - Union Party candidate for Co treas (3/26/68); partner in new Tharp & Neal Grocery on E side of Square (6/2/69); 1869 sells a Marion lot (1/5/70); CW vet (1/19/70); att Old Settlers meeting (6/8/70); of Marion; 29 Sep 1870 in Delaware Co m Mrs. Lucy G. Bradford of Delaware Co (10/5/70)

THOMAS, Daniel - is att Marion Public Sch (1/12/70); Marion HS student (12/23/70)

THOMAS, Dick - of Thomas & Beshores; owns the first velocipede to be in Marion (3/3/69)

THOMAS, Eli - a dir, Liberty Twp Pike Co (4/28/69); viewer for a rd in Franklin Twp (7/23/69)

THOMAS, Elijah - 1867 buys 3 ac in Mill Twp from John C. Macy for & 1868 sells 3 ac in Mill Twp (3/26/68)

THOMAS, Enoch - 23 Apr 1860 lays out Thomas' Addn, Marion (4/16/68)

THOMAS, Hannah B. - 1869 Mill Twp landowner (12/21/70)

THOMAS, Henley - Franklin Twp landowner (1/8/68)

THOMAS, Henry - 1868 Center Twp landowner (1/12/70)

THOMAS, Henry D. - 8 Apr 1869 m Mary 'Mollie' E. Clunk (4/14/69; 5/5/69)

THOMAS, Jesse - is att Marion Public Sch (1/12/70)

THOMAS, John - 1869 Van Buren Twp landowner (12/21/70)

THOMAS, John J., Jr. - his wife committed suicide last Aug; 4 Dec 1870 his 3y old child d when his 5y old s caused the 3y old to strangle on cinnamon drops (12/7/70)

THOMAS, Loruhama - sells 34 ac in Mill Twp (1/26/70)

THOMAS, Marcus - is att Marion Sch (11/6/67; 1/12/70)

THOMAS, Martha A. - 1868 Center Twp landowner (1/12/70)

THOMAS, Mary Ann [(Kelly)] - lived on Strawtown rd 2 mi from Marion; age 38; wife of John J. Thomas; mbr Friends; apparent suicide by morphine 19 Aug 1870 (8/24/70)

THOMAS, Milly - 1867 buys a Marion lot (1/8/68)

THOMAS, Milton - sells 4 ac in Center Twp (11/2/70)

THOMAS, Nelson - Fairmount Twp landowner (1/6/69)

THOMAS, Noah - sells 10 ac in Center Twp (4/2/68); buys 7.54 ac in Marion (2/2/70); sells 15 ac in Center Twp (2/9/70); sells a lot in Marion to M. Josephy for $1,500 (11/2/70)

THOMAS, Philander - Sims Twp landowner (1/8/68)

THOMAS, Sarah - 1864 buys 1 lot in Marion from George N. Eckfield (4/16/68); 1869 owns Fairmount property (12/21/70)

THOMAS, Seruhama - Mill Twp landowner (1/8/68)

THOMAS, William - is att Marion Public Sch (1/12/70)

THOMAS, William - 1867 sells 80 ac in Center Twp to Jesse D. Wright (2/12/68); buys/sells Fairmount property (2/2/70)

THOMASON, Absolem - of Monroe Twp (12/25/67); organizes Monroe Twp support for the proposed GR,W&C RR (11/3/69)

THOMPSON, Franklin - organizes Washington Twp support for the proposed GR,W&C RR (11/3/69)

THOMPSON, H. Clay - Washington Twp landowner (1/6/69)

THOMPSON, G.K. - 1866 buys 160 ac in Van Buren Twp from Amos Mullen (2/26/68); sells Van Buren Twp ac (3/4/68)

THOMPSON, George - buys 1 Washington Twp ac (12/21/70)

THOMPSON, H.D. - 1869 owns property in Marion (12/21/70)

THOMPSON, James - att Old Settlers meeting (6/8/70)

THOMPSON, Mary - 1869 owns land in Mill Twp & in Monroe Twp (12/21/70)

THOMPSON, Matilda - tchr, Morris Chapel SS (5/26/69)

THOMPSON, Samuel R. - buys 40 ac in Monroe Twp from David M. Fine (1/22/68); organizes Monroe Twp support for the proposed GR,W&C RR (11/3/69)

THOMPSON, William - 1867 sells a lot in Jonesboro to John Q. Jennings (3/12/68); 1869 owns Jonesboro property (12/21/70)

THORNBURG, Shadrack - 1869 Monroe Twp landowner (12/21/70)

THRAILKILL, Henry - Sims Twp landowner (1/8/68)

THRASHER, Elizabeth - 1868 Green Twp landowner (1/12/70)

THRASHER, Josiah - farmer in Green Twp near Independence; d recently (7/1/68); his personal property will be sold 27 Aug 1868 (8/12/68)

TIBBITS, Charles S. - 1864 is a Grant Co Comm (6/9/69); 19 Oct 1867 lays out Tibbits' Addn, Marion (4/16/68); 1867 sells Marion property to Joseph Wilcuts (1/15/68), & to William Poole (3/4/68); sells 40 ac in Franklin Twp (4/2/68); has controlling interest in Hub & Spoke Factory (7/13/69); v pres, bd of dir, LM,W&C RR (3/3/69); mbr, Marion M.E. Ch (7/23/69); sells 95 ac in Franklin Twp & buys 10 ac in Center Twp & buys Marion lots (1/26/70); sells Marion lots (2/9/70; 5/11/70)

TIBBITS, Edward - a Rep of Franklin Twp (6/8/70)

TIBBITS, Emma E. - is att Marion Public Sch (11/6/67)

TIBBITS, John - is att Marion Public Sch (12/18/67)

TIBBITS, William - is att Marion Public Sch (11/6/67)

TIMONY, John - 1869 sells 80 ac in Monroe Twp (1/5/70)

TIMONY, John D. - buys Marion property from Jacob G. Eby (12/29/69), & from James A. Sizemore (1/26/70)

TINGLEY, Marshall F. - f of Fayette Co; ed, Marion Weekly Chronicle (10/1/67; 10/26/71); secy, Marion Literary Soc (1/15/68)

TINKLE, S.A. - SS tchr, Salem Ch (5/5/69)

TINNEY, John M. - owns property in Jonesboro (1/8/68); sells 1 lot in Marion to Rachel Whisler (5/14/68)

TIPPEY, Henderson - sells 40 ac in Van Buren Twp (1/22/68); Rep Party candidate for Land Appraiser of Grant Co (3/4/68)

TIPPY, J.J. - is att Marion Public Sch (11/6/67)

TITUS, Samuel - admin estate of Hugh Hamilton, dec (3/24/69)

TITUS, Samuel W. - 1869 buys 40 Green Twp ac (1/5/70); CW vet of Green Twp(1/19/70); buys 40 Green Twp ac (10/19/70)

TOBIN, Mary - owns property in Farmington (1/6/69)

TODD, Jane H.H. - 1867 sells 80 ac in Van Buren Twp (1/8/68)

TO-KUNG-YAH, Robert - a Miami Indian of Somerset; his mare & McClellan saddle were stolen on the night of 16 Jul 1869; $25 reward for its return (6/23/69)

TOLLE, Nancy - sells 1 ac in Green Twp to Elijah Tolle (4/6/70)

TOWNSEND, J[ames] B. - May 1868 buys a license to m J[ulia] A. Noe (6/4/68)

TRADER, Arthur - 1867 buys 40 ac in Liberty Twp from Nelson Conner (1/22/68); 1867 sells Liberty Twp ac (4/30/68)

TRADER, Robert - Fairmount Twp landowner (1/6/69)

TRASK, Town of - has 1 'played-out' blacksmith shop and a deserted house, the Post Office is 0.25 mi outside of town (9/14/70)

TRASK, Ezra S. - 1838 lays out Trask's Addn of Out-Lots to Marion (4/16/68)

TRIBBY, Ruth E. - 1869 Sims Twp landowner (12/21/70)

TRIMBLE, James K. - sells 40 ac in Jefferson Twp (12/25/67)

TRIMBLE, William F. - Liberty Twp landowner (1/6/69)

TRIPP, Elder __ - pastor, Lugar Creek Christian Ch (7/22/68)

TRIPP, A.W. - mbr Grant Lodge of F&AM (4/30/68)

TROOK, John - buys 40 ac in Washington Twp (1/22/68)

TROWBRIDGE, Hiram - is att Marion Public Sch (1/12/70)

TROWBRIDGE, Hyatt - is att Marion Public Sch (1/12/70); Marion HS student (12/23/70)

TROXELL, M.M - buys 20 ac in Monroe Twp from Ambrose Huffman & sells 20 ac in Monroe Twp to Isaac Parks (3/30/70)

TRUSLER, John N. - 1868 Van Buren Twp landowner (1/12/70)

TUCKER, Fieman - 1867 sells Franklin Twp property (1/8/68)

TUCKER, Miles - May 1868 buys license to m Eliza A. Youse (6/4/68)

TULLY, Bell - is att Marion Public Sch (1/12/70)

TURNER, Elizabeth - 1869 Green Twp landowner (12/21/70)

TURNER, Harrison - att Marion Public Sch (11/6/67; 1/12/70)

TURNER, James N. - 13 Jan 1842 lays out Turner's Addn to Marion (4/16/68); Mar 1868 buys license to m Hannah Nixon (4/2/68); treas, Grant Co Agric Soc Fair (7/29/68; 8/3/70); grows ca 7 varieties of grapes (8/31/70)

TURNER, James P. - a blacksmith for past 17 yr; prop, Turner Blacksmith Shop located on Adams St 1 blk above Spencer House (4/7/69)

TURNER, John Nelson - 1850 is Democrat candidate for Grant Co delegate to State Constitutional Conv (8/18/69); buys 80 ac in Liberty Twp from Co Sheriff (12/29/69); att Old Settlers meeting (6/8/70)

TURNER, Lemuel - drives a mule team hitched to his dray wagon (12/16/70)

TURNER, Margaret 'Maggie' - is att Marion Sch (11/13/67)

TYSOR, Gabriel - Monroe Twp landowner (1/8/68)

TYSOR/TYSER, Samuel - engineer for Roseburg steam sawmill; 11 Nov 1870 is killed when boiler exploded (11/16/70)

UNDERHILL, Phinneas S. - 1867 sells 2 Marion lots (3/12/68)

UNION TOWNSHIP - in 1847 was an area of 4 mi by 7 mi, and occupied the E part of what is now Fairmount Twp & the SE part of what is now Mill Twp (7/20/70)

UPLAND, Town of - 30 Sep 1867 is laid out with 48 lots by Jacob Bugher (4/23/68)

VAIL, Dr. M.S. - a prop, Tripp & Vail; buys out the interest of I.C. Kelley in Tripp & Kelley (3/3/69)

VALL, Mary A. - Fairmount Twp landowner (1/8/68)

VAN BUREN TOWNSHIP - John F. Swann, Trustee (9/18/67; 10/19/70); no Post Office is in this Twp (11/30/70)

VAN BUREN TOWNSHIP, Schools of - 441 school children are in Twp (11/17/69)
District # 4 Sch - mentioned (5/7/68)
ROOD SCH - is 12.5 mi from Marion (9/21/70; 12/28/70)

VanCANNON, Elias - 1867 sells 1 lot in Fairmount (6/25/68)

VANCE, Jackson - of Franklin Twp; recently found a stray white heifer (1/8/68)

VanDEVANTER, Isaac - and James F. McDowell are attys with offices in the Spencer House (9/18/67); 1867 sells 2 Marion lots to U&L RR Co (6/25/68); owns property in Marion (1/8/68)

VANGUNDY, Henry - Monroe Twp landowner (1/8/68)

VANMINDEN/VANNURSDEN, John - Feb 1868 buys license to m Judy May (3/4/68)

VANVALKENBURG, James - 1869 Green Twp landowner (12/21/70)

VEACH, Joel J. - viewer for a rd between Grant Co & Miami Co (7/23/69); 1868 Sims Twp landowner (1/12/70)

VEACH, John J. - losing candidate for JP, Washington Twp (10/19/70)

VERNON, Ira - sells 80 ac in Monroe Twp (12/29/69)

VINCENT, Nathan - Fairmount Twp landowner (1/8/68)

VINNEDGE, J.W. - 7 Jul 1870 at Xenia m Eunice E. Haisley/ Hazely (7/20/70)

VOOR(H)IS, W.R. - of Pleasant Twp; CW vet (1/26/70)

WADE, Henry - 1850 is in the drug business (8/28/69); 1867 sells a Marion lot (1/8/68); buys 40 ac in Franklin Twp (4/2/68); buys property in Marion (4/13/70)

WADE, John - now of Albany, NY; f publ, Marion Journal; is now visiting Marion (10/23/67)

WAITS, Erastus - Mar 1869 buys a license to m Frances Smith (4/7/69)

WALKER, Cornelius - sells 80 ac in Richland Twp (5/14/68)

WALKER, W[infield] S. - Feb 1869 buys license to m [Eliza] A. Abbott (3/3/69)

WALL, David - Monroe Twp delegate to State Rep Conv (2/9/70)

WALL, Rebecca - dec; owned property in Marion (1/6/69)

WALL, Thomas - dec; owned property in Marion (1/8/68)

WALLACE, Aaron T. - 1869 Liberty Twp landowner (12/21/70)

WALLACE, Benjamin F. - JP, Center Twp (10/19/70)

WALLACE, Benjamin P. - of 3 mi E of Jonesboro; 6 Jan 1869 found a stray white bull (3/3/69)

WALLACE, Catherine - owns property in Marion (1/6/69)

WALLACE, Lewis - Liberty Twp landowner (1/8/68)

WALLACE, Milton - is att Marion Public Sch (11/6/67)

WALLACE, Price - buys 2 lots in Harrisburg (7/6/70)

WALLACE, Samuel L. - 11 Nov 1870 m Malinda Haleman (11/16/70)

WALNUT CREEK - bd of County Comm gave the Mill Twp Trustee $75.00 to aid in bldg bridge over Walnut Creek on Mill Twp & Monroe Twp line (3/11/69)

WALTON, J[ames] C. - Dec 1869 buys license to m S[usan] M. Powell (1/5/70)

WARD, John - Liberty Twp landowner (1/6/69)

WARD, Leander - of Jonesboro; mbr Jonesboro F&AM; partner in Ward & Bond Sawmill; killed 7 Aug 1868 when the sawmill boiler exploded; bur Richmond (8/12/68; 8/19/68); L.L. Bond admin his estate (7/20/70)

WARD, Simon - sells 40 ac in Liberty Twp (2/2/70)

WARD, William - 1869 Jefferson Twp landowner (12/21/70)

WARD & BOND SAWMILL - is 3 mi N of New Cumberland; its boiler exploded 7 Aug 1868 killing Leander Ward & Mr. ___ Shelton, the boiler engineer; Mr. Bond and an unnamed employee were injured; loss to sawmill is ca $3,000 (8/12/68)

WARRENBURG, Frederick - f of Richland Twp; moved to Clinton, IL; is convicted of stealing & selling 2 of James Highley's horses, is sentenced to 5 yr in Ind penitentiary (4/7/69)

WASHINGTON TOWNSHIP - James Phillips, Trustee (9/18/67); Frank M. Helm, Trustee (4/7/69); John Otis is appointed Constable (7/23/69)

WASHINGTON TOWNSHIP, Schools of - 372 school children are in Twp (11/17/69)
CENTER SCH - site of meeting of local Reps (2/2/70)
SALEM SCH - mentioned (5/7/68)
SCH No. 9 - Tom C. Neal, tchr (12/16/70)

WATKINS, Joseph - buys 144 ac in Richland Twp (4/13/70)

WATKINS, Dr. Nathaniel D. - dental surgeon; office is in Spencer House Blk (9/7/70)

WATSON, Henry - Oct 1870 buys a license to m Caroline Crow (11/2/70)

WEASNER, Allen - 1869 Richland Twp landowner (12/21/70)

WEASNER, Micajah - buys property in Center Twp (4/27/70)

WEAVER, Henry - Liberty Twp landowner (1/6/69)

WEAVER, John W. - 1868 Liberty Twp landowner (1/12/70)

WEAVER, Philander - May 1869 buys license to m C[atharine] Burden (6/2/69)

WEAVER, Pleasant - 1868 Mill Twp landowner (1/8/68)

WEBB, Anderson - Center Twp Assessor (10/19/70)

WEBB, Catharine E. - 1869 owns property in Marion (12/21/70)

WEBB, John T. - dec; owned property in Marion (1/6/69)

WEBSTER, Dr. E.C. - partner in Marion group of Dr.'s Jay, Webster & Hogin (1/12/70); is an eclectic physician; office is on SW corner of Square (9/7/70)

WEBSTER, G.L. - is asst Grant Co Clerk (11/16/70)

WEBSTER, G.W. - Marion contractor; is bldg the Universalist College Bldgs. in Logansport; owns the lots on the S side of the Square in Marion (8/24/70)

WEBSTER, George - is att Marion Public Sch (11/6/67)

WEBSTER, Mary - is att Marion Public Sch (1/12/70)

WEBSTER, Mollie - is att Marion Public Sch (11/6/67; 1/12/70)

WEBSTER, William C. - treas, Grant Co Live Stock Assn (8/5/68); Dec 1868 buys license to m Callie Hall (1/6/69)

WEDDINGTON, Dr. Samuel C. - is a candidate for the State Legislature (8/31/70)

WEEKS, Hiram P. - native of Vermont; 1851 lives in Marion (8/17/70); of Marion; mbr Presbyterians; & wife celebrated their 50th wedding anniv recently (2/9/70)

WEIMER, Abraham - 1867 buys 79 ac in Green Twp (4/16/68)

WELCH, Alice - Marion HS student (12/23/70)

WELCH, H[arrison] - Dec 1869 buys license to m Lucinda Middleton (1/5/70)

WELKER, Adam - buys 3 ac in Sims Twp (3/30/70)

WELKER, Miles - dec; owned land in Green Twp (1/6/69)

WELLER, William - buys a blacksmith shop in Marion from Joel Reece (5/11/70)

WELLS, Emily - of NE Madison Co; wife of John Wells; 5 Mar 1868 started to home of her son-in-law, James Dickey, from the home of Joseph Dickey; going through a 1.5 mi-long woods, she lost her way; searchers found her at 1 AM at the home of J.M. Huston where she had sought shelter (3/12/68)

WELLS, Capt. Jacob M. - sells 2 lots in Marion to James S. Jennings (1/22/68); CW vet (1/19/70)

WELLS, James A. - in Liberty Twp 25 Feb 1869 m Emeline Powell (3/3/69)

WELLS, John B. - buys 20 ac in Liberty Twp from Mahlon Harvey (12/15/69); of Liberty Twp; CW vet (1/19/70); raises Chester White hogs (11/2/70)

WELLS, Robert T. - Green Twp landowner (1/6/69)

WESNER, Micajah - 1867 buys land in Center Twp (1/29/68)

WEST, Spencer R. - 1867 sells 20 ac in Franklin Twp (3/4/68)

WESTERFIELD, Cyrus - buys 120 ac in Green Twp (12/29/69), & sells 40 ac in Green Twp to Samuel W. Titus (1/5/70)

WESTERFIELD, W.D., Esq - of Green Twp; is a Notary Public (11/3/69); sells part of 40 ac in Green Twp to Abraham Covalt (4/13/70); lives in Rigdon (9/7/70)

WESTFALL, Charles - 1868 Franklin Twp landowner (1/12/70)

WESTFALL, James - of 1.5 mi W of Marion; age 42; m; d 21 Dec 1867 (1/8/68)

WHARTON, William - 1868 Jefferson Twp dir, Grant Co Agric Soc Fair (7/29/68); Jefferson Twp delegate to State Rep Conv (2/9/70); Rep candidate for Co Comm (7/13/70)

WHINNERY, Mills - Van Buren Twp taxpayer (1/26/70)

WHINNERY, William M. - buys Van Buren Twp ac (9/28/70)

WHIPPLE, B.W. - Sims Twp landowner (1/8/68)

WHIPPLE, George W. - 1869 Liberty Twp landowner (12/21/70)

WHISLER, J.C. - a Marion butcher (8/18/69)

WHISLER, Jacob - of Marion; declares bankruptcy (10/23/67)

WHISLER, Leroy M. - 8 Jun 1870 m Tilla McKinney (6/8/70)

WHISLER, Molly - is att Marion Public Sch (11/6/67)

WHISLER, Rachel - buys 1 lot in Marion (5/14/68)

WHITAKER, William - Apr 1869 buys license to m Nancy J. Dunwoody (5/5/69)

WHITE, Callie - of Jalapa; sells Elias Howe Sewing Machines (11/30/70)

WHITE, George W. - viewer for a new rd in Pleasant Twp (3/11/69); sells 80 ac in Pleasant Twp to Samuel Bechtel & sells property in Marion to Tharp & Neal (11/10/69); 1869 owns property in Jalapa (12/21/70); Center Twp taxpayer (1/26/70)

WHITE, Hiram - sells 2 lots in Marion (10/26/70)

WHITE, James C. - is att Marion Public Sch (11/6/67)

WHITE, Joel O. - 1866 buys 1 lot near Fairmount (4/30/68); sells 1 lot near Fairmount to Patrick H. Dean (4/30/68)

WHITE, Lindsey - 1869 Liberty Twp landowner (12/21/70)

WHITE, William - sells 303 ac in Van Buren Twp to Jacob Crist (1/15/68); Liberty Twp landowner (1/6/69)

WHITSON, David M.V. - sells 40 ac in Liberty Twp (3/12/68)

WHITSON, Martin V. - buys part of lot in Jonesboro (4/16/68)

WHORTON, William - Jefferson Twp dir, 1870 Grant Co Fair (8/3/70)

WIAND, Israel - Jul 1868 buys license to m Celissa A. Taylor (8/5/68)

WIAND/WIANT, Harrison - Nov 1867 buys license to m Pelina Stalker (12/11/67); Center Twp landowner (1/6/69)

WIGHT, Leroy W. - of South Pomfret, VT; 22 Feb 1869 m Helena A. Huffman of Marion (2/24/69; 3/3/69)

WIGGER, John H. - prominent Marion citizen (8/18/69), & businessman (9/29/69)

WILDLIFE - 20 years ago, 'D.C.S.' successfully hunted wolf, deer and turkey in Liberty Twp (4/2/68); 1850, Grant Co pays a bounty of $19.50 or more for wolf scalps (8/18/69); quail are "quite plenty in some parts of Grant County" (11/16/70)

WILEY, Harrison H. - buys 1 lot in Jonesboro (6/25/68)

WILKINSON, Henry J. - sells 100 Van Buren Twp ac (1/29/68)

WILLCUTS, Aura - is att Marion Public Sch (11/6/67)

WILLCUTS, Clark - 6 Nov 1849 lays out Willcuts Addn to Marion; dec; his heirs 10 Oct 1867 lay out Willcuts' 2nd Addn to Marion (4/16/68)

WILLCUTS, Clarkson - 1867 sells 2 lots in Marion (2/12/68)

WILLCUTS, Enos - 1867 buys 40 ac in Fairmount Twp (4/2/68)

WILLCUTS, James - 1867 sells 2 lots in Jonesboro (1/29/68)

WILLCUTS, John - sells property in Marion (1/15/68)

WILLCUTS, Jonathan - Franklin Twp landowner (1/8/68); owns property in Marion (1/6/69)

WILLCUTS, Joseph - 1867 buys property in Marion (1/15/68); sells 2 lots in Marion to Clarkson Willcuts (4/13/70)

WILLCUTS, Libbie - is att Marion Public Sch (11/6/67)

WILLCUTS, Thomas - sells a Marion lot (1/8/68); 1867 sells 1 lot in Marion to C&IC RR (6/25/68); 1867 sells property in Marion (1/15/68; 2/12/68; 2/26/68); 1868 Franklin Twp landowner (1/12/70); sells 7.54 ac in Marion (2/2/70); buys 15 ac in Center Twp (2/9/70); buys 10 ac in Center Twp (4/6/70)

WILLIAMS, A.H. - 1868 Washington Twp landowner (1/12/70)

WILLIAMS, B.F. - Liberty Twp landowner (1/8/68)

WILLIAMS, Garrett - 1869 Franklin Twp landowner (12/21/70)

WILLIAMS, Isaac J. - buys/sells Jefferson Twp ac (9/14/70)

WILLIAMS, J[ames] H. - Mar 1870 buys license to m N[ancy] J. Walker (4/6/70)

WILLIAMS, James L. - 1867 sells 6 ac in Jefferson Twp to U&L RR Co for $1 (6/25/68)

WILLIAMS, J[ohn] - Dec 1868 buys license to m S[usannah] Middleton (1/6/69)

WILLIAMS, Dr. L[ewis] - 1851 is prop, Indiana House, Marion (8/17/70); physician & surgeon with offices over Swayzee & Co Store, W side of Square (9/18/67); mbr, Grant Co Medical

Soc (11/20/67); & wife celebrated their 20th wedding anniv 28 Mar 1868 (4/2/68); organizes support for the proposed GR,W&C RR (11/3/69); buys 20 ac in Franklin Twp (4/27/70)

WILLIAMS, William - buys 40 ac in Fairmount Twp from Samuel Bowers (1/26/70)

WILLIS, Jacob - Green Twp landowner (1/6/69)

WILLSON, Jason - a dir, Grant Co Live Stock Assn (8/5/68); prop, Exchange Bank (9/7/70)

WILMORE, Martha J. - buys 40 ac in Franklin Twp from Joshua Marshall (3/12/68); sells 40 ac in Franklin Twp (1/26/70)

WILSON, Francina - 1864 sells land in Pleasant Twp (3/26/68)

WILSON, Henry - of Fairmount Twp recently found a stray sorrel horse (6/22/70)

WILSON, J.W. - JP, Monroe Twp (10/19/70)

WILSON, James S. - Fairmount Twp taxpayer (1/26/70)

WILSON, Jasper - Liberty Twp landowner (1/6/69)

WILSON, Jesse - buys a lot in Fairmount (11/24/69)

WILSON, John M. - Liberty Twp landowner (1/8/68; 1/6/69); 1869 Mill Twp landowner (12/21/70)

WILSON/McWILSON, John - Fairmount Twp landowner (1/8/68); dec; 1868 his heirs owned land in Fairmount Twp & in Jefferson Twp (1/12/70)

WILSON, Mrs. Keziah - officer in Rebekah Lodge, Jonesboro (4/28/69)

WILSON, Lindsey - sells 60 ac in Fairmount Twp (11/3/69)

WILSON, Micajah - organizes Fairmount Twp support for proposed GR,W&C RR (11/3/69); buys property in Fairmount from Eli Neal (11/10/69)

WILSON, Michael - 1869 Sims Twp landowner (12/21/70)

WILSON, Nathan D. - 10 Nov 1867 his home near Fairmount burned (11/13/67); is exor of estate of David Stanfield, dec (1/13/69); Fairmount Twp delegate to State Rep Conv (2/9/70); sells ac near Fairmount to Micajah Wilson (4/27/70), & to Enoch Beals (12/7/70)

WILSON, Rhoda - Franklin Twp landowner (1/8/68)

WILSON, Samuel S. - Liberty Twp landowner (1/8/68); May 1869 buys license to m Rachel Hall (6/2/69)

WILSON, William - Liberty Twp landowner (1/6/69)

WILSON/WILLSON, William G. - Trustee for 3rd Ward, Jonesboro (5/11/70)

WIMMER, Isaac - viewer for a rd between Grant Co & Miami Co (7/23/69)

WIMPY, Robert - buys 17 ac in Mill Twp from Loruhama Thomas (1/26/70), & sells 16 ac in Mill Twp (7/20/70)

WINANS, David A. - 27 Dec 1868 m Cynthia A. Broaderick of 4 mi E of Jonesboro (1/6/69)

WINCHELL, George N. - 1867 buys/sells Marion lots (1/8/68); prop with Miles Murphy of Winchel & Co Drygoods (8/18/69)

WINCHELL, Reuben A. - Nov 1867 buys license to m Sarah E. Lewis (12/11/67)

WINE, George - sells to Michael Beck 2 lots in Marion & an adjoining 2.23 ac (4/2/68)

WINE, George W. - Washington Twp landowner (1/8/68)

WINE(S), M.G. - age 84; d 6 Aug 1870 (8/17/70)

WINE, William H. - Feb 1868 buys license to m Mary Jackson (3/4/68)

WINSLOW, Aaron - Jan 1869 buys license to m Hannah A. Brooks (2/3/69)

WINSLOW, Allen - 1867 buys Jonesboro property (1/15/68); mbr Amana Lodge, IOOF; 15 Mar 1869 d at his home in Jonesboro (3/31/69); 1868, Mill Twp landowner (1/12/70)

WINSLOW, Daniel - a v pres, Old Settlers meeting (6/8/70)

WINSLOW, Jesse - buys 2 lots in Fairmount (8/17/70)

WINSLOW, John - Dec 1869 buys license to m M[ary] L. Shugart (1/5/70)

WINSLOW, Jonathan P. - Trustee, Fairmount Twp (9/18/67); buys property near Fairmount (1/22/68); 1867 sells a lot in Fairmount (3/4/68); buys 17.5 ac in Fairmount Twp (4/30/68); organizes Fairmount Twp support for proposed GR,W&C RR (11/3/69); is on committee to fight alcohol in Fairmount (12/29/69); Fairmount Twp delegate, State Rep Conv (2/9/70)

WINSLOW, Milton - buys 42 ac in Mill Twp (10/27/69)

WINSLOW, Miss Mary 'Mollie' M. - Fairmount HS tchr, fall session 1870 (8/3/70)

WINSLOW, Nixon - 1867 buys Fairmount Twp ac (2/26/68); admin estate of James Redden, dec (6/2/69), & of Jesse Reece, dec & of John Foust, dec (7/30/74); ; sells 1 ac in Fairmount (2/9/70); produced 120 bushels of flax-seed on 7 ac this season (8/24/70)

WINSLOW, Sarah - buys a lot near Jonesboro (2/2/70)

WINSLOW, Selah - 1867 buys property in Marion (1/15/68)

WINSLOW, Thomas - dec; 1869 owned land in Fairmount Twp (12/21/70)

WINSLOW, Dr. W.L. - dental surgeon in Marion (8/18/65)

WINTERS, Josiah - viewer for a rd between Jonesboro & Harrisburg (7/23/69)

WISE, Henry - buys 150 ac in Mill Twp (7/20/70)

WISER, Adelia - is att Marion Public Sch (1/12/70); Marion HS student (12/23/70)

WISER, Clara B. - is att Marion Public Sch (1/12/70)

WITT, Dr. C. - 1851 is a Marion MD (8/17/70)

WOLF(E), Adam - buys 40 ac in Jefferson Twp (6/8/70)

WOLF, J[ames] N.D. - Jan 1869 buys license to m Mary R.B. Roney (2/3/69)

WOOD, Daniel - sells 21 ac in Fairmount Twp (12/15/69)

WOOD, George - of Xenia, Miami Co; Oct 1867 his black mare is stolen (10/23/67); Sims Twp landowner (1/8/68); sells 126 ac in Sims Twp to Evan Bell (4/9/68)

WOOD, Joseph - owns property in Mier (1/6/69)

WOOD, Luke - of Evansville; 10 Jun 1869 m Lizzy Hiatt of Somerset, f of Marion (6/16/69)

WOOD, Capt. William - admin estate of Silas Braffit, dec (9/25/67; 4/2/68); organizes support in Richland Twp for proposed GR,W&C RR (11/3/69); of Richland Twp; CW vet (1/19/70); sells 144 ac in Richland Twp to Joseph Watkins & buys 152 ac in Sims Twp from John Murray (4/13/70)

WOODARD, Emily - 1869 Franklin Twp landowner (12/21/70)

WOODARD, James H. - sells 10 ac in Monroe Twp (12/25/67)

WOODY, Lewis - 1850 is Whig candidate for Grant Co Assessor (8/18/69)

WOODYARD, Emily - 1868 Franklin Twp landowner (1/12/70)

WOODYARD, James - 1868 Franklin Twp landowner (1/12/70)

WOOLEN, Edward - buys 60 ac in Fairmount Twp (11/3/69)

WOOLEN, Jacob - Jan 1869 buys license to m Penina Wilson (2/3/69)

WOOLEN, William R. - sells 40 ac in Liberty Twp (1/29/68)

WOOLMAN, Benjamin - 1847 is ed, 'Marion Telegraph' (7/6/70)

WOOLMAN, Elizabeth R. - SS tchr, Salem Ch (5/5/69)

WORK, Elvira - is att Marion Public Sch (11/13/67)

WRIGHT, Asa K. - is given 40 ac in Liberty Twp by John Wright & sells that 40 ac to David W. Gillimore (9/7/70)

WRIGHT, Charles L. - Fairmount Twp landowner (1/6/69); sells 54 ac in Fairmount Twp to David C. Lucas (11/2/70)

WRIGHT, Hannah C. - is att Marion Sch (11/13/67)

WRIGHT, Isabel - is att Marion Sch (11/6/67)

WRIGHT, Jacob - assesses lands for constructing Marion & Liberty Twp Turnpike 6/23/69)

WRIGHT, James - 1867 buys 40 ac in Liberty Twp (4/16/68)

WRIGHT, Jesse - buys a Fairmount lot (12/15/69)

WRIGHT, Jesse D. - 1867 buys 80 ac in Center Twp (2/12/68)

WRIGHT, Joab - is bldg a large barn on his farm near Marion (5/5/69); Center Twp taxpayer (1/26/70)

WRIGHT, Joel B. - buys Fairmount Twp property (12/25/67); sells part ownership in a Fairmount woolen factory to Rees & Haisley (4/27/70); buys/sells a lot in Fairmount (11/30/70)

WRIGHT, John - sells a lot near Jonesboro (2/2/70)

WRIGHT, John E. - 1868 Richland Twp landowner (1/12/70)

WRIGHT, Marion - of Richland Twp; CW vet (1/19/70)

WRIGHT, Milton J. - is att Marion Public Sch (11/13/67)

WRIGHT, Mollie - is att Marion Public Sch (11/6/67)

WRIGHT, Nathan - 1862 sells property in Jonesboro (1/15/68)

WRIGHT, Dr. Peter Harmon - practice is in Fairmount (2/9/70)

WRIGHT, Robert - buys an Upland lot (4/13/70)

WRIGHT, Samuel K.G. - of Brownsville, MI; 18 Feb 1868 m Mariah, dt William Neal (2/26/68; 3/4/68)

WRIGHT, Zenas J. - Liberty Twp landowner (1/6/69)

YARNELL, William C. - in Marion 25 Sep 1870 m Mary A. Hooper, both of North Grove, Miami Co (10/5/70)

YORK, Aaron S. - Apr 1869 buys license to m Lillie A. Dean (5/5/69)

YORK, A[lfred] Y. - viewer, new Pleasant Twp rd (3/11/69)

YOUNG, Benjamin - prop, Young Ice Cream Saloon (6/2/69)

YOUNG, Benjamin F. - 15 May 1870 m Ella Hodge (5/25/70)

YOUNG, H. - prop of a Marion taylor shop (7/13/70)

YOUNG, Henry L. - injured while plastering a room (6/16/69)

YOUNG, John - is att Marion Sch (12/18/67)

YOUNG, Samuel - of Van Buren Twp; has a crippled hand; Rep Party candidate for Land Appraiser of Grant Co (3/4/68)

YOUNG, Scott - is att Marion Sch (1/12/70)

ZAHN, E.S. - & Co are on Adams St where they manuf wagons, carriages, & buggies to order (7/8/68); sells a lot in Marion to Benjamin R. Norman (11/2/70)

ZAHN, John H. - Recorder, Grant Co (10/1/67)

ZEEK, Adelia - mbr IOGT Lodge, Jonesboro (6/22/70)

ZEEK, John - Trustee, 2nd Ward, Jonesboro (5/11/70)

ZELLER, Morgan H. - dec at age 25; mbr, Masons & IOOF; prop., clothing store in Marion; his heirs sell store to S.L. Bayless (8/18/65)

ZELLER, Reuben - Washington Twp landowner (1/6/69)

ZIMMERMAN, John - sells 80 ac in Monroe Twp (4/27/70)

ZIRKLE, Willis - buys 40 ac in Sims Twp (11/10/69)

ZUCK, Hiram - Van Buren Twp landowner (1/6/69)

MAIDEN NAME INDEX

ABBOTT, Eliza A.   177
ACHOR, Sarah Jane   117
ADAMS, Ellen Adelia   61
ALLEN, Mary   2   17
ANDERSON, Elizabeth   33   Martha   146
ANTRIM, Sarah A.   34
ARNETT, Achsah T.   102
ARTHURHULTZ, June   62   Martha   145
ASBERY, Esther   3
BALDWIN, Emily   133   Jennette   22   Louisa   69
BALLINGER, Elizabeth   57   Emily   32
BARNARD, Mary C.   90
BARRETT, Rachel   147
BARTLETT, __   31
BAUGH, Anna C.   86
BEAM, Margaret J.   78
BEATTY, Rachel A.   74
BEAUCHAMP, Rachel   103
BECHTEL, Margaret   101
BECK, Mary C.   7
BEHYMER, Mary J.   71
BENNETT, Nancy E.   16
BENOY, Harriett   159
BERRY, Jane   153   Martha   62
BEVARD, Hannah   107
BLACKBURN, Elvira   61
BLINN, Sarah E.   44
BLOXIN, Naomi   51
BOCOCK, Victoria   66
BOGUE, Elmina   65
BOLE, Lorinda   33   Matilda E.   163
BOND, Margaret   80
BONE, Martha J.   135
BOOKOUT, Rachel M.   135
BOOTH, Mary   130
BOWMAN, Elvira   43
BRADFIELD, Fanny   97   Phebe   7
BRANDON, Minerva   139
BRILEY, __   152
BROADRICK, Cynthia A.   185
BROCHT, Catherine   140
BROOKS, Hannah   186   Millie   26   97

MAIDEN NAME INDEX

BROWN, Margaret 69
BROWNLEE, Laura 95
BRUSHWILLER, Martha B. 62
BRYANT, Mary J. 149
BUCHANAN, Hattie A. 46 Laura J. 67
BURAKER, Lydia 29 Mary 42
BURDEN, Catharine 179 Melissa 14 Rebecca 162
BURSON, Jane 20 133
CAMBLIN, Margaret 140
CAMPBELL, Amanda 6
CANDY, Frances R. 89
CAREY, Celia 102 Lizzie 169
CARMINE, Martha 154
CARPENTER, Lucinda 132
CARRIENS, Lucinda 118
CLARK, Cynthia A. 57 Frances D. 46
CLESTER, Martha J. 84
CLOUD, Nancy J. 9
CLUNK, Mary E. 170
COCHRAN, Mary C. 4
COLEMAN, Anna 117 Mahala 117
CONGER, Emma J. 73
CONNELLY, Ann M. 99 Rebecca 128
CONNER, Asenath 162
CONNOTY/CONNATY, Mariah 64
COREY, Margaret 121
CORNER, Mildred 94
COVALT, Angeline 37
CRAIG, Caroline 85
CREVISTON, Martha A. 39
CROW, Caroline 178
CROWELL, Mary E. 130
CULBERTSON, Sarah 16
DANIELS, Elizabeth 49
DAY, Sarah E. 144
DEAN, Lillie A. 189
DILLON, Julia Ann 41 107
DINART, Elizabeth J. 160
DOLMAN, Theresa 101
DOUGLASS, Emma W. 130
DOVE, Eliza 107
DULING, Eliza J. 84

MAIDEN NAME INDEX 193

DUNWOODY, Nancy J.   181
EAKINS, Elizabeth A.   136
EARLY, Sarah E.   51
EBY, Sarah C.   12
ECHELBARGER, Phoebe C.   44
ELLIOTT, Nancy   150
ELLIS, Lydia Ann - 85   Mary A.   168
ENDSLEY, Mary E.   118
ENTZMINGER, Sarah H.   128
EVANS, Eliza R.   117   Sarah P.   116
EYESTONE, Florence O.   88
FANKBONER, Sarah F.   131
FARR, Mary   165   Susannah   49
FELTON, Ellen   25   Keziah   38
FISHER, Jennie   34   Sarah   146
FITZSIMMONS, Annie   6   Elizabeth   92
FLEMING, Amanda   160
FLOYD, Mahala A.   75
FOUTCHE, Lydia   55
FRANTZ, Louisa   129
FUTRELL, Mary J.   60
GALBREATH, Millie   163
GARDNER, Josephine   152   Nancy   152
GENNEY, Catherine   60
GLASGOW, Mariah   99
GODFREY, Nancy   144
GOSSETT, Phoebe   147
GRAY, Rebecca J.   129
GREEN, Patience   122
GRIFFIN, Margaret   134
GRINDLE, Anna C.   50   Esther A.   64
GUTELIUS, Emma   37
HAHN, Mary A.   32
HAINES, Mary   41   Rebecca   88   Sarah   4   Susannah 13
HAISLEY, Eunice E.   176
HALEMAN, Malinda   177
HALL, Callie   180   Rachel   185   Sarah J.   63
HAMAKER, Dulcena H.   15
HAMILTON, Charlotte   106   Hannah   134   Laura   31
HANMORE/HANNON, Mary A.   19
HARDACRE, Mary J.   101
HARL/HARBOLD, Rebecca   32

MAIDEN NAME INDEX

HARMON, Melissa A.   44
HARPER, Angeline   35
HARRIS, Arrelia   160   Rachel   144
HARVEY, Angelina   136   Avis   128
HAYDEN, Mary   48
HAYS, Sarah J.   42
HERRON, Sarah   148
HIATT, Lizzy   187   Rachel   52   Sarah   137
HITE, Mary E.   14   149
HODGE, Ella   189
HOGIN, Emily E.   104
HOLLIDAY, Anabell   121
HOLLIS, Sarah   65
HOOPER, Mary A.   189
HORNER, Cynthia A.   144
HORTON, Jane   66   Laura J.   167
HUFFMAN, Helena A.   182
HUGHES, Lucetta   92
HUGGINS, Mollie E.   53
HULSE, Sarah E.   84
HUTCHINS, Sarah A.   20
ISENHOUR, Drucilla   101
JACKS, Martha Jane   5
JACKSON, Mary   186
JAMES, Bernice   94   Mary   81   162
JEFFRIES, Harriett   116
JENKINS, Jane B.   159
JOHNSON, Ann E.   9   Mary   34   97   Perlina E.   84
   Susan J.   16   Susannah   86
JOLLY, Catherine   150
JORDON, Mahala   124
JOSLIN, Nancy   168
JUNKEN, Mary J.   67
KELLEY, Susan   42
KELLY, Mary Ann   171
KENNEDY, Mattie   81
KIDNER, Amanda   100
KIMES, Amanda   149
KINNEY, Sarah E.   76
KNIGHT, Beauley   163   Martha   125   Mary   127
KUNKEL, Mary A.   11
LACKEY, Martha J.   125

MAIDEN NAME INDEX

LACY, Catharine   23
LANE, Jennie   89
LANSBERRY, Katurah E.   140
LAWSON, Sarah E.   157
LEE, Dianna   102
LENNET/TENNET, Sarah   90
LEWELLEN, Martha J.   163
LEWIS, Sarah E.   185
LINE, Lucinda   60
LIVINGOOD, Harriett L.   133
LLOYD, Mary   43
LOWE, Mary   24
LUCAS, Anna M.   149
LUGAR, Minerva   153
LYON, Mary   154
McCAN(N), Mary A.   141
McCOY, Hannah E.   95   Mary   126
McCRACKEN, Asenath   159
McDANIEL, Mary A.   127
McGEE, Rebecca   11
McKINNEY, Tilla   181
McNAMARA, Mary   6
MABERRY, Emma   147
MALONE, Hester A.   23
MARINE, Alcha A.   104
MARSH, Mary M.   40   139
MATCHETT(E), Mary A.   44
MAULLER, Mary H.   63
MAXWELL, Nancy M.   167
MAY, Judie/Judy   176
MEEKS, Jemima J.   119
MIDDLETON, Lucinda   180   Susannah   183
MILES, Mary L.   49
MILLER, Mary A.   15
MILLHOLLEN, Caroline   146   Eliza   121
MITCHENER, Elizabeth E.   54
MODLIN, Mariah   95
MOORE, Angelina   97   Martha   1
MOORMAN, Mahala J.   48
MORGAN, Tabitha   130
MULLEN, Mary A.   126
MURRAY, Nancy   37

MAIDEN NAME INDEX

NEAL, Mariah   189
NEEDLER, Emeline   72
NELSON, Cerelda A.   95
NIXON, Hannah   175
NOE, Julia A.   173
NOSE, Bathsheba   135
OGLE, Abigail   69   Nellie   54
OLIVER, Elizabeth   137
OSBORN, Rachel E.   16
PAGE, Mary   94
PALMER, Mary   20   143
PARKER, Mary E.   82
PARKS, Sarah   80
PARSON, Nancy A.   55
PATTERSON, Abbie   127   Anna   71   Mary   36   Salina   121
PAXTON, M. Victoria   154
PAYNE, Louisa   68   Margaret   12
PENCE, Sarah E.   49
PHILLIPS/PHILIPS/PHELPS, Lousena E.   91
PIERCE, Evaline   30   Martha   54
POWELL, Emeline   180   Mary   133   Susan   177
PRICE, Delight   56   Hannah   126   Lydia   117
PULLEY, Emily   6   Josephine   161
RADLEY, Alice C.   26   45
RANDOLPH, Sarah A.   106
REDFORD, Sarah   88
REECE, Matilda   66
REEVES, Minerva   55
RICHARDS, Mary A.   17   Sarah E.   53
ROBERTS, Mary A.   117
ROGERS, Sarah F.   52
RONEY, Mary R.B.   187
ROOD, Marinda   48
ROUSH, Mary C.   43
RULEY, Sarah E.   163
RUSH, Margaret E.   142   150
SAID, Mary E.   100
SANFORD, Amanda   6
SCOTT, Lydia C.   19   Rachel E.   30
SEFORD, Sarah   6
SEWARD, Louise   119   154
SHERWOOD, Amanda M.   78   Mary   150

MAIDEN NAME INDEX

SHINHOLT, Elizabeth V. 5
SHIVELY, Theresa 83
SHUFF, Anna E. 131
SHUGART, Mary 13 186
SIRTINE, Maris E. 69
SKILLMAN, Delila 155
SMALL, Anna 92 Margaret 85 Mary 132
SMITH, Frances 161 177 Mary 46
SNORF, Jennie 153 163
SNYDER/SAIDER, Rebecca J. 14
STAIR, Sarah V. 71
STALKER, Pelina 182
STANDISH, Mary 144
STEBBINS, Anna M. 121
STEPHENS, Rosella A. 155
STEWART, Mary C. 143
STOUT, Sarah 11
STRAIN, Mary J. 132
STUART, Jane 149
SULLIVAN, Mary A. 20
TAYLOR, Celissa A. 182
THOMAS, Janetta 164 Nancy 131 Ruth A. 152
THORN, Catharine 24
THRASHER, Sarah 128
TROXELL, Mary E. 103
TUCKER, Margaret J. 33
TURNER, Rosetta 10
VERTRICE, Caroline 86
WALKER, Harriet 107 Nancy J. 183
WALL, Amanda 139
WEAVER, Ellen 86
WELCH, Louisa J. 55 Sarah 152
WESTFALL, Angeline C. 16
WHINNEY, Lida A. 35
WHITE, Barbara A. 30
WILLCUTS, Auracy 20
WILLIAMS, Catherine 54 Effa Ann 123 Mariah 128
   Sarah A. 76
WILLIS, Mahala 97
WILSON, Margaret J. 123 Nancy 12 Penina 188
WINSLOW, Jennie 85
WINTERS, Nancy M. 75

MAIDEN NAME INDEX

WISE, Sarah A.   55   Susannah   145
WOOD, Mary   1   168   Nancy   105
WRIGHT, Bathsheba   54
WRIGHT, Mary E.   107
WYANT, Eva   152
YOUNG, Angeline   79
YOUSE, Eliza A.   174

Other Heritage Books by Ralph D. Kirkpatrick, Ph.D.

*Back Creek Friends Cemetery Burial Records
Revised Edition*

*Burial Records of Four Grant County, Indiana
Quaker Cemeteries*

Local History and Genealogy Abstracts from
Fairmount News, *Fairmount, Indiana, 1888–1900*

Local History and Genealogy Abstracts from
Fairmount News, *Fairmount, Indiana, 1901–1905*

*Local History and Genealogical Abstracts from
Jonesboro and Gas City, Indiana Newspapers, 1889–1920*

*Local History and Genealogy Abstracts from
Marion, Indiana Newspapers, 1865–1870*

*Local History and Genealogy Abstracts from
Marion, Indiana Newspapers, 1871–1875*

*Local History and Genealogy Abstracts from
Marion, Indiana Newspapers, 1876–1880*

*Local History and Genealogy Abstracts from
Marion, Indiana Newspapers, 1881–1885*

*Local History and Genealogical Abstracts from
Upland, Indiana Newspapers, 1891–1901*

www.ingramcontent.com/pod-product-compliance
Lightning Source LLC
Chambersburg PA
CBHW071417160426
43195CB00013B/1727